Public Sector Financial Management

This series brings together cutting edge research in public administration on the new budgeting and accounting methodologies and their impact across the public sector, from central and local government to public health care and education. It considers the need for better quality accounting information for decision-making, planning and control in the public sector; the development of the IPSAS (International Public Sector Accounting Standards) and the EPSAS (European Public Sector Accounting Standards), including their merits and role in accounting harmonisation; accounting information's role in governments' financial sustainability and crisis confrontation; the contribution of sophisticated ICT systems to public sector financial, cost and management accounting deployment; and the relationship between robust accounting information and performance measurement. New trends in public sector reporting and auditing are covered as well. The series fills a significant gap in the market in which works on public sector accounting and financial management are sparse, while research in the area is experiencing unprecedented growth.

More information about this series at
http://www.palgrave.com/gp/series/15782

Francesca Manes-Rossi
Rebecca Levy Orelli
Editors

New Trends in Public Sector Reporting

Integrated Reporting and Beyond

palgrave
macmillan

Editors
Francesca Manes-Rossi
Department of Economics
Management and Institutions
University of Naples Federico II
Napoli, Italy

Rebecca Levy Orelli
Department of Management
Alma Mater Studiorum
University of Bologna
Bologna, Italy

Public Sector Financial Management
ISBN 978-3-030-40055-2   ISBN 978-3-030-40056-9 (eBook)
https://doi.org/10.1007/978-3-030-40056-9

This Palgrave Macmillan imprint is published by the registered company Springer Nature Switzerland AG.
The registered company address is: Gewerbestrasse 11, 6330 Cham, Switzerland

Contents

Contributors

Caroline Aggestam Pontoppidan Department of Accounting and Auditing, Copenhagen Business School, Copenhagen, Sweden

Chiara Di Gerio University of Rome "Tor Vergata", Rome, Italy

Spiridione Lucio Dicorato University of Rome "Tor Vergata", Rome, Italy

Teodora Viorica Farcas Babeş-Bolyai University of Cluj-Napoca, Cluj-Napoca, Romania

Gloria Fiorani University of Rome "Tor Vergata", Rome, Italy

Judith Frei Institute of Management Accounting, Johannes Kepler University, Linz, Austria

Dorothea Greiling Institute of Management Accounting, Johannes Kepler University, Linz, Austria

James Guthrie Macquarie Business School, Macquarie University, Sydney, NSW, Australia

Ellen Haustein Center for Accounting and Auditing, University of Rostock, Rostock, Germany

Sanja Korac German University of Administrative Sciences, Speyer, Germany

Peter C. Lorson Center for Accounting and Auditing, University of Rostock, Rostock, Germany

Melanie Lubinger Institute of Management Accounting, Johannes Kepler University, Linz, Austria

Francesca Manes-Rossi Department of Economics, Management and Institutions, University of Naples Federico II, Napoli, Italy

Ann Martin-Sardesai School of Business and Law, CQ University, Sydney, NSW, Australia

Tudor Oprisor Babeş-Bolyai University of Cluj-Napoca, Cluj-Napoca, Romania

Rebecca Levy Orelli Department of Management, Alma Mater Studiorum, University of Bologna, Bologna, Italy

İsmail Çağrı Özcan Department of Aviation Management, Ankara Yıldırım Beyazıt University, Ankara, Turkey

Giuseppe Paciullo University of Rome "Tor Vergata", Rome, Italy

Pasquale Ruggiero University of Siena, Siena, Italy
Brighton Business School, Brighton, UK

Iris Saliterer University of Freiburg, Freiburg, Germany

Amanda Sonnerfeldt School of Economics and Management, Lund University, Lund, Sweden

Adriana Tiron-Tudor Babeş-Bolyai University of Cluj-Napoca, Cluj-Napoca, Romania

Gianluca Zanellato Babeş-Bolyai University of Cluj-Napoca, Cluj-Napoca, Romania

List of Tables

Determinants of Environmental, Social, and Governance Reporting of Rail Companies: Does State Ownership Matter?

Contemporary Challenges in Public Sector Reporting

James Guthrie and Ann Martin-Sardesai

Background

Public sector accounting scholarship has witnessed enormous developments over the last three decades (e.g. Broadbent and Guthrie 1992, 2008; Lapsley 1988; Steccolini 2019). One area of scholarship is public sector accountability and public service accounting and reporting. Accountability in the public sector is a different, complex, chameleon-like and multifaced concept encompassing several dimensions (Barberis 1998; Mulgan 2000; Sinclair 1995). The public sector with its multiple stakeholders requires a much broader set of accountability forms which goes beyond the scope of financial dimensions, by also including political (or democratic), public, managerial, bureaucratic, professional and personal accountability (Sinclair 1995). Public services are created in a complex

J. Guthrie (✉)
Macquarie Business School, Macquarie University, Sydney, NSW, Australia
e-mail: james.guthrie@mq.edu.au

A. Martin-Sardesai
School of Business and Law, CQ University, Sydney, NSW, Australia
e-mail: a.sardesai@cqu.edu.au

F. Manes-Rossi, R. Levy Orelli (eds.), *New Trends in Public Sector Reporting*, Public Sector Financial Management,
https://doi.org/10.1007/978-3-030-40056-9_1

environment, haunted by wicked problems (Jacobs and Cuganesan 2014) and faced by diminishing resources, as well as the emergence of unexpected events and crises, such as the global financial crisis in 2008 (Bracci et al. 2015).

In contemporary times the public sector needs to consider global and emerging issues such as climate change, sustainable economic development, modern-day slavery, taxation avoidance, biodiversity and ecological accounts (Bebbington and Unerman 2018; Kastberg and Lagstrom 2019; Steccolini 2019). These issues have been identified as being the guiding principles bridging environmental and human developmental concerns (Bebbington and Larrinaga 2008, 2014). Interdisciplinary accounting scholars should explore how public sector accounting and accountability can respond to the challenges posed by a shifting and increasingly intangible publicness (Steccolini 2019); for instance, calling for alternative accountability mechanisms such as integrated reporting (IR) (e.g. de Villiers et al. 2014; Guthrie and Parker 1990; IIRC 2016), whereby accounting provides the processes and operational ways in which the public interest and public value are decided upon, planned and accounted for in an abstract public space (Miller and Rose 2008).

In addition, in recent decades with the influence of new public management (NPM) doctrines and related neoliberal ideologies, public sector systems have adopted a variety of hybrid governance and organisational forms in their activities (Guthrie 1993). It has thus become common to provide public services (such as infrastructure, utilities, education, port, health care, art, culture and social services) through hybrid organisations operating at the intersection of the public sector and the market (Grossi et al. 2019). Hybrid governance is the inter-organisational relationships, roles, calculative practices, performance measurement systems and accountability and reporting systems that operate in the area between public, private and non-profit sectors and have conflicting goals, institutional pressures, complexity and accountabilities related to different institutional logics (Hopwood 1996; Kastberg and Lagstrom 2019).

These significant advancements of NPM, neoliberalism, publicness and hybridisation provide a context in which the following brief discussion on contemporary challenges in public sector and services reporting, integrated reporting and beyond take place. The purpose of this chapter is to provide an overview of developments over the past decades and highlight seven frameworks that have been used by the public sector for reporting. In this introduction to the book, we do not engage with the contributions as this is done in the last chapter.

Seven Critical Public Sector Reporting and Accountability Frameworks

Seven critical reporting and accountability frameworks are identified, and the chapter proceeds as follows. First, traditional financial reporting as represented by financial statements is discussed. Second, management accounting systems as described by performance management systems, budgets and various output and outcome metrics are covered. Third, the general area of non-financial reporting is represented by the European Commission directive. Fourth, the IR framework and the practices of IR are presented. Fifth, the area of reporting in social and environmental accounting is described. Sixth, the United Nations sustainability goals and the various mediums used to disclose this information are explained. Finally, the area of public value reporting is analysed. Of course, this is not exclusive and the only reporting models available, as cultural norms, laws and regulations and previous practice would determine which frameworks are used at certain points in time within nation states and the public sector and services organisations.

The purpose of this introduction is to highlight several of the issues and challenges facing public sector interdisciplinary accounting researchers and these reporting frameworks.

Financial Reporting

For the public sector, with the influence of NPM and the neoliberalism ideology, a private sector accrual model of financial reporting has become popular over the past decades. The traditional financial statements included four basic financial statements: balance sheet, income statement, statement of changes in equity and cash flow statement. Different countries have developed their accounting principles over time: for instance, the American gap principles—Generally Accepted Accounting Principles (GAAP)—that set guidelines for the preparation of financial statements. However, the volume of information available has reached levels not previously seen and continues to grow as reporting requirements become more extensive and voluntary disclosures are made for a variety of reasons.

The global movement to standardising accounting rules was made by the International Accounting Standards Board (IASB). The IASB developed the International Financial Reporting Standards (IFRS), which have been adopted by Australia, Canada and the European Union (for public sector organisations). These financial statements and reports are based on accrual of information. Accrual-based financial statements contain a range of accounting-based information different from traditional cash accounting systems (Guthrie et al. 1999). Some research has criticised the adoption of accrual accounting to the whole government sector, especially when it comes to budgets, financial reporting by departments and accountability for public services (Guthrie et al. 1998; Gigli and Mariani 2018).

Over the years, various financial reporting models have emerged, and public sector financial reporting has evolved into many different forms. For instance, Kuroki et al. (2018) provide evidence of different perspectives of the International Public Sector Accounting (IPSA) conceptual framework model indicating the changes in accounting practice in the public sector space. An analysis of these findings reveals that the accounting profession, as an integral part of the capital market system, exerts pressure to drive standardisation of financialised accrual accounting practices. In contrast, government agencies support accounting systems aligned with conventional accountability principles aligned with jurisdiction-specific contexts (Vivian and Maroun 2018). The interaction of these opposing perspectives is a primary determinant of changes in an accounting practice and financial reporting in the public sector space. Research studies make a strong representation that concentration on just the traditional financial accrual report underrepresents the value and contribution of the public sector and this should be supplemented by developing standards and reports on social benefits and public value (Brown et al. 2018).

Public Sector Management Accounting

Guthrie's (1998) critique of NPM and the adoption of accrual accounting identified two streams in management accounting. The first—accrual management systems (AMS)—identified that internal information systems needed to create and record information about revenues, expenses, assets and liabilities. This was important as calculative practices of public sector moved from cash and fund basis to accrual basis. The second—accrual budgeting (AB)—traditionally required government agencies to prepare budgets and seek appropriations on a cash basis. There is a suggestion that these should now move to an accrual basis, which would imply the inclusion of such costs as depreciation or accrued employee entitlements in the annual government budget. This would result in an emphasis on resource allocation based on accrual numbers and not on appropriations of cash by parliaments. A critical reporting and accountability document for the public sector is public budgets and various budgeting activities.

Saliterer, Sicilia and Steccolini (2018), in their excellent review of the changing nature of public budgets over the last decades, have observed how this vital reporting tool has altered. Traditionally, budgeting has involved the processes through which governments decide how much to spend on what, limiting expenditures to the revenues available and avoiding overspending. Over time, budgeting has increasingly been expected to perform different roles and functions, becoming an essential political medium, a tool for providing stimulus to the economy and to society, a fundamental governance and management device, and a central accountability channel. This multiplicity of functions has translated into a variety of different budget accounting and reporting formats and increasingly complex budgeting processes.

The idea of 'more with less' has become a slogan, as managers seek to maintain or improve the quality of public service delivery. This has been an international trend and there has been no escape for public service managers (Arnaboldi et al. 2015). The financial crisis of 2008 intensified the need for making best use of reduced resources in public services, and accentuated the longstanding need for effective performance management of public services. It has attracted the attention of key world institutions such as the Organization for Economic Cooperation and Development (OECD) (Curristine 2008; Perrin 2003) on the fostering of performance budgeting and monitoring systems and the World Bank. However, the sheer complexity of and the over-simplistic approach to performance management in the public sector makes performance management quite difficult. This is a big challenge facing public services.

European Commission Non-financial Reporting Directive

Directive 2014/95 of the European Union regulates the disclosure of certain practices and organisational performances. The Directive provides that non-financial information helps measuring, monitoring and managing the undertakings performance and their impact on society (EU 2014). The non-financial reporting directive requires public disclosure documents such as annual reports, sustainability reports and integrated reports to include five topics: (1) environmental matters; (2) social and employee aspects; (3) respect for human rights; (4) anti-corruption and bribery issues; and (5) diversity on board of directors (Martin-Sardesai and Guthrie 2020).

The Directive requires organisations to report on impacts, developments, performance and position relating to a set list of non-financial issues. Organisations are given the freedom to disclose this information in any reporting model they wish to use or in a separate report. In preparing their statements, companies may use national, European or international guidelines, such as the UN Global Compact, the OECD guidelines for multinational enterprises or the ISO 2600 according to the EU Commission. An important point here is that while countries encourage the use of voluntary frameworks, now organisations are required to disclose which framework was used if any. These standards have increased the awareness and the importance in the public sector as well as improved internal processes (Habek and Wolniak 2013). Many voluntary frameworks exist which can be followed to report on these topics. Notably, the Global Reporting Initiative (GRI) standards can be used for each topic and are globally the most commonly used framework (Dumay et al. 2010).

Integrated Reporting

IR is gaining popularity among public sector organisations. The International Integrated Reporting Council (IIRC) claims that more than 1000 businesses worldwide have prepared a form of integrated report (IIRC 2016). As of March 2017, the IIRC lists 477 organisations (including some public sectors) whose reports refer to the IIRC. The IIRC and its supporters predict that IR represents the future of corporate reporting and will become the "corporate reporting norm" (IIRC 2013, p. 2).

At the heart of IR Framework is a belief that a wide range of factors determines the value of an organisation—some of these are financial and are accounted for in financial statements (e.g. property, cash), while many such as intellectual capital, greenhouse risks and energy security are not. The belief is that if the IR Framework is used to construct an IR, it will articulate ways to generate and preserve value in the short, medium and long term, helping investors to manage risks (Guthrie et al. 2020).

It is, therefore, necessary, to extend the reporting of not only financial data with ecological data, for example, about carbon dioxide emissions that an organisation generates. The 2015 Paris climate agreement requires that carbon dioxide emissions need to be reduced. IR, therefore, needs two sides—the financial data as well the non-financial ecological data—and it must aim at two achievements: annual financial profit as well as accounting for nature (e.g. reductions in CO_2 emissions) (Parvez et al. 2020).

Social and Environmental Accounting

Social and environmental accounting (SEA) is a process of accounting for social and environmental effects of organisations' actions to particular stakeholder groups within society and to society at large (Guthrie and Parker 1990). SEA emphasises the notion of corporate accountability. It is an approach to reporting an organisation's activity which stresses the need for the identification of socially appropriate behaviour, the determination of those to whom the organisation is accountable for its social performance and the development of appropriate measures and reporting techniques (Adams and Guthrie 2005).

Modern forms of SEA first produced widespread interest in the 1970s. Its concepts received severe consideration from professional and academic accounting bodies (e.g. the Accounting Standards Board's predecessor, the American Accounting Association and the American Institute of Certified Public Accountants). Interest in social accounting cooled off in the 1980s and was resurrected in the mid-1990s, partly nurtured by growing social, ecological and environmental awareness. SEA is a broad field that can be divided into narrower fields. Environmental accounting may account for an organisation's impact on the natural environment. Sustainability accounting is the analysis of social and economic sustainability. The International Standards Organization (ISO) provides a standard, ISO 26000, of the seven core areas to be assessed for social accounting.

SEA challenges conventional accounting, in particular financial accounting, which provides a small image of the interaction between society and organisations, and thus artificially constraining the subject of accounting. It points to the fact that organisations influence their external environment (sometimes positively and many times negatively) through their actions and should, therefore, account for these effects as part of their standard accounting practices and reporting (Guthrie and Parker 1989). SEA offers an alternative account and reporting for public sector entities. SEA for accountability purposes is designed to support and facilitate the pursuit of social objectives, such as public good. These objectives can be manifold but can typically be described in terms of social and environmental desirability and sustainability. SEA for management control is designed to support and facilitate the achievement of an organisation's objectives (Farneti and Guthrie 2009).

The Sustainable Development Goals

The role of accounting in furthering sustainable development has expanded and become more sophisticated. In 2015, 193 countries of the UN General Assembly adopted the 2030 Development Agenda titled "Transforming our world: the 2030 Agenda for Sustainable Development" and selected 17 Sustainable Development Goals (SDGs) that are intended to stimulate action in areas of critical importance for humanity and the planet. As a framework, the SDGs extend the previous Millennium Development Goals (MDGs) in many ways, but particularly by seeking to profoundly link the social, economic and environmental aspects of goals. Nations need to take action in their own ways to help ensure that the implementation is coordinated, and provide a far greater chance of success in this lofty and vital endeavour (Stafford-Smith et al. 2017).

The idea of SDGS has quickly gained ground because of the growing urgency of sustainable development for the entire world. Although specific definitions vary, sustainable development embraces the so-called triple bottom line approach to human well-being (Sachs 2012). The SDGs have recently emerged into the policy arena as an exposition of how development ambitions and environmental limits can be integrated into a coherent framework. The SDGs are connected to the work of academic accountants and have rapidly gained traction among stakeholders, including corporations and the accounting profession (United Nations 2019).

Source: United Nations (**2019**)

Bebbington and Unerman (2018) are raising awareness of the SDGs among accounting academics to help in the initiation, scoping and development of high-quality research projects in this area. The SDGs need the unprecedented mobilisation of global knowledge operating across many sectors and regions. Governments, international institutions, private businesses, academia and civil society will need to work together to identify the critical pathways to success, in ways that combine technical expertise and democratic representation (Sachs 2012). The SDG framework provides both an opportunity and a need for accounting and reporting in this area to advance, refocus and become more impactful, especially in the public sector (Bebbington and Unerman 2018; Guthrie et al. 2020).

Public Value Accounting and Reporting

Public value is value for the public. Value for the public is a result of evaluations about how basic needs of individuals, groups and the society as a whole are influenced in relationships involving the public. The definition that remains equates managerial success in the public sector with initiating and reshaping public sector enterprises in ways that increase their value for the public in both the short and the long run (Moore 1995).

Public value accounting and reporting describe the value that an organisation contributes to society. The concept of public value is widely discussed in the literature (see Alford and O'flynn 2009; Moore 1995), as is its realisation, measurement and reporting (Moore 2002; 2014; Talbot 1998, 2010, 2011). Since late last century, the debate on public sector reform has been marked by the emergence of theories, concepts and values around the paradigm of NPM (see Broadbent and Guthrie 1992; Guthrie et al. 1999) and now on network governance and public services (Broadbent and Guthrie 2008). The concept of public value has been increasingly associated usually within the expression 'public value management' with public administration.

There have been two significant recent developments in the literature. First is Moore's (2013) book, which poses several basic questions (and answers many of these using North American case studies) about how, when and why public agencies can and should use public value performance measurement and management systems to enhance organisational performance, strengthen public accountability and create conditions that allow citizens, elected officials and public managers to align and pursue a vision of public value creation. Second is the number of calls for more studies of the application of public value in practice (Van Helden and Northcott 2010) and adopting action research (Cuganesan et al. 2014). The combined view of how public value is conceptualised and practised is an important question (Cuganesan et al. 2014). Therefore, the contemporary debate has shifted to how the public sector can meet community expectations regarding issues of fiscal crisis, sustainability and providing public services. However, an equally important topic is how public value is identified, managed, measured and reported.

Conclusions

The purpose of the chapter was to provide an overview of several developments in the past decades and briefly review seven frameworks used for public sector reporting. We outlined the importance of context in which public sector organisations and governments must engage with critical global issues such as climate change and social inequality. We propose that public sector accounting and reporting provide one means by which processes and operational ways can be decided upon, planned and accounted for in the public space. As indicated in the various chapters within the current book, there is much work that has been done. However, there is still a lot of accounting academic research into essential topics that needs to be undertaken.

References

Adams, C., & Guthrie, J. (2005). *Social and Environmental Reporting*. London: Palgrave Macmillan.

Alford, J., & O'flynn, J. (2009). Making Sense of Public Value: Concepts, Critiques and Emergent Meanings. *International Journal of Public Administration, 32*(3–4), 171–191.

Arnaboldi, M., Lapsley, I., & Steccolini, I. (2015). Performance Management in the Public Sector: The Ultimate Challenge. *Financial Accountability & Management, 31*(1), 1–22.

Barberis, P. (1998). The New Public Management and a New Accountability. *Public Administration, 76*(3), 451–470.

Bebbington, J., & Larrinaga, C. (2008). Carbon Trading: Accounting and Reporting Issues. *European Accounting Review, 17*(4), 697–717.

Bebbington, J., & Larrinaga, C. (2014). Accounting and Sustainable Development: An Exploration. *Accounting, Organisations and Society, 39*(6), 395–413.

Bebbington, J., & Unerman, J. (2018). Achieving the United Nations Sustainable Development Goals: An Enabling Role for Accounting Research. *Accounting, Auditing & Accountability Journal, 31*(1), 2–24.

Bracci, E., Humphrey, C., Moll, J., & Steccolini, I. (2015). Public Sector Accounting, Accountability and Austerity: More Than Balancing the Books? *Accounting, Auditing & Accountability Journal, 28*(6), 878–908.

Broadbent, J., & Guthrie, J. (1992). Changes in the Public Sector: A Review of Recent "Alternative" Accounting Research. *Accounting, Auditing & Accountability Journal, 5*, 2.

Broadbent, J., & Guthrie, J. (2008). Public Sector to Public Services: 20 Years of Contextual Accounting Research. *Accounting Auditing and Accountability Journal, 21*(2), 129–169.

Brown, R., Ellwood, S., & Conrath-Hargreaves, A. (2018). The Conceptual Underpinnings of Recent Advances in International Public Sector Accounting Standards: Developing a Standard for Social Benefits, *22nd Annual Conference Financial Reporting and Business Communication*, Bristol.

Cuganesan, S., Guthrie, J., & Vranic, V. (2014). The Riskiness of Public Sector Performance Measurement: A Review and Research Agenda. *Financial Accountability & Management, 30*(3), 279–302.

Curristine, T. (2008). Performance Budgeting in OECD Countries, *6th Annual Meeting of Latin American Senior Budget Officials*, Santiago, Chile, 28–31.

de Villiers, C., Rinaldi, L., & Unerman, J. (2014). Integrated Reporting: Insights, Gaps and an Agenda for Future Research. *Accounting, Auditing & Accountability Journal, 27*(7), 1042–1067.

Dumay, J., Guthrie, J., & Farneti, F. (2010). GRI Sustainability Reporting Guidelines for Public and Third Sector Organizations: A Critical Review. *Public Management Review, 12*(4), 531–548.

European Union. (2014). Amending Directive 2013/34/EU as Regards Disclosure of Non-financial and Diversity Information by Certain Large Undertakings and Groups, 2014/95/EU. Available at http://eur-lex.europa.eu/legal-content/EN/TXT/PDF/?uri=CELEX:32014L0095&from=EN/. Accessed 22 Oct 2019.

Farneti, F., & Guthrie, J. (2009). Sustainability Reporting in Australian Public Sector Organisations: Why They Report. *Accounting Forum, 33*(2), 89–98.

Gigli, S., & Mariani, L. (2018). Lost in the Transition from Cash to Accrual Accounting. *International Journal of Public Sector Management, 31*(7), 811–826.

Grossi, G., Kallio, K., Sargiaconomo, M., & Skoog, M. (2019). Accounting, Performance Management Systems, and Accountability Changes in Knowledge-Intensive Public Organizations: A Literature Review and Research Agenda. *Accounting, Auditing & Accountability Journal, 32*, 23.

Guthrie, J. (1993). Australian Public Business Enterprises: Analysis of Changing Accounting, Auditing and Accountability Regimes. *Financial Accountability & Management, 9*(2), 101–114.

Guthrie, J. (1998). *Can Markets Save the Public Sector?* Scotland: University of Edinburgh.

Guthrie, J., & Parker, L. (1989). Corporate Social Reporting: A Rebuttal of Legitimacy Theory. *Accounting and Business Research, 19*(76), 343–352.

Guthrie, J., & Parker, L. (1990). Corporate Social Disclosure Practice: A Comparative International Analysis. *Advances in Public Interest Accounting, 3*(1), 159–175.

Guthrie, J., Humphrey, C., & Olson, O. (1998). International Experiences with New Public Financial Management Reforms: New World? Small World? Better World? In *Global Warning: Debating International Developments in New Public Financial Management.* Norway: Cappelen Adademisk Forlag.

Guthrie, J., Olson, O., & Humphrey, C. (1999). Debating Developments in New Public Financial Management: The Limits of Global Theorising and Some New Ways Forward. *Financial Accountability & Management, 15*(3–4), 209–228.

Guthrie, J., Rossi, F., Nicolo, G., & Orelli, R. (2020). Investigating Risk Disclosures in Italian Integrated Reports: Integrating Reporting and Risk Disclosure – Italian Experience. *Meditari Accountancy Research*, Forthcoming.

Habek, P., & Wolniak, R. (2013). European Union Regulatory Requirements Relating to Sustainability Reporting. The Case of Sweden. *Scientific Journals, 34*(106), 40–47.

Hopwood, A. G. (1996). Looking Across Rather Than Up and Down: On the Need to Explore the Lateral Processing of Information. *Accounting, Organizations and Society, 21*(6), 589–590.

IIRC, The International Integrated Reporting Council. (2013). *International Framework.* http://www.theiirc.org/wp-content/uploads/2013/12/13-12-08-THE-INTERNATIONAL-IR-FRAMEWORK-2-1.pdf. Accessed 29 Dec 2013.

IIRC, The International Integrated Reporting Council. (2016). *When? Advocate for Global Adoption.* https://integratedreporting.org/when-advocate-for-global-adoption/. Accessed 21 June 2017.

Jacobs, K., & Cuganesan, S. (2014). Interdisciplinary Accounting Research in Public Sector: Dissolving Boundaries to Tackle Wicked Problems. *Accounting, Auditing & Accountability Journal, 32*, 3.

Kastberg, G., & Lagstrom, C. (2019). Processes of Hybridization and de-Hybridization: Organizing and the Task at Hand. *Accounting, Auditing & Accountability Journal, 1*(1), 21–33.

Kuroki, M., Hirose, Y., & Motokawa, K. (2018). Research on Local Government Reporting: Literature Analysis Using Text Mining. *SSRN 3140932.*

Lapsley, I. (1988). Research in Public Sector Accounting: An Appraisal. *Accounting, Auditing & Accountability Journal, 1*(1), 21–33.

Martin-Sardesai, A., & Guthrie, J. (2020). Social Report Innovation: Evidence from a Major Italian Bank 2007–2012. *Meditari Accountancy Research.*

Miller, P., & Rose, N. S. (2008). *Governing the Present: Administering Economic, Social and Personal Life.* London/Cambridge, UK: Polity Press.

Moore, M. (1995). *Creating Public Value: Strategic Management in Government.* Cambridge, MA: Harvard University Press.

Moore, M. (2002). *The Public Value Scorecard: A Rejoinder and an Alternative to Strategic Performance Measurement in Nonprofit Organizations,* Hauser Center for Nonprofit Organizations, MA, USA.

Moore, M. (2013). *Recognizing Public Value.* Cambridge, MA: Harvard University Press.

Moore, M. (2014). Public Value Accounting: Establishing the Philosophical Basis. *Public Administration Review, 74*(4), 465–477.

Mulgan, R. (2000). Comparing Accountability Intech Public and Private Sectors. *Australian Journal of Public Administration, 59*(1), 87–97.

Parvez, M., Hazelton, J., & Guthrie, J. (2020). *Integrated Reporting of Greenhouse Gases: Lessons from City-Based Greenhouse Gas Measurement and Reporting.* London: Routledge.

Perrin, B. (2003). *Implementing the Vision: Addressing Challenges to Results Focused Management and Budgeting.* Paris: OECD.

Sachs, J. (2012). From Millennium Development Goals to Sustainable Development Goals. *The Lancet, 379*(9832), 2206–2211.

Saliterer, I., Sicilia, M., & Steccolini, I. (2018). *Public Budgets and Budgeting in Europe: State of the Art and Future Challenges.* London: Palgrave Macmillan.

Sinclair, A. (1995). The Chameleon of Accountability: Forms and Discourses. *Accounting Organisations and Society, 20*(2/3), 219–237.

Stafford-Smith, M., Griggs, D., Gaffney, O., Ullah, F., Reyers, B., Kanie, N., Stigson, B., Shrivastava, P., Leach, M., & O'Connell, D. (2017). Integration: The Key to Implementing the Sustainable Development Goals. *Sustainability Science, 12*(6), 911–919.

Steccolini, I. (2019). Accounting and the Post-New Public Management: Reconsidering Publicness in Accounting Research. *Accounting, Auditing & Accountability Journal,* 32 (1), 255–276.

Talbot, C. (1998). Output and Performance Analysis – Time to Open Up the Debate. *Public Money & Management, 18*(2), 4.

Talbot, C. (2010). *Theories of Performance – Organizational and Service Improvement in the Public Domain.* Oxford: Oxford University Press.

Talbot, C. (2011). *Strategy in Government – The UK Experience of Medium-Term and Outcome Centered Budgeting 1997–2010.* London: Edward Elgar.

United Nations. (2019). *Sustainable Development Goals.* Available at https://www.un.org/sustainabledevelopment/. Accessed 29 Oct 2019.

Van Helden, G. J., & Northcott, D. (2010). Examining the Practical Relevance of Public Sector Management Accounting Research. *Financial Accountability and Management, 26*(2), 213–240.
Vivian, B., & Maroun, W. (2018). Progressive Public Administration and New Public Management in Public Sector Accountancy. *Meditari Accountancy Research, 26*(1), 44–69.

James Guthrie, MA, FCPA, is Distinguished Professor of Accounting, Macquarie Business School Macquarie University, Australia. He is the joint founding editor of *Accounting, Auditing and Accountability Journal* consistently ranked in the top five. Guthrie has published 180 articles, 20 books and 45 chapters in books. As a researcher, he has had a significant impact in his fields of particular expertise—audit, non-financial reporting, public sector, intellectual capital, knowledge management, and social and environmental accounting. He has over 25,000 citations to his work as measured by Google Scholar. Guthrie has been actively involved with the OECD, European and wider academic communities.

Ann Martin-Sardesai, CPA, is Senior Lecturer in Accounting at CQ University, Sydney, Australia. She has been serving on the editorial board of *Accounting, Auditing and Accounting Journal* since 2017. Her research interests are in the area of management accounting with a specific focus on performance management systems in the higher education sector. Her other areas of research interest include integrated reporting, intellectual capital, and social and environmental accounting.

The Rise of Integrated Reporting in the Public Sector: An Analysis of Transnational Governance Interactions

Caroline Aggestam Pontoppidan and Amanda Sonnerfeldt

Introduction

The global political agenda is today dominated by discussions on financial stability and sustainable development.[1] The quest for new reporting models incorporating environmental, social, and governance (ESG) performance has been driven forward through debates on the role and accountability of corporations in society. This debate is also becoming

[1] As an example research, already a decade ago, considered voluntary sustainability reporting (SR) in public sector organisations using the Global Reporting Initiative (GRI) Sustainability Reporting Guidelines (Guthrie and Farneti 2008).

C. Aggestam Pontoppidan (✉)
Department of Accounting and Auditing, Copenhagen Business School, Copenhagen, Sweden
e-mail: cap.acc@cbs.dk

A. Sonnerfeldt
School of Economics and Management, Lund University, Lund, Sweden

F. Manes-Rossi, R. Levy Orelli (eds.), *New Trends in Public Sector Reporting*, Public Sector Financial Management,
https://doi.org/10.1007/978-3-030-40056-9_2

increasingly prominent within the public sector. Biondi and Bracci (2018) highlight that "despite the attempts to harmonize and improve public sector accounting, traditional financial reporting is not considered capable of fulfilling the accountability needs of the wider non-expert citizenry" (p. 1). Public sector accountability has been characterised by its complex, elusive, and multifaceted character, which goes beyond the financial and stewardship dimensions (Almquist et al. 2013; Sinclair 1995). While governments in recent years have become more dependent on societal actors to achieve their goals due to the complexity of the challenges they face (Klijn 2012), broader forms of accountability and enhanced transparency are in turn being demanded by their stakeholders. As such, we observe new multidimensional external reporting being embraced by the public sector to provide relevant decision-useful information to its different stakeholders using methods such as sustainability reporting (SR), popular financial reporting (PFR), and more recently integrated reporting (IR).

The IR framework defines six 'capitals', with each representing forms of value for an entity's value creation process.[2] These capitals are classified as financial capital, manufactured capital, intellectual capital, social and relationship capital, human capital, and natural capital. IR is founded on the premise of integrated thinking that results in a periodic integrated report by an organisation about value creation across these capitals. The framework provides guidance on thinking holistically regarding the resources an entity uses as well as the connectivity and trade-offs between them as value is created for both the entity and others. Though the primary purpose of an integrated report is to explain to financial capital providers how an entity creates value over time, the multi-capital, long-term approach and the guiding principle of connectivity both facilitate a focus on a broader set of values, including sustainability development. Although IR has thus far been largely oriented towards corporate reporting needs, the idea of IR has recently been included in a global agenda to strengthen the performance of government agencies and entities such as cities, local governments, health and educational institutions, as well as non-governmental organisations (Manes-Rossi 2017). IR has been put forward as a framework to help public sector entities address diverse, and often conflicting, accountability requirements while gaining a greater understanding of the

[2] Note that the concept of value creation in itself is worthy of examination. Haller (2016) has examined the literature on the value concept, arriving at a comparison and analysis of: shareholder value, stakeholder value, shared value, and, what is more relevant to this chapter, public value.

ways in which they create value. Furthermore, the IR approach provides more holistic disclosures and a sharper focus on how sustainable outcomes will be delivered for a range of stakeholders over time (IIRC 2016).

In the course of public sector reforms focused on the modernisation of governments, private sector actors, foundations, and other agencies have come to be involved in determining the requirements for new governance and accountability mechanisms (Almquist et al. 2013; Christensen and Lægreid 2007). The emergence of IR in the public sector can be seen as a component of regulatory governance and an outcome of a multi-stakeholder, public-private initiative targeted at shaping public sector conduct and, more specifically, public sector reporting.

This chapter has a strong focus on this multi-stakeholder approach from a governance perspective in relation to IR. More specifically, the chapter is to deepen our understanding from a governance perspective of how governing mechanisms from the private sector diffuse into the public sector. In support of this goal, the study analysed the roles and interactions of various actors included in relevant policy-making or the process of transferring IR to the public sector. Additionally, attending to how governance interactions embed IR in the public sector serves to highlight the meaning of the term 'public value' and how this meaning is orchestrated in governance interactions. Meynhardt (2009) suggests that the notion of public value attracts a need to engage in dialogue about values, value conflict, and the role of the public sector in changing societal contexts.

Drawing on the theoretical perspective of transnational business governance interactions (depicted more accurately in this chapter as transnational governance interactions, TGI), focus is placed on how the governance actors and networks engage with and react to one another; the driving forces, mechanism, and modalities of interaction; as well as the character of such interaction in the process of construing and shaping a private sector tool to fit the public sector (Eberlein et al. 2013). This chapter contributes to a discussion on the role of networks and partnerships within networks, especially their role in terms of an emblematic shift from 'government' to 'governance', or from hierarchical to networked governance (Bäckstrand 2008) in public sector reporting. In doing so this sheds further light on "network-type patterns of collaboration" (Almquist et al. 2013) that drive forward new reporting initiatives such as IR.

The chapter is structured as follows: a brief review of literature pertaining to IR in the public sector, an introduction to the transnational governance interaction analytical framework, an analysis addressing the agenda-setting for IR as a governance tool for non-financial reporting in the public sector, and finally, the conclusion.

Integrated Reporting in the Public Sector

The broader practice of IR has been situated within the broad organisational field of corporate reporting (Humphrey et al. 2017). A predominant focus in the literature on IR has been on studying this, admittedly rather new reporting phenomena, in a private sector context. However, an emerging body of research has attended to the latest key developments and implementation of IR in the public sector (Veltri and Silvestri 2015; Cheng et al. 2014; Bartocci and Picciaia 2013; Cohen et al. 2014). This has extended the debate on the future form of reporting in the public sector by examining alternative forms of reporting, hereunder the framework of integrated reporting, by exploring whether and how these reports could be related to each other in order to fulfil the needs of a core user group, namely citizen. As an example of the foregoing, Oprisor et al. (2016) address IR in the context of public sector accountability, teasing out dimensions which are embedded in public value[3] creation before addressing questions on the suitability of IR for public sector entities and its potential to enhance accountability for such entities. Researches have also raised the need for a focus on the accounting change processes that drive integrated reporting in the public sector (Katsikas et al. 2017). It is argued in this regard that examining integrated reporting as an integral part of accounting change processes and as a driver for change can stimulate a deeper understanding of the challenges and benefits in terms of public value creation.

The public sector has for the past few decades been subjected to multitudinous processes of change, such as is typified by the New Public Management (NPM) agenda[4] (Hood 1991). Despite stark criticism of NPM (English et al. 2005) the movement has continued to evolve, more recently being labelled as in a 'transitory stage' (Osborne 2006) and thus giving rise to another designation as 'New Public Governance' (NPG)

[3] For a definition and elaboration of public value see, as an example, Moore's text on 'Creating Public Value'.

[4] The first New Public Management (NPM) developments can be traced back to the late 1970s and early 1980s under Prime Minister Margaret Thatcher in the United Kingdom ('the Financial Management and Next Steps initiatives'). In addition to this, it also had a start among selected municipal governments in the United States (Groot and Budding 2008).

(ibid.) as well as New Domestic Governance (NDG) (Schleifer 2013), with the latter promoting a shift towards private regulatory instruments. Both NDG and NPG thus thrust public administration into an era that seeks to strengthen its sensitivity to citizens' needs and to ensure greater transparency and flexibility, which ultimately support greater citizen engagement in political administration and governance (Manes-Rossi 2017; see also Almquist et al. 2013). The NPG movement has been described as having a multi-organisational focus, which has led to furthering research interest in how public sector organisations are managed, in how they perform, and more recently, in understanding their impact on the environment (Manes-Rossi 2017). It is thus concerned with raising questions relating to the role of reporting that goes beyond its traditional financially centred role within the public sector. Scrutinising accounting and financial reporting reforms within the public sector has been a long-standing research focus in the literature (Lapsley 1999; Lapsley et al. 2009). Recent contributions have, for example, addressed the accounting reform carried out by the European Commission, elucidating how it evolved over time and the drivers behind the reformed accounting systems' embrace of an NPG perspective (Grossi and Soverchia 2011).

More recently, ESG in the public sector has generated considerable interest among scholars in the field. Studies have echoed that public sector organisations can play an influential role in a more sustainable future (Jones 2010; Miller and Loman 2014). The role and relevance of sustainability accounting and accountability, as well as the legitimating role such reports can play, have also been addressed. Manes-Rossi (2017) even puts forward that although there is heightened informative power to these new forms of non-financial reporting, information on sustainability issues alone does not completely satisfy the accountability needs for different groups of stakeholders. She argues that additional reporting in the form of "future strategies and plans, alliances and partnerships, networking activities, governance mechanisms in place all combined with forms of citizens' engagement" would strengthen the accountability of the public sector (ibid., p. 2). Indisputably in this regard, IR can provide information on the different types of tangible and intangible resources involved in the value creation processes with which the public sector engages. This chapter thus seeks to meaningfully contribute to the literature on IR in the public sector by providing a specific focus on the role of transnational governance interactions for placing IR on the public sector agenda.

Transnational Governance Interactions

A reporting field once characterised by voluntary action, corporate social responsibility (CSR), and other non-financial components of reporting is increasingly becoming subject to public regulation (Buhmann 2013). This takes place through regulatory modalities ranging from hard public law to standards, frameworks, incentives, and reporting (Buhmann 2013). The transnational governance interactions (TGI) framework proposed by Eberlein et al. (2013) offers an approach to the conceptualisation and analysis of schemes applying non-state authority to govern organisational conduct across borders. Given that initiatives to regulate non-financial reporting and information are not limited to non-state standards and frameworks, the scholarly need to understand interactional aspects of how frameworks that can operate as governance tools embed themselves within the public sector, even though emanating from private organisations, is important to fill the knowledge gap on the evolution and effects of such standards or frameworks. This gives weight to Almquist et al.'s (2013) reasoning that "'governance' has become one of the buzz-words in modern social sciences", explaining that in a general sense, "governance deals with the steering and coordination of various actors, often in network-type patterns of collaboration" (p. 1). To delve deeper into the substance of interaction, TGI sheds light on the complexity of interactions at various levels of governance work. This enables an analysis that seeks out the role of key actors and their influence, thus providing insights on the debates, issues as well as tensions within and between actors in the space.

Eberlein et al. (2013) put forth that interactions take place at multiple levels: the "micro" level of individuals and organisations that create and act within transnational governance schemes, the "meso" level of schemes themselves, and the "macro" level of regulatory complexes. Similarly, units of analysis can also vary from dyadic interactions to wider interactions within public-private regimes. Interactions can be studied as both outcomes and causal factors. As outcomes, one would ask what drives and shapes the interactions under consideration; as causal factors, the question turns to what effects interactions have on transnational governance schemes, regulatory complexes and outputs, as well as outcomes and impacts. In both of the above approaches to studying outcomes, varied mechanisms and pathways of influence may come into play. In addition, it should be noted that interactions are dynamic, meaning that patterns in the early stages of a scheme may differ significantly from those that appear once it is firmly institutionalised and where the entry of new players will also modify interaction patterns.

In the TGI analytical framework, regulatory governance is the starting point and is itself disaggregated into six components:

(i) Framing the regulatory agenda and setting objectives;
(ii) formulating rules or norms;
(iii) implementing rules within targets;
(iv) gathering information and monitoring behaviour;
(v) responding to non-compliance via sanctions and other forms of enforcement; and
(vi) evaluating policy and providing feedback, including review of rules.

This chapter is delimited to address the first component, namely framing the regulatory agenda and setting objectives, specifically in this case regarding moving IR as a reporting tool from the private sector reporting agenda to the public sector agenda. For each component of the regulatory governance process, six questions that are crucial in analysing interactions are addressed: (i) Who or what is interacting, (ii) what drives and shapes the interactions, (iii) what are the mechanisms and pathways of interaction, (iv) what is the character of the interactions, (v) what are the effects of interaction, and (vi) how do interactions change over time?

The analysis is structured around three key dimensions of the first component of the TGI model, namely framing the regulatory agenda. These three dimensions include who and what interacts, mechanisms and pathways of interaction and the character of interaction. The 'who and what interacts' are the institutions (private, public, professional associations) and key individuals holding specific institutional tasks. The drivers and shapers are understood to be the background interests that actors pursued or which motivated actors to engage in the interaction. When referring to 'mechanisms and pathways' this chapter's perspective is that these are the specific communicative modalities, including networks, discursive strategies, and technical forms of communication, employed. The 'character of interaction' is the degree of competition, co-optation, chaos, or alignment between interacting instruments or institutions. The framework is actor-centred in that it emphasises interactions between actors in for one or several transnational governance frameworks or schemes.

Setting an Agenda for IR

In the late 2000s, the financial and sustainability crises galvanised a growing number of policy and regulatory initiatives by state and non-state actors at the international, transnational, regional, and national levels to address regulatory gaps that would promote greater financial stability and more sustainable societies (UNEP 2014). On 11 September 2009, the Accounting for Sustainability (A4S) and the Global Reporting Initiative (GRI) convened a high-level meeting comprising investors, standard setters, companies, accounting bodies, and UN representatives with the purpose of creating an internationally consistent approach to 'connect' the separate pillars of financial and sustainability reporting. This skilful configuration included actors with regulatory power, expertise, networks and resources, as well as reporting organisations and their beneficiaries, and was sufficient to generate the critical mass needed to legitimise and pave the way for the establishment of the International Integrated Reporting Council (IIRC) to oversee the creation of the IR framework. The need for integrated reporting was framed in the context of the well-established climate change and sustainability crisis as well as the ongoing problems pertaining to reporting practices. The founding documents established the need for international cooperation to reduce duplication of current fragmented initiatives in the corporate reporting field and stressed the importance of cohesiveness and consistency in reporting. The collaborative approach was adopted not to compete with or set standards for existing systems, but to provide strategic oversight and vision through creating a framework for reporting (A4S 2009). A steering committee and a workgroup were formed comprising members from the accountancy profession (IFAC, IASB, accountancy firms, professional associations), standard-setters (GRI, AccountAbility, A4S, CDSB,[5] corporations, civil society organisations, the UN, stock exchanges, investors groups, and others (academics, consultants). This formation served as an arena for members to interact and coordinate their actions, share expertise, and consolidate recommendations on IR. These developments formed the basic platform of interactions that opened up the possibility for the establishment of mechanisms and pathways that allowed for the spread of IR from the private into the public sector.

The concept of IR more recently has been referred to, and in some instances 'endorsed', in a number of initiatives aimed at institutionalising ESG reporting and disclosures. Examples of this can be found in, but are

[5] Climate Disclosure Standards Board.

not limited to, the United Nations (UN) Global Compact,[6] the Organisation for Economic Co-operation and Development (OECD) Guidelines for Multinational Enterprises as well as the GRI. In addition, legislative-driven regulatory initiatives, such as the King Code of Governance Principles for South Africa, that require IR as mandatory for specific entities are also worth mentioning.

Mechanisms and Pathways Enabling the Rise of IR as a Governance Tool for Non-financial Reporting

The idea of IR was first introduced by the IIRC in a 2011 discussion paper titled 'Towards Integrated Reporting – Communicating Value in the 21st Century'. The paper states: "Integrated Reporting brings together material information about an organization's strategy, governance, performance and prospects in a way that reflects the commercial, social and environmental context within which it operates. It is intended to provide a clear and concise representation of how an organization demonstrates stewardship and how it creates and sustains value" (IIRC 2011, p. 2). Although IR was presented as equally applicable to a broad range of organisations, including public sector entities, the IIRC's initial focus was on large companies (IIRC 2011, p. 8). The IIRC's attempt to institutionalise IR as a practice in the corporate reporting field has shifted its purpose towards promoting a more cohesive and efficient approach to corporate reporting. This entails the IIRC's focus on improving the quality of information available to financial capital providers on how an organisation creates value over time (IIRC 2013).[7]

In 2013 the International Federation of Accountants (IFAC) issued a consultation draft of the then proposed International Framework: Good Governance in the Public Sector, which had been developed jointly by itself and the Chartered Institute of Public Finance and Accounting (CIPFA).[8] This consultation draft stated, "All entities depend on a variety of resources and relationships for their success. These resources and relationships can be regarded as different forms of capital that flow into, throughout (conversion process), and out of the public sector entity" and

[6] See https://www.unglobalcompact.org/library/2991

[7] IIRC (2013) The International IR framework, p. 4.

[8] See http://www.ifac.org/system/files/publications/files/Good-Governance-in-the-Public-Sector.pdf (accessed 15 March 2019).

suggested that they can be categorised following the capitals defined in the then IIRC's 'Consultation Draft of the International Integrated Reporting Framework' of 2013 (p. 9). The final International Framework: Good Governance in the Public Sector (2014) maintains this strong link to the IR framework. Indeed, Mervyn King highlights this in the foreword to the International Framework: Good Governance in the Public Sector, where he states:

> Another aspect of public sector governance highlighted in this publication is the need for integration in both the reporting of and thinking about organizational performance. The International Integrated Reporting Council's release of its Framework for Integrated Reporting (December 2013) makes this publication especially timely, as these two documents complement each other extremely well. (2014)

The IIRC and its networking efforts with a number of influential organisations, including the Chartered Institute of Public Finance and Accounting (CIPFA), the CCAB (Consultative Committee of Accounting Bodies), IPSASB (International Public Sector Accounting Standards Board), and the World Bank, have been important in promoting IR in the public sector. In 2012 and 2013, the IIRC and CCAB hosted an IR round table and a number of workshops, which provided a forum to discuss IR in the public sector. Following on from this, CIPFA published a paper, with input from IPSASB, which considered the relevance of IR to the public sector (CIPFA 2013). The paper discursively deployed the concepts of similarity and differences between the public and private sector reporting obligations. It drew on the challenges of public sector reporting, highlighting the complexity, patchwork nature, and short-term focus of such reporting, and in doing so, sought to pave the way for the introduction of the IR framework into the sector. It then established a pathway for the work needed to develop a public sector perspective on integrated reporting, taking into account the distinctive nature of public sector accountability, the greater stakeholder diversity than often exists in the private sector, and the need to better understand both value and value creation in the public sector context. While the stated mission of the IIRC is "to establish integrated reporting, and thinking within mainstream business practice as the norm in the public and private sectors",[9] the IR

[9] See http://integratedreporting.org/the-iirc-2/

framework, according to the first chairperson of the Public Sector Pioneer Network (PSPN), was not overly focused on public sector entities even though its broad agenda does not preclude such applicability. Initially, while a number of the more commercial-oriented type of public sector organisations and entities showed an interest in IR, adoption in the public sector was nevertheless rather slow to gather momentum (Oprisor et al. 2016).

IR in the public sector context became construed as

> a way for public service organizations to enhance their strategic planning and consider the long-term fiscal (as well as social and environmental) sustainability of the organization … an opportunity to consider and review the interconnectedness of complex multi-service delivery and to clarify goals and identify preferred outcomes within the wider context of promoting public wellbeing. (CIPFA 2013, p. 8)

It was also advanced as a framework that could be applied alongside the Good Governance in the Public Sector Framework published by the International Federation of Accountants (IFAC) to promote a holistic approach to public sector governance.

The idea to apply the IR framework in the public sector was further pushed along by accountancy firms and the work of individuals holding leadership positions in key organisations, including IIRC, IFAC, IPSASB, and CIPFA, involved in public sector reporting. For example, the CEO of IFAC from 2002 to 2013, Ian Ball, was appointed Chairman of CIPFA International in 2013. At the same time he served as a principal adviser, albeit in a volunteer capacity, representing IFAC as a member of the Chair of the IIRC Working Group in 2013. Ian Carruthers, who joined CIPFA in 2006, had been involved in the development of the 'International Framework: Good Governance in the Public Sector' with IFAC before being appointed Chair of the IPSASB in 2016.

The value of IR was further promoted by accountancy firms and the work of individuals holding leadership positions in key organisations such as the IIRC, IFAC, IPSASB, and CIPFA, all of which are involved in public sector reporting.

Subsequently, in May 2014, CIPFA and the IIRC announced the plan to establish the PSPN. The establishment of the PSPN illustrates a networking entity, as members of the PSPN come from the World Bank Group, United Nations Development Programme (UNDP), the City of

London Corporation, the Wales Audit Office, and UK government departments, among others.

The PSPN launched on 17 November 2014[10] was funded by IIRC reserves and participant contributions and staffed using secondments from accounting firms. It served as a forum for public sector organisations to identify and address key aspects pertaining to the relevance and adoption of IR in their sector. Amongst PSPN's activities was a meeting held in London on 27 May, 2015, attended by 34 organisations, where interested parties met to explore the ideals and ideas of IR in the public sector. Throughout the meeting, the notion of integrated reporting being relevant in the public sector was developed and promoted in key speeches by the IIRC, CIPFA, the World Bank, all organisations that already utilised the IR framework. The speeches were focused on specific themes: stakeholders and accountability, value creation in the public sector, and business models in the public sector context. The Chair of IIRC in 2013, Mervyn King, highlighted that many public sector organisations were already run as integrated institutions and construed 'public value' as "the impact of the product created on society and the environment to create the right conditions for the 21st century".

In 2016 the interactions between the IIRC, CIPFA, and the World Bank, which had been taking place since 2012, culminated in a publication titled 'Integrated Thinking and Reporting – Focusing on Value Creation on the Public Sector', which was co-authored by the IIRC and CIPFA, with funding from the World Bank. This publication places emphasis on the notion of public value and specifically states that

> to explain to public sector leaders and their teams how integrated thinking and reporting can help the sector consider how to make the most of resources, encourage the right behaviours and demonstrate to stakeholders how they are achieving the strategy and creating value over the short and longer term. (p. 4)

This elaboration on public value provides a glimpse into a value dichotomy extant in the public sector that has come to exist as a result of the NPM agenda. One the one hand, value is construed from an economic perspective, but at the same time, the IIRC and CIPFA (2016) draw on

[10] See http://www.cipfa.org/about-cipfa/press-office/archived-press-releases/2014-press-releases/pioneering-public-sector-integrated-reporting-network-launched

more non-tangible and ethical characteristics in their writing when assessing public value.

The process that took place from 2012 until the issuance of the 2016 co-authored publication illustrates the numerous interactions that took place at multiple levels, ranging from the micro level of individuals conversing through to organisations that create and act within transnational governance schemes. By drawing out 'mechanisms and pathways' this section has established an understanding of the specific communicative modalities, hereunder networks, discursive strategies, and technical forms of communication (cf. Buhman 2013), that enabled IR to enter the agenda of non-financial reporting and disclosures in the public sector.

Discussion

Thus, in scrutinising the pathways through which IR emerged and became topical in formal publications regarding non-financial reporting in the public sector, the study found the involvement of multiple partnerships. These partnerships, which can be conceptualised as networks, can be identified through the agenda-setting process of bringing IR into the public sector and categorised into three types, namely public-private (hybrid), intergovernmental-governmental and private-private. The partnerships formed also reflect the global nature of governance of ESG reporting and, as illustrated in this chapter, IR. Attending to the formation of these partnerships highlights the increased variation and complexity of governing ESG reporting. The process of bringing IR from the private reporting sphere into the public reporting sphere demonstrates the seminal role of non-governmental actors such as CIPFA, IFAC, and the World Bank, among others, in shaping public sector reporting developments and governance.

A consideration of the character of interaction (cf. Eberlein et al. 2013, p. 16) entails looking at the process that came to develop a degree of coordination towards an agenda in a way that combined interests within an overall goal of governance. The character of interaction thus refers to the degree of competition, chaos, or alignment between interacting instruments or institutions.

In the case of bringing IR into the public sector reporting domain, the mechanisms and pathways established partnerships, or networks, that worked to produce alignment between interacting instruments. For example, alignment between the IIRC's IR framework and IFAC's International

Framework: Good Governance in the Public Sector. Following the TGI model, transnational interactions "strive for legitimacy and policy relevance, learn from one another, and copy proven 'recipes for success'" (p. 12). In the case of IR's move into the public sector, there was an evident discursive articulation of the IR principles. We have witnessed those principles being reproduced in a number of key policy documents, as illustrated in the section on mechanisms and pathways.

The interactional nature of governance seen at play in introducing IR into the public sector has created arenas where governments lack their traditional levels of overall control and where common rules and norms govern policy developments, something that is exemplified in the alignment between IFAC's: International Framework: Good Governance in the Public Sector and the IR framework. In addition, what is also worthy of note at this point is that this serves to highlight the relationship between various levels of governance (cf. Jacobsson et al. 2003).

This chapter has categorised and mapped the landscape of transnational interactions between professional organisations, semi-governmental institutions, and private-public partnerships that ultimately mobilised the forces that successfully propelled IR onto the reporting agenda in the public sector. Research on the NPM movement has, at least in accounting literature, been extended to address 'New Public Financial Management' (Guthrie et al. 1999; Olson et al. 1998), where a key focus has been on accounting technologies as a dominant part of NPM (Christensen and Yoshimi 2003; Lapsley 1999; Olson et al. 1998). This chapter adds to the broader literature on IR as a reporting 'technology' within the NPM movement and more specifically addresses its evolvement from a New Public Governance perspective.

This chapter has also illustrated the numerous partnerships extant in the New Public Governance era. More specifically it highlights how such partnerships, which have been shown to be diverse in nature, were established and that these created the mechanisms and pathways required to place IR onto the public sector reporting agenda. Thus we can conceptualise these partnerships as a broad network, where we observe various forms of joint action within the network: from public-private (hybrid), governmental and private-private to professional associations in accounting. The network established by the partnerships is characterised by heterogeneous actors, all possessing varying standard-setting or other capacities and acting within diverse institutional contexts. In the case of bringing IR into the public sector, the network created mechanisms and opened up pathways that sought to influence the exercise of voluntary governance of non-financial reporting in the public sector, a process that was reliant on this multi-stakeholder approach. The expanding reach and influence of this public sector IR network through its partnerships can be tied to the rise of transnational-networked governance. Thus governance is increasingly characterised by involving multi-sectoral collaboration between civil society, government or intra-governmental entities, and other market actors.

Conclusion

There has been a growing amount of academic research focused on IR (Dumay et al. 2016). Early studies in this field took a normative character focused on the arguments for IR (Eccles and Krzus 2010). This chapter contributes to the broader literature on IR by seeing IR from being used as a governing instrument adopted by IIRC to then being embedded in the public sector governance space, which represents a unique journey in several respects. As illustrated in this chapter, the rise of IR in public sector governance adds to our understanding of the emerging dynamics of multi-stakeholder involvement and interactions in NPG. It has been noted throughout this analysis that the IIRC actively engaged in and enrolled other actors to assist in embedding IR within the public sector regulatory space for reporting. The analysis has also shown that interactional transnational governance suggests that IR offers very beneficial prospects for public institutions as a means towards governing global concerns for non-financial information and reporting.

Furthermore, the research done here indicated that for IR to be embedded as a tool for non-financial reporting in the public sector, the IIRC had to work around the political and institutional constraints of existent state-centred governance of reporting by actively involving or 'enrolling' private non-state actors to promulgate IR. Importantly, it also denotes the role of the IR framework as a governance tool without built-in implementation or enforcement modalities.

The application of the transnational governance interaction framework (Eberlein et al. 2013) to the IR framework in the public sector demonstrates how non-enforceable transnational governance initiatives are not only deployed by state or private standard-setters (such as the IPSASB or the IASB), but can and do involve numerous other organisations (cf. Young 1994). This current analysis of the emergence of the IR framework within the public sector governing space, seen through the lens of interactional governance, shows that this form of governance is capable of migrating from deployment by specialised private or public-private groups in specific sectors, to be embraced by public institutions which see its value in addressing global concerns with regard to non-financial reporting. The implications of this migration of a governance tool from the private to the public sector are potentially very significant considering IR's potential contributions to the global regulation of sustainable development.

The transnational interaction approach shows the IR framework has cut across the divide separating public and private regulatory spaces, drawing on both sectors in concert to promote the use of IR in the public sector. By combining a range of actors, drivers, mechanisms, and forms of interaction, transnational governance interaction offers governmental, non-governmental and intergovernmental authorities new opportunities to shape private sector action outside their formal regulatory boundaries.

Networks have been described as emblematic of the shift from 'government' to 'governance', or from hierarchical to networked governance (Bäckstrand 2008). Clearly understanding the migration of IR from the private to the public sector from a TGI perspective also reveals the emergence of networked governance of ESG reporting. Networked governance has gained attention in studies on transnational advocacy networks consisting of state and non-state actors (ibid.). This indicates that ESG reporting in the public sector is starting to be built on the premise of non-hierarchical steering and therefore is becoming increasingly characterised by a decentralised, voluntary, market-oriented interaction between public and private actors. This can be contrasted with the 'old governance' style, which builds on hierarchical top-down modes of steering and traditional regulation of reporting. As is often the case with change, a measure of caution must be exercised. In this regard one particular area of concern raised in this research is that public and private arrangements frequently remain "poorly aligned" (Schleifer 2013, p. 534). Attending to such alignment in future research is thus of relevance. With this rapidly evolving new landscape being formed by IR's migration to the public sector, further research needs to be devoted to addressing and evaluating the accountability of different types of interactions and partnerships as well as the interplay between these.

Further research on the interactional aspects of the rise of the IR framework in the public sector could uncover the regulatory perspectives through a detailed analysis of the ways in which the IR framework could potentially influence other reporting schemes (EU directives, the GRI, the Global Compact, etc.). In addition, further research perspectives on the potential for regulation of global ESG reporting, and hereunder IR, need to include a detailed elucidation of transnational governance features relating to an analysis of the effectiveness of implementation of IR through interaction with other non-financial reporting frameworks, standards, and schemes, issues that are highly relevant for practice.

This chapter has shown how integrated reporting, through transnational interactions and partnerships, was de-contextualised from the corporate reporting context and abstracted into a global template made translatable to the public sector. Terminology specific to corporate reporting was revised and a broader range of outputs (services, regulation, infrastructure, financial transfers) and outcomes (economic, social and environmental), and accountability that catered to the broader stakeholder groups were re(introduced). An analysis of the mechanisms and pathways required for IR to be inserted into the public sector agenda also showed a focus among stakeholders on public value, something Berg emphasised when discussing the role of public value in public sector reforms and pointed to the increased use of concepts of value in the discourse regarding public sector reform.

References

Accounting for Sustainability. (2009). *Governance and Collaboration – Establishing an "International Connected Reporting Committee"*. London: Accounting for Sustainability.

Almquist, R., Grossi, G., van Helden, G. J., & Reichard, C. (2013). Public Sector Governance and Accountability. *Critical Perspectives on Accounting, 24*(7–8), 479–487.

Bäckstrand, K. (2008). Accountability of Networked Climate Governance: The Rise of Transnational Climate Partnerships. *Global Environmental Politics, 8*(3), 74–102.

Bartocci, L., & Picciaia, F. (2013). Towards Integrated Reporting in the Public Sector. In *Integrated Reporting* (pp. 191–204). Cham: Springer.

Biondi, L., & Bracci, E. (2018). Sustainability, Popular and Integrated Reporting in the Public Sector: A Fad and Fashion Perspective. *Sustainability, 10*(9), 1–16.

Buhmann, K. (2013). The Danish CSR Reporting Requirement as Reflexive Law: Employing CSR as a Modality to Promote Public Policy. *European Business Law Review, 13*(2), 187–216.

Cheng, M., Green, W., Conradie, P., Konishi, N., & Romi, A. (2014). The International Integrated Reporting Framework: Key Issues and Future Research Opportunities. *Journal of International Financial Management & Accounting, 25*(1), 90–119.

Christensen, T., & Lægreid, P. (2007). Introduction—Theoretical Approach and Research Questions. In T. Christensen & P. Lægreid (Eds.), *Transcending New Public Management*. Aldershot: Ashgate.

Christensen, M., & Yoshimi, H. (2003). Public Sector Performance Reporting: New Public Management and Contingency Theory Insights. *Government Auditing Review, 10*(3), 71–83.

CIPFA (2013). *Integrated Reporting and Public Sector Organisations – Issues for Consideration July 2013*. CIPFA.

Cohen, S., Karatzimas, S., & Venieris, G. (2014). The Informative Role of Accounting Standards in Privatising State-Owned Property: Comparing Greek Governmental Accounting Standards and IPSAS. *Global Business & Economics Review, 17*(1), 51–62.

Dumay, J., Bernardi, C., Guthrie, J., & Demartini, P. (2016). Integrated Reporting: A Structured Literature Review. *Accounting Forum, 40*(3), 166–185.

Eberlein, B., Abbott, K. W., Black, J., Meidinger, E., & Wood, S. (2013). Transnational Business Governance Interactions: Conceptualization and Framework for Analysis. *Regulation & Governance, 8*(1), 1–22.

Eccles, R. G., & Krzus, M. P. (2010). *One Report: Integrated Reporting for a Sustainable Strategy*. New York: Wiley.

English, L., Guthrie, J., & Parker, L. (2005). Recent Public-Sector Financial Management Change in Australia: Implementing the Market Model. In C. Greve, J. Guthrie, O. Olson, & L. Jones (Eds.), *International Public Financial Management Reform: Progress, Contradictions and Challenges* (pp. 23–54). Greenwich: Information Age Press.

Groot, T., & Budding, T. (2008). New Public management's Current Issues and Future Prospects. *Financial Accountability & Management, 24*(1), 1–13.

Grossi, G., & Soverchia, M. (2011). European Commission Adoption of IPSAS to Reform Financial Reporting. *Abacus, 47*(4), 525–552.

Guthrie, J., & Farneti, F. (2008). GRI Sustainability Reporting by Australian Public Sector Organizations. *Public Money & Management, 28*, 361–366.

Guthrie, J., Olson, O., & Humphrey, C. (1999). Debating Developments in New Public Financial Management: The Limits of Global Theorising and Some New Ways Forward. *Financial Accountability & Management, 15*(3–4), 209–228.

Haller, A. (2016). Value Creation: A Core Concept of Integrated Reporting. In C. Mio (Ed.), *Integrated Reporting*. London: Palgrave Macmillan.

Hood, C. (1991). A Public Management for All Seasons? *Public Administration, 69*(spring), 3–19.

Humphrey, C., O'Dwyer, B., & Unerman, J. (2017). Re-Theorizing the Configuration of Organizational Fields: The IIRC and the Pursuit of 'Enlightened' Corporate Reporting. *Accounting and Business Research, 47*(1), 30–63.

IFAC. (2014). *International Framework: Good Governance in the Public Sector.* Available at https://www.ifac.org/knowledge-gateway/contributing-global-economy/publications/international-framework-good-governance-public-sector

IIRC. (2011). Discussion Paper "*Towards Integrated Reporting – Communicating Value in the 21st Century*". https://integratedreporting.org/wp-content/uploads/2011/09/IR-Discussion-Paper-2011_spreads.pdf.

IIRC. (2013). *The International Integrated Reporting Framework.* IIRC. https://integratedreporting.org/resource/international-ir-framework/

IIRC. (2016). Focusing on value creation in the public sector, http://integratedreporting.org/wp-content/uploads/2016/09/Focusing-on-value-creation-in-the-publicsector-_vFINAL.pdf. Accessed 22 September 2018.

Jacobsson, B., Lægreid, P., & Pedersen, O. K. (2003). *Europeanization and Transnational States: Comparing Nordic Central Governments.* London and New York: Taylor & Francis.

Jones, M. J. (2010). Accounting for the Environment: Towards a Theoretical Perspective for Environmental Accounting and Reporting. *Accounting Forum, 34*, 123–138.

Katsikas, E., Manes-Rossi, F., & Orelli, R. (2017). *Towards Integrated Reporting Accounting Change in the Public Sector*, Switzerland: Springer.

Klijn, E. H. (2012). Public Management and Governance: A Comparison of Two Paradigms to Deal with Modern Complex Problems in D. In L. Faur (Ed.), *The Handbook of Governance* (pp. 201–214). Oxford: Oxford University Press.

Lapsley, I. (1999). Accounting and the New Public Management: Instruments of Substantive Efficiency or a Rationalising Modernity? *Financial Accountability and Management, 15*(3 & 4), 201–207.

Lapsley, I., Mussari, R., & Paulsson, G. (2009). On the Adoption of Accrual Accounting in the Public Sector: A Self-Evident and Problematic Reform. *European Accounting Review, 18*(4), 719–723.

Manes-Rossi, F. (2017). Integrated Reporting and the Public Domain – Engagement with Practice, Foreword in Towards Integrated Reporting: Accounting Change in the Public Sector. In E. Katsikas, F. Manes-Rossi, & R. Orelli (Eds.), *Towards Integrated Reporting Accounting Change in the Public Sector.* Switzerland: Springer.

Meynhardt, T. (2009). Public Value Inside: What Is Public Value Creation? *International Journal of Public Administration, 32*(3), 192–219.

Miller, C. A., & Loman, M. (2014). *Measuring and Reporting Sustainability: The Role of the Public Sector.* White Paper #2, Columbia University Academic Commons.

Olson, O., Guthrie, J., & Humphrey, C. (1998). *Global Warning! Oslo: Cappelen Akademisk Forlag.*
Oprisor, T., Tiron-Tudor, A., & Nistor, C. S. (2016). The Integrated Reporting System: A New Accountability Enhancement Tool for Public Sector Entities. *Audit Financier, 14*(139), 747–760.
Osborne, S. P. (2006). The New Public Governance? *Public Management Review, 8*(3), 377–387.
Schleifer, P. (2013). Orchestrating Sustainability: The Case of European Union Biofuel Governance. *Regulation & Governance, 7*(4), 533–546.
Sinclair, A. (1995). The Chameleon of Accountability: Forms and Discourses. *Accounting, Organizations and Society, 20*(2), 219–237.
UNEP. (2014). *Integrated Governance – A New Model of Governance for Sustainability.* A Report by the Asset Management Working Group of the United Nations Environment Programme Finance. Initiative June. https://www.unepfi.org/publications/investment-publications/integrated-governance-a-new-model-of-governance-for-sustainability-2/
Veltri, S., & Silvestri, A. (2015). The Free State University Integrated Reporting: A Critical Consideration. *Journal of Intellectual Capital, 16*(2), 443–462.
Young, J. (1994). Outlining Regulatory Space: Agenda Issues and the FASB. *Accounting, Organizations and Society, 19*(1), 83–109.

Caroline Aggestam Pontoppidan holds a PhD in Business Administration and is an associate professor at the Department of Accounting and Auditing at the Copenhagen Business School. Her research pertaining to public sector accounting and non-financial reporting takes an interest in the governance and instutionalisation of standards and frameworks in different contexts.

Amanda Sonnerfeldt holds a PhD in Business Law and is a senior lecturer at the Department of Business Administration at the School of Economics and Management, Lund University, Sweden. Her work focuses on transnational standard setting and the regulation of corporate reporting and auditing from both historical and contemporary perspectives.

Assessing Universities' Global Reporting Initiative G4 Sustainability Reports in Concurrence with Stakeholder Inclusiveness

Judith Frei, Melanie Lubinger, and Dorothea Greiling

Motivation and Research Questions

In the public and private sectors, stakeholder accountability demands have increased considerably, leading to many forms of obligatory and voluntary reporting practices. New Public Management (NPM) has been a main driver in the public sector for the increased accountability pressures. The managerial drive of NPM reforms has affected the role and functions of public universities as well as values of higher education (Parker 2011). As a result, universities across the globe are moving towards a market-driven enterprise culture (Parker 2011; Lucas 2006). Universities are confronted with rather pluralistic accountability demands by a broad spectrum of

J. Frei (✉) • M. Lubinger • D. Greiling
Institute of Management Accounting, Johannes Kepler University, Linz, Austria
e-mail: Judith.Frei@jku.at; Melanie.Lubinger@jku.at; Dorothea.Greiling@jku.at

F. Manes-Rossi, R. Levy Orelli (eds.), *New Trends in Public Sector Reporting*, Public Sector Financial Management,
https://doi.org/10.1007/978-3-030-40056-9_3

stakeholders. To address their main stakeholders, universities engage in a variety of accountability activities. Sustainability reporting is one of them.

Sustainability reporting has gained relevance especially amongst multinational private sector companies and to a lesser degree for the public and the non-profit sector (Cho et al. 2015; Manetti and Toccafondi 2014; Guthrie and Farneti 2008). Sustainability reporting is a reaction to stakeholder pressures, resulting in reputational, competitive, political and market opportunities (Burritt and Schaltegger 2010). Proponents of sustainability reporting stress its contribution to an increase in transparency and accountability (James 2015; Malik 2015; Burrell and Roberts 2014; Baker 2010). Critical accounting scholars are sceptical as to whether sustainability reporting does improve stakeholder accountability. It is seen as a public-relation endeavour without substance, a greenwashing attempt or a strategic impression management tactic (Burritt and Schaltegger 2010; Gray 2010; Hopwood 2009). The voluntary nature of sustainability reports (SRs) provides room for presenting an organisation in a too positive way by selective, incomplete and biased disclosures (Cho et al. 2015).

As a remedy for the improving stakeholder accountability of SRs, stakeholder inclusiveness (SI) is advocated by sustainability reporting guidelines. Organisations have to establish a stakeholder engagement (SE) process in order to understand what key stakeholders want to know. A well-advanced SE process is seen as a core requirement for a higher quality of sustainability reporting and towards SRs that focus on stakeholder-material aspects.

However, whether SI leads to improved stakeholder accountability is an open question. On the one hand, meeting the information needs of relevant stakeholders under resource-providing aspects is in line with strategic stakeholder theory. On the other hand, prior research on sustainability reporting practices, using neo-institutionalism as a theoretical lens, provides arguments that SRs are not focused on stakeholder-relevant aspects and therefore stakeholder accountability is most likely low (Shabana et al. 2017; Higgins and Larrinaga 2014; Bebbington et al. 2009).

Concerning the institutional field, this chapter concentrates on universities, which are an interesting field to study because of their complex social mandate (Ntim et al. 2017). Compared to other sectors, studies evaluating the state of the art of sustainability reporting are still at an early stage (Ferrero-Ferrero et al. 2017; Ceulemans et al. 2015). Combining this with a focus on SE is an even lesser addressed topic (Ferrero-Ferrero et al. 2017; Hinson et al. 2015). Universities are also interesting to study because the number of key stakeholders who hold universities accountable has increased considerably in the past decades.

Based on a systematic literature review and an empirical study the following research questions (RQs) are addressed:

RQ 1. What are the main stakeholder groups and topics of universities identified by SE indicators of Global Reporting Initiative (GRI) G4?
RQ 2. To what extent do universities comply with the GRI G4 Guidelines (general and specific standard disclosures) and how are the documented main topics of the SE process covered by G4 reports?

To address RQ1, the findings from a systematic literature review on the key stakeholder groups and their information needs are combined with the results of what is documented in the most recent GRI G4 reports. The GRI Guidelines are chosen because they are still the most widely applied sustainability reporting guidelines and allow a global comparison. To gain an insight into RQ2, prior studies in GRI G4 Guidelines compliance serve as a basis for analysing the extent to which public and private universities of our sample comply with the GRI G4 Guidelines in order to evaluate whether the information disclosure in the SRs is a comprehensive or superficial one.

The remainder of the paper is structured as follows:

In Section "Theoretical Background", strategic stakeholder theory and neo-institutionalism are introduced to identify arguments for and against comprehensive stakeholder accountability in universities' SRs. After a very brief introduction to sustainability reporting frameworks in the university context, Section "Sustainability Reporting at Universities and Prior Empirical Studies" presents the main results of a systematic literature review and discusses main stakeholders, their information needs and the adoption of sustainability reporting guidelines. Section "Methodology, Sample Description and Findings" then presents the research design of the study along with the findings. A concluding assessment of the research questions is presented in Section "Conclusions and Directions for Further Research" together with a short discussion, as well as limitations and implications of this research project.

Theoretical Background

Although there is a broad stream of literature of theoretical reflections on general motives, implementation levels in and across countries and factors driving the implementation of SRs (Shabana et al. 2017; Cho et al. 2015), studies focusing on sustainability reporting in universities are not always theory-based (Sassen and Azizi 2018b; Gamage and Sciulli 2017; Bice and Coates 2016; Larrán et al. 2016; Lopatta and Jaeschke 2014; Ralph and Stubbs 2014; Lozano et al. 2013; Siboni et al. 2013; Fonseca et al. 2011; Lozano 2011). The theory-based ones primarily use three theories concerning the relationship between universities and their stakeholders: stakeholder theory, legitimacy theory and neo-institutionalism (Brusca et al. 2018; Larrán et al. 2019; Sassen and Azizi 2018a; Dagilienė and Mykolaitienė 2016; Hinson et al. 2015; Larrán et al. 2012; Mainardes et al. 2012).

In this chapter, strategic stakeholder theory and neo-institutionalism are used for formulating contradictory expectations about high or low guideline compliance and for assessing the extent to which SRs are guided by the results from the SE process.

Strategic stakeholder theory, introduced by Freeman (1984) to a wider audience, is used for making a pro-argument. Strategic stakeholder theory stresses that a cooperative relationship of an organisation with its most relevant stakeholders is essential (Freeman et al. 2004). In strategic stakeholder theory, the stakeholder focus is limited to co-operations based on economic usefulness. An excellent relationship with key stakeholders creates a win-win situation that unlocks an additional potential for value creation (Harrison et al. 2010; Freeman et al. 2004). Two essential preconditions for stakeholder-oriented SRs (in the university sector and outside) are that the reporting entity knows who the most relevant stakeholders are and understands the main information needs these key stakeholders require. Meeting the information needs of key stakeholders is an integral part of strategic stakeholder management. In line with strategic stakeholder theory, it can be argued that SRs of universities should be focused on the information needs of key stakeholders. To know who the key stakeholders are is one main aim of the SE process; the second aim is to know what information key stakeholders regard as relevant. The GRI G4 Guidelines demand that the preparer lists the information needs and classifies them as low, medium or highly relevant. Moreover, SRs should be focused on the stakeholder-relevant aspects in order to unlock the value potential suggested by strategic stakeholder theory. Under the resource-securing aspects, it is therefore essential that universities' SRs show high compliance with the information needs of key stakeholder groups. This reasoning is in line with the 'outside-in' approach of Burritt and Schaltegger (2010) towards sustainability reporting.

Knowing and prioritising the information needs of key stakeholders is not a simple task for universities because substantial changes in the university sector have led to a situation in which universities are nowadays confronted with a wide range of heterogeneous accountability demands of internal and external stakeholders. The stakeholder audiences which hold universities' management accountable have increased considerably (e.g., ministries, other public research funders, private foundations, current and potential students and staff, business partners, employers of graduates, alumni) in the last two decades (Ntim et al. 2017).

For a counterargument resulting in low stakeholder orientation and low stakeholder accountability, neo-institutionalism is used. This theory focuses on the influences of societal pressures on organisations. Coercive, normative and mimetic isomorphisms are drivers for complying with societal pressures for legitimacy and survival reasons (Higgins and Larrinaga 2014; DiMaggio and Powell 1991). Coercive isomorphism requires compliance with external norms imposed by the state and other powerful actors with sanctioning rights. In the case of normative isomorphism, professional standards are the driver for management practice (DiMaggio and Powell 1991). When organisations imitate seemingly more successful peer organisations, DiMaggio and Powell (1991) label such behaviour as mimetic isomorphism.

So far sustainability reporting and in particular guideline-compliant SRs are still an emerging practice for universities, although there have been a few voluntary endeavours towards SRs. The institutionalisation process of sustainability reporting is not well advanced. In addition, universities are starting to integrate information on selected aspects of their sustainability performance, mostly in an unsystematic way. In the past years, the guideline compliance has been low. Sustainability reporting is not yet a relevant professional practice for universities. A decent position in international ranking or accreditations in business schools is much more important than sustainability reporting for most universities under the strategic position aspects. Mimetic isomorphism requires that the non-complying universities regard it as risky not to adopt this practice. This can also be ruled out due to the low number of universities publishing SRs. Coercive isomorphism requires external stakeholders with powerful sanctioning rights. Only the Spanish province of Andalusia has introduced an obligation to implement SRs in the university sector. Sustainability reporting is a voluntary endeavour in nearly all regions of the world and sustainability standard setters have de facto no sanctioning power. Therefore, coercive isomorphism can also be ruled out as a strong pressure.

Summing up these counterarguments, it is likely that sustainability reporting guidelines can be classified as a weak pressure and therefore most likely lead to low compliance. Stakeholder orientation, and in consequence stakeholder accountability, is most probably superficial and far removed from holistic stakeholder accountability. The GRI Guideline compliance in this case will most likely be low.

Sustainability Reporting at Universities and Prior Empirical Studies

Universities play a fundamental role in contributing to a more sustainable society and in the integration of sustainable development in society. Sustainability assessment and reporting are regarded by some authors as a relevant part of sustainability efforts by universities (Alonso-Almeida et al. 2015; Lozano et al. 2015; Lozano 2006). For evaluating the content of universities' SRs, quite a few normative assessment frameworks exist (for an overview, see Larrán et al. 2016; Ceulemans et al. 2015). Frequently referred to university sector–specific assessment frameworks are those by Lozano (2006), Fonseca et al. (2011) and frameworks which augment the GRI Framework with additional sector-specific indicators (e.g., Lopatta and Jaeschke 2014; Sassen et al. 2014). All sector-specific frameworks have the disadvantage that they were developed in a particular institutional context, predominately in North America and Europe, which makes them less suitable for international comparison. Only the GRI and the International Integrated Reporting Council (IIRC) have developed voluntary worldwide reporting guidelines, which are also used in the university sector. The drawback of both is that they are not sector-specific.

The majority of empirical studies focusing on the status quo of sustainability or integrated reporting in universities use various versions of the GRI Guidelines (Larrán et al. 2016). Despite the rising relevance of integrated reporting, the GRI Guidelines are still the most widely used ones for preparing and assessing the current state of an organisation's economic, environmental and social performance for universities (Alonso-Almeida et al. 2015; Lopatta and Jaeschke 2014; Lozano 2006).

To achieve transparent, stakeholder-oriented accountability, the GRI Guidelines define reporting principles concerning the report quality and report content (GRI 2013). The principles for defining the content of SRs consist of SI, sustainability context, materiality and completeness. To apply the principle of SI, GRI requires that "the organization should identify its stakeholders, and explain how it has responded to their reasonable expectations and interests" (GRI 2013: 16). The importance of SE within universities is also stressed by scholars and is seen as a demanding process due to the plethora of key stakeholders, which might also be a barrier for integrating sustainability in universities (Blanco-Portela et al. 2017; Disterheft et al. 2015).

Prior Empirical Studies

Empirical studies on the state of the art of sustainability reporting practices of universities are on the rise, but so far, it is still an under-researched field as the systematic literature review resulted only in 22 studies. The search period was from 2000 to 2018, limited to peer-reviewed English journal articles.

Content-wise three main clusters were identified, namely single case studies on the SI, studies addressing stakeholder expectations and studies on the guideline compliance of SRs. While the first two clusters refer to RQ1, the third cluster provides some insight into RQ2.

SI in Selected Sustainability Reports/Integrated Reports (Three Studies)

Regarding RQ1, the literature review revealed three single case studies dealing with SI. Brusca et al. (2018) analysed the implementation of sustainability and integrated reporting at the University of Cadiz by applying the framework of Secundo et al. (2016). As the most important stakeholder group, the university's social council could be identified as a representative of other stakeholders with the aim of enhancing competitiveness and attaining third mission objectives. In addition, auditors represented an important stakeholder group, based on the fact that they supported the integrated reporting implementation process. According to the Spanish case, SI plays a key role in the value-creation and strategic-management processes. Veltri and Silvestri (2015) investigated the integrated report (IR) of the Free State University in South Africa to answer the question as to whether intellectual and non-intellectual capital content was included and interconnected within one single report to enhance stakeholders' information needs. Due to the results, content elements of the IIRC Framework were mentioned but there was neither any capital-specific reporting nor any reporting on the interconnectedness of the capitals. When defining report content, managers of the university did not consider stakeholder interests; furthermore, there were no references concerning a stakeholder dialogue. Lozano et al. (2013) described the SR preparation process of the University of Leeds as an 'inside-out' approach. It was a management decision not to consider stakeholders' interests.

A common finding of the three identified single case studies is that different stakeholder groups should be engaged to develop and validate SRs, but with the exception of the Andalusian case, external stakeholders' interests were not considered in a systematic way.

Internal and External Stakeholder Expectations (Five Studies)

Referring to the main topics identified by SE, five studies were found. Ferrero-Ferrero et al. (2017) analysed the SE techniques in SRs in depth. Surveys, stakeholder workshops and panels have been mostly applied by more than the half of the analysed G4 SRs. For an in-depth analysis of stakeholder expectations, a case study was conducted in a Spanish university. Economic and environmental issues, labour practices and decent work, human rights, local communities and ethical issues were the most mentioned expectations of stakeholders. Furthermore, the compliance rate between the expectations of internal stakeholders and the documented material aspects has been analysed. In Andalusia, sustainability reporting of universities is obligatory. In a working group with senior managers of eight public Andalusian universities, stakeholder material aspects for a sustainability assessment and reporting tool were identified (Larrán et al. 2016). A total of 155 material aspects clustered into seven categories were found: corporate governance, students, staff, society, environment, companies and continuous improvement. The categories of corporate governance and environment showed the highest relevance, followed by students, staff and society. In a prior study, Larrán et al. (2012) analysed expectations of stakeholder groups of ten public universities in Andalusia. All stakeholder groups required more information on governance of universities, employability and value education for students, universities' commitment to society, transferability of university research to companies and the allocation of resources. Ralph and Stubbs (2014) investigated factors that influence the integration of environmental sustainability at four English and four Australian universities. Stakeholder pressure was identified as the second most important driver for providing information on the environmental sustainability in the eight SRs. In the analysis of students' expectations at 11 public universities in Portugal, the 'academic level of demand' or employability played the most important role, but also improvement of partnership with the university staff, employability, personal fulfilment and the current environmental conditions were mentioned (Mainardes et al. 2012).

A common finding of all five papers is that stakeholder information needs are quite extensive. The four papers focusing on more than one stakeholder group also revealed the great heterogeneity of stakeholder expectations.

Based on the systematic literature review the following can be concluded with respect to RQ1. The small number of studies shows that this is still an under-researched field. Prior literature primarily focuses on the plethora and variety of information needs of key stakeholders. Studies analysing SE-activities of universities and empirically investigating and ranking the main stakeholder groups and topics within universities are far less frequent.

(Coverage) Analysis of SRs/IRs Based on the GRI Guidelines (14 Studies)

Moving on to RQ2, few studies exist which focus on a quantitative guideline compliance. As displayed in Table 1, ten studies report on total coverage rates (TCRs) or specific coverage rates of performance dimensions, while two out of them provide additional insights into SE.

Table 1 Studies reporting on TCRs of specific coverage rates

Author(s) (year)	*TCR*	*Economic*	*Environmental*	*Social*	*Educational*	*SE*
Fonseca et al. (2011)	36%	19%	63%	21%	25%	57%
Lozano (2011)		11%	17%	7%	6%	
Lopatta and Jaeschke (2014)	26%	25%	29%	14%	30%	
Sassen et al. (2014)		40%	31%	11%	27%	
Hinson et al. (2015)	57%					67%
Romolini et al. (2015)		64%	49%	53%		
Gamage and Sciulli (2017)		9%	63%	31%	52%	
Larrán et al. (2019)	44%	54%	41%	44%		
Sassen and Azizi (2018a)		4%	15%	1%	13%	
Sassen and Azizi (2018b)		11%	30%	7%	21%	

Additionally, four studies provide insights into selected aspects, for example, selective triple bottom line (TBL) indicators of universities' SRs (Bice and Coates 2016) or selected TBL indicators of the GRI G3 Guidelines in Lithuania's tertiary sector institutions (Dagilienė and Mykolaitienė 2016). In nine Italian university SRs, Siboni et al. (2013) found a low consistency with the GRI Guidelines. Italian universities applied Italian and international guidelines. Zorio-Grima et al. (2018) found that nearly one third of 49 public Spanish universities reported on the GRI indicators, but only 6 out of 49 registered their reports to the GRI.

The (quantitative) coverage of SE in SRs was an issue in four studies in this cluster. Sustainability reporting is seen as a communication instrument to satisfy stakeholder demands (Sassen and Azizi 2018a, b; Lozano 2011) with the ability to improve stakeholder relations (Gamage and Sciulli 2017) and to lower information asymmetries (Lopatta and Jaeschke 2014). Bice and Coates (2016) revealed that all ten universities included in the analysis provided information on internal and external stakeholders. Hinson et al. (2015) found that four out of six universities included information on their SE process. Four of the nine examined Italian universities engaged with their stakeholders at different levels within the sustainability reporting process (Siboni et al. 2013). Fonseca et al. (2011) state that four out of seven analysed universities reported on SE. Coercive pressure from resource-providing societal key stakeholders was mentioned as a possible reason for including information about sustainability in annual reports of universities (Hinson et al. 2015; Fonseca et al. 2011).

Summing up, the following can be concluded: Although the potential of sustainability and integrated reporting for the improvement of stakeholder accountability is emphasised in many papers of the systematic literature review, detailed information on the SE process and SI is not well addressed, with the exception of one study which analyses SE techniques, stakeholder groups and stakeholder expectations (Ferrero-Ferrero et al. 2017). Studies analysing universities which address main stakeholder groups and main communication topics are scarce. Only selected aspects of the information needs of stakeholder groups were analysed and the stakeholder focus of the studies was unbalanced. The findings of Ceulemans et al. (2015) that the importance of SE within the sustainability reporting process is under-researched is still valid. There is no study analysing the fit between the documented topics and the coverage rates of universities' SRs in the SE process analysed. What is missing is a systematic analysis of the main stakeholder groups as well as additional information on the communication topics universities focus on in their stakeholder dialogue. Additionally, there is no study analysing whether the relevant topics identified in the SE process are indeed reported in the GRI G4 SRs. Addressing this research gap is a relevant issue if one recalls that nowadays universities have to position themselves strategically within a broader group of stakeholders.

Methodology, Sample Description and Findings

Methodology and Sample Description

The assessment of SRs is based on G4 Guidelines. The sample consists of 33 SRs in line with G4 that have been uploaded until April 2018. Therefore, we excluded all other kinds of SRs of universities that are not in line with the GRI G4 Framework.

Regarding the geography of the analysed universities, they are distributed in the following way: two universities are from North America, eight from Europe, eight from Asia and two from Australia. Twenty universities are private and 13 are public. Besides this, the numbers of students per analysed university varies from 42% under 15,000 students to 49% between 15,001 and 55,000 students, to 9% over 55,000 students. Of these, 36% were ranked by one of the following major ranking institutions: Times Higher Education (THE), QS World University Ranking (QS)], Academic Ranking of World Universities (ARWU).

For empirically investigating the two research questions, a mixed-method research design was used. It included two different content analyses—a qualitative one and a quantitative one—followed by a correlation analysis. Two persons coded them independently and the discrepancies were discussed and reconciled.

A qualitative content analysis was completed to analyse the documented SE of universities based on the reported G4 SE indicators. For this the G4-24 to G4-27 indicators of the 33 SRs were analysed. These indicators give an overview of the SE activities of the universities including a list of addressed stakeholders and the main topics universities communicate to their stakeholders. In a first step of the qualitative content analysis, the stated topics and stakeholders of each university were identified. In a second step, the stakeholders and identified topics were clustered and summarised into stakeholder groups and main communication topics.

In the quantitative content analysis, compliance rates for the Standard Disclosures of G4 SRs as well as for the Specific Standard Disclosures such as economic, environmental and social with its subcategories of labour and decent work, human rights, society and product responsibility were calculated. For each category, a compliance level was calculated as shown in the following example.

Example: Category Economic
Number of economic performance indicators: 13
University 1 reports 7 of 13
Compliance level: $7/13*100 = 53.85\%$
The classification of the compliance levels is the following: no coverage = 0, > 0–33.33% = 1, > 33.33–66.66% = 2 and > 66.66% = 3.

In a final step, a correlation analysis between the main topics universities communicate to their stakeholders and the compliance rate was performed. This was done to evaluate the fit between the topics documented in G4-26 and G4-27 and the indicator-based parts of the SRs. To evaluate this fit, the indicators and their extension of coverage in the form of the calculated coverage rate of the GRI reports were used. For strategic management the General Standard Disclosures—for finance the coverage rate of the category economic and for sustainability the TCR that is in line with the triple-bottom-line principle—were used. The other high-scoring SE topics identified, such as research information, education programmes and campus life, could not be included in the regression analysis because GRI G4 does not cover these topics.

To test the correlation, the following hypotheses were formulated:

H0: There is no correlation between the two groups. The identified main communication topic has no influence on the coverage of this topic in the report content of G4 SRs.

H1: There is a correlation between the two groups. The identified main communication topic has an influence on the coverage of this topic in the report content of G4 SRs.

To interpret the results of these correlations, the Spearman correlation coefficient was used. If the p value is under the significance level of 0.05

the null hypothesis is rejected and a correlation between the two groups exists. A positive correlation means that the extension of reporting on the identified main communication topic in the stakeholder process of G4 SRs is aligned with the value of this topic according to the SE process. For example, if an identified main communication topic of the SE process such as strategic management issues, sustainability and finance is valued as highly important, the coverage of this topic in the SR is also at a high level. If there is a negative correlation or no correlation, the identified main communication topics of the SE process are not reported accordingly in the SRs.

Findings

Concerning the main stakeholder groups addressed by certain universities, the analysis shows that 93.33% of the investigated universities report to the university assembly. This group includes the head of the university, head of departments as well as the university council. Other frequently mentioned stakeholder groups are university staff (scientific and non-scientific), students and government. Only 36.67% of the analysed universities mentioned parents and public media partners (33.33%) as important stakeholders.

The most important communication topics that are addressed to the certain stakeholder groups are issues concerning strategic management like vision, strategic objectives as well as upcoming strategic changes of the reporting universities. Information on sustainability, education programmes, research information and campus life are also very relevant topics in the communication of universities towards their main stakeholders. Other important topics that have been identified are finance and legal issues.

Considering the results of the quantitative content analysis, there are differences within certain categories. In terms of the General Standard Disclosure compliance, which includes strategic management information as well as information on the universities' profile, it can be stated that 30% of the universities have a rate between 80% and 100%, 30% a rate between 79% and 60%, and 40% a rate between 59% and 40%. No university that was analysed has a coverage rate of the General Standard Disclosures under 40%.

We further analysed the coverage rates within the six GRI categories. The results are represented in the form of pie charts and tables. There are pie charts for every GRI category that show the detailed coverage of each indicator. The additional tables show the general coverage of the category.

A criterion for this analysis was the question of whether the investigated universities report more than 50% of indicators of certain categories. As for the Economic category, 46.67% of the universities that have been investigated report more than 50% of all indicators. Eleven out of the 33 (33.33%) universities report more than 50% of the indicators in the Environmental category. As for the Social – Labour Practices and Decent Work category, 50% of all reports have a coverage rate of over 50%. In terms of the categories of Social – Human Rights, Society and Product Responsibility, 26.67% of the investigated universities report more than 50% of the indicators. Summing up, this means that 10 out of 33 universities use more than 50% of the stated indicators of the GRI Framework and 23 universities report less than 50% in these three categories (Human Rights, Society, Product Responsibility). Consequently, the categories with the top coverage rates are the Standard Disclosures, and in the social dimension, the subgroup Labour Practices and Decent Work followed by the Economic and Environmental performance.

The TCR of the analysed SRs are the following: 8 universities (24.24%) have a coverage rate between 80% and 100%, 2 universities (6.06%) between 79% and 60%, 4 universities (12.12%) between 59% and 40% of all indicators, 16 universities (48.48%) between 39% and 20% and 3 universities (9.09%) report less than 20% of the indicators from the G4 line.

However, the mere quantitative coverage rates do not allow an assessment if the main communication topics that are identified in the SE process are in fact reported in the G4 SRs. The correlation analysis of the main communication topics identified of the SE process had no statistical significance. The main communication topics of the SE process are not reported at an adequate coverage level in the G4 SRs. Therefore, the G4 SR is not a main reporting tool for the identified topics of the SE process.

Conclusions and Directions for Further Research

The findings are based on the results of a systematic literature review and an analysis of the most recent 33 GRI G4 SRs worldwide uploaded in the GRI database. The low number of relevant prior studies as well as the fact that only 33 reports were uploaded clearly limits the generalisability of the results. Therefore, our results only provide a first insight into an under-researched field.

With respect to RQ1, the results of the systematic literature review showed that prior studies focused primarily on information needs of university stakeholders. Less systematic was the evaluation of main stakeholder groups. Moreover, the analysis of the relevant stakeholder groups had a narrow focus because they were limited either to one single case (Brusca et al. 2018) or to a small sample number of universities (Ferrero-Ferrero et al. 2017). Although the multitude and the interests of different stakeholder groups are emphasised in the studies, only Brusca et al. (2018) identified the university's social council as the main stakeholder group and a key driver for sustainability reporting. Ferrero-Ferrero et al. (2017) identified stakeholder groups of ten SRs worldwide to answer the question of whether material aspects mentioned by internal stakeholders are aligned with the documented aspects in the SRs. Our own empirical study showed that universities clearly document who their main stakeholders are. The findings reveal that a mixture of internal and external stakeholder groups are in line with the expectations of the heterogeneity of main stakeholder groups in the university context. Seven different stakeholder groups were classified in the analysed 33 SRs as highly relevant. While the systematic literature review identified a rather unstructured and wide list of potential information needs concerning topics such as corporate governance and environment, employability or university quality standards for degrees (e.g. Larrán et al. 2012, 2016; Mainardes et al. 2012), our own study showed that universities are able to identify main communication topics with their main stakeholders as required by the GRI G4 Guidelines. The topics are a mixture of general management topics (strategic management issues, sustainability, finance and legal issues) and university-specific aspects (education programmes, research information and campus life). Information on sustainability is regarded as highly relevant. A caveat is that the reports are quite vague regarding what is meant by sustainability.

Regarding RQ2, the results are far less positive. The systematic literature review revealed ten studies analysing quantitative guideline compliance by reporting on total or special coverage rates. Two studies out of them report on SE (Hinson et al. 2015; Fonseca et al. 2011). None of these studies analysed the coverage of main communication topics of the SE process. Our empirical study showed that the coverage of these categories in the 33 analysed G4 SRs is not in line with the relevance of the main communication topics identified in the SE process. There is no statistical correlation between the relevance of main communication topics which universities document as the outcome in the SE process and the coverage of these topics in the analysed G4 SRs. Therefore, the main topics of the SE process that are addressed are not covered in an adequate way in the G4 SRs.

Besides this, the findings indicate that sustainability reporting, in particular the guideline-driven one, is still in its early stage in the university sector. The literature review revealed TCRs and coverage rates of selected performance indicators are on average less than 50% (with the exception of the study of Hinson et al. 2015, with an average of 57%). This is in line with our result: in our global sample of all GRI G4 registered SRs, 19 out of 33 universities have a TCR of less than 40%. The findings can be interpreted as a clear sign that SRs of universities are far removed from comprehensive guideline compliance. While low levels of coverage might be tolerated for the time being, it might fire back if the practice matures in the sector. Then selective reporting might be seen as a greenwashing attempt.

As shown by the systematic literature review, the small number of SRs available for an analysis is something we share with other quantitative content analyses in the university sector (between 6 and 28 reports). Only Larrán et al. (2019) had a larger sample size, as they analysed 138 SRs published from 58 universities on the GRI website, following the G3, G3.1 or G4 Guidelines.

Theoretically, the reporting behaviour is more in line with the expectations of neo-institutionalism than with strategic stakeholder theory, which stresses the value-adding potential of a stakeholder-oriented reporting as an essential part of the stakeholder management process. The small number of reports available and the poor coverage rates of the three triple-bottom-line dimensions are signs that sustainability reporting is not an institutionalised practice.

A closer look at the three isomorphistic pressures might give some indications as to why this is the case, despite the societal relevance universities should attribute towards a more sustainable world. Due to the low implementation rates, universities are not under any mimetic pressure to imitate sustainability reporting as a practice implemented by successful peers. The coercive pressure of GRI (and other sustainability reporting standards) is very low because GRI does not have any direct sanctioning power if universities show low compliance. So far, universities are not under any legal pressures to implement sustainability reporting in line with GRI. Although universities classify seven different stakeholder groups as highly relevant and sustainability is classified as a highly relevant communication topic, stakeholder pressures are not strong enough to cover sustainability issues sufficiently. Neither national legislators nor main funders require SRs. Powerful resource-providers use their power to demand accountability reports from universities tailor-made for their specific information needs. The accountability requirements of public funders of universities vary from country to country, sometimes with different funding categories, for example if it is funding for research or for student programmes. The idea to develop a sector-neutral worldwide relevant sustainability reporting standard might not work under the very specific accountability requirements powerful university funders have. The scope of GRI is likely too broad for meeting the specific information need of powerful stakeholders of universities.

In comparison with other voluntary reputation signals universities can select from, GRI is a weak one. While under reputation-enhancing aspects, best performing accreditation requirements for universities have quite high entrance barriers and require obligatory peer visits, which can result in no accreditation or frequently lead to accreditation with recommendations, the implementation costs of GRI are low, especially if one takes into account the low levels of guideline compliance.

From strategic stakeholder management perspectives, the low focus of the SRs on the topics, which universities document as highly relevant for their communications with main stakeholders, is problematic. Stakeholder orientation is not taken seriously enough. While universities abide by fulfilling a certain coverage rate of GRI SE indicators, this is not mirrored in other parts of the SRs. Universities might not be clear about the role SRs could play in the sustainability performance related to the communication process. To comply with the GRI, G4-24 to G4-27 indicators do not lead sufficiently to SRs addressing the main communication topics.

For improving the relevance of SRs in universities, standard setters of GRI SRs might want to consider whether their sector- and industry-neutral approach leads to the desired outcomes. If standard setters are convinced of the need of a high-quality framework for university sustainability reporting, it might be worthwhile considering the development of a sector-specific university supplement.

On a more fundamental level, the question can be raised as to whether sustainability reporting is an appropriate instrument for universities. The benefits of sustainability reporting are far less obvious for universities than in the case of stock-listed companies where sustainability reporting has become a major trend.

Our study gives rise to a number of future research areas. Future research could investigate the reasons and motives for such a low fit between the main communication topics and the SRs. This would require interviews with preparers and powerful stakeholders under resource-providing aspects. Furthermore, our study focuses on universities' SRs based on G4 Guidelines. Only a very small number of universities across the globe prepare and publish SRs based on GRI Guidelines. It might be worthwhile to investigate if sector-specific guidelines lead to higher adoption and compliance rates in those areas which are regarded by the main stakeholders as highly relevant.

As our study has focused on the documented outcome of the SE process and therefore only on the preparer-declared outcome, it might also be interesting to investigate the quality of the SE process from the perspective of the main users of SRs.

References

Alonso-Almeida, M. D. M., Marimon, F., & Casani, F. (2015). Diffusion of Sustainability Reporting in Universities: Current Situation and Future Perspectives. *Journal of Cleaner Production, 106*(12), 144–154.

Baker, M. (2010). Re-conceiving Managerial Capture. *Accounting, Auditing & Accountability Journal, 23*(7), 847–867.

Bebbington, J., Higgins, C., & Frame, B. (2009). Initiating Sustainable Development Reporting: Evidence from New Zealand. *Accounting, Auditing and Accountability Journal, 22*(4), 588–625.

Bice, S., & Coates, H. (2016). University Sustainability Reporting: Taking Stock of Transparency. *Tertiary Education and Management, 22*(1), 1–18.

Blanco-Portela, N., Benayas, J., Pertierra, L. R., & Lozano, R. (2017). Towards the Integration of Sustainability in Higher Education Institutions: A Review of Drivers of and Barriers to Organizational Change and Their Comparison Against Those Found of Companies. *Journal of Cleaner Production, 166*, 563–578.

Brusca, I., Labrador, M., & Larran, M. (2018). The Challenge of Sustainability and Integrated Reporting at Universities: A Case Study. *Journal of Cleaner Production, 188*, 347–354.

Burrell, N. E., & Roberts, R. E. (2014). The Public Interest Imperative in Corporate Sustainability Reporting Research. *Accounting and The Public Interest, 14*, 79–86.

Burritt, R. L., & Schaltegger, S. (2010). Sustainability Accounting and Reporting: Fad or Trend? *Accounting, Auditing & Accountability Journal, 23*(7), 829–846.

Ceulemans, K., Lozano, R., & Alonso-Almeida, M. D. M. (2015). Sustainability Reporting in Higher Education: Interconnecting the Reporting Process and Organisational Change Management for Sustainability. *Sustainability, 7*(7), 8881–8903.

Cho, C. H., Laine, M., Roberts, R. W., & Rodrigue, M. (2015). Organized Hypocrisy, Organizational Façades, and Sustainability Reporting. *Accounting, Organizations and Society, 40*, 78–94.

Dagilienė, L., & Mykolaitienė, V. (2016). Sustainability Reporting in the Higher Education Sector – Case Study of Lithuania. *ZögU/Journal for Public and Nonprofit Services, 39*(1–2), 163–174.

DiMaggio, P. J., & Powell, W. W. (1991). The Iron Cage Revisited: Institutional Isomorphism and Collective Rationality. In W. W. Powell & P. J. DiMaggio (Eds.), *The New Institutionalism in Organizational Analysis* (pp. 63–82). Chicago: University of Chicago Press.

Disterheft, A., Caeiro, S., Azeiteiro, U. M., & Leal Filho, W. (2015). Sustainable Universities – A Study of Critical Success Factors for Participatory Approaches. *Journal of Cleaner Production, 106*, 11–21.

Ferrero-Ferrero, I., Fernández-Izquierdo, M. Á., Muñoz-Torres, M. J., & Bellés-Colomer, L. (2017). Stakeholder Engagement in Sustainability Reporting in Higher Education, an Analysis of Key Internal Stakeholders' Expectations. *International Journal of Sustainability in Higher Education, 19*(2), 313–336.

Fonseca, A., Macdonald, A., Dandy, E., & Valenti, P. (2011). The State of Sustainability Reporting at Canadian Universities. *International Journal of Sustainability in Higher Education, 12*(1), 22–40.

Freeman, R. E. (1984). *Strategic Management: A Stakeholder Approach*. Cambridge: Cambridge University Press.

Freeman, R. E., Wicks, A. C., & Pramar, P. (2004). Stakeholder Theory and "The Corporate Objective Revisited". *Organization Science, 15*(3), 364–369.

Gamage, P., & Sciulli, N. (2017). Sustainability Reporting by Australian Universities. *Australian Journal of Public Administration, 76*(2), 187–203.

Global Reporting Initiative GRI. (2013). *G4 Sustainability Reporting Guidelines*. https://www.globalreporting.org/. Accessed 9 Jan 2019.

Gray, R. (2010). Is Accounting for Sustainability Actually Accounting for Sustainability and How Would We Know? An Exploration of Narratives of Organisations and the Planet. *Accounting, Organizations and Society, 35*(1), 47–62.

Guthrie, J., & Farneti, F. (2008). GRI Sustainability Reporting by Australian Public Sector Organizations. *Public Money & Management, 28*(6), 361–366.

Harrison, J. S., Bosse, D. A., & Phillips, R. A. (2010). Managing for Stakeholders, Stakeholder Utility Function and Competitive Advantage. *Strategic Management Journal, 31*(1), 58–74.

Higgins, C., & Larrinaga, C. (2014). Sustainability Reporting. Insights from Institutional Theory. In J. Bebbington, J. Unerman, & B. O'Dwyer (Eds.), *Sustainability Accounting and Accountability* (pp. 273–289). London: Routledge.

Hinson, R., Gyabea, A., & Ibrahim, M. (2015). Sustainability Reporting Among Ghanaian Universities. *Communication, 41*(1), 22–42.

Hopwood, A. G. (2009). Accounting and the Environment. *Accounting, Organization and Society, 34*(3), 433–439.

James, M. L. (2015). The Benefits of Sustainability and Integrated Reporting: An Investigation of Accounting Majors' Perceptions. *Journal of Legal, Ethical and Regulatory Issues, 18*(1), 1–20.

Larrán, M. J., López Hernández, A., & Calzado Cejas, M. Y. (2012). Stakeholder Expectations in Spanish Public Universities: An Empirical Study. *International Journal of Humanities and Social Science, 2*(10), 1–13.

Larrán, M. J., Madueño, J. H., Calzado, Y., & Andrades, J. (2016). A Proposal for Measuring Sustainability in Universities: A Case Study of Spain. *International Journal of Sustainability in Higher Education, 17*(5), 671–697.

Larrán, M. J., Peña, F. J. A., & Madueño, J. H. (2019). An Analysis of University Sustainability Reports from the GRI Database: An Examination of Influential Variables. *Journal of Environmental Planning and Management, 62*(6), 1019–1044.

Lopatta, K., & Jaeschke, R. (2014). Sustainability Reporting at German and Austrian Universities. *International Journal of Education Economics and Development, 5*(1), 66–90.

Lozano, R. (2006). A Tool for a Graphical Assessment of Sustainability in Universities (GASU). *Journal of Cleaner Production, 14*(9–11), 963–972.

Lozano, R. (2011). The State of Sustainability Reporting in Universities. *International Journal of Sustainability in Higher Education, 12*(1), 67–78.

Lozano, R., Llobet, J., & Tideswell, G. (2013). The Process of Assessing and Reporting Sustainability at Universities: Preparing the Report of the University of Leeds. *Revista Internacional de Tecnología, Sostenibilidad y Humanismo, 8*, 85–112.

Lozano, R., Ceulemans, K., Alonso-Almeida, M., Huisingh, D., Lozano, F. J., Waas, T., & Hugé, J. (2015). A Review of Commitment and Implementation of Sustainable Development in Higher Education: Results from a Worldwide Survey. *Journal of Cleaner Production, 108*, 1–18.

Lucas, L. (2006). *The Research Game in Academic Life*. Maidenhead: Open University Press.

Mainardes, E., Raposo, M., & Alves, H. (2012). Public University Students' Expectations: An Empirical Study Based on the Stakeholders Theory. *Transylvanian Review of Administrative Sciences, 8*(35), 173–196.

Malik, M. (2015). Value-Enhancing Capabilities of CSR: A Brief Review of Contemporary Literature. *Journal of Business Ethics, 127*(2), 419–438.

Manetti, G., & Toccafondi, S. (2014). Defining the Content of Sustainability Reports in Nonprofit Organizations: Do Stakeholders Really Matter? *Journal of Nonprofit & Public Sector Marketing, 26*(1), 35–61.

Ntim, C. G., Soobaroyon, T., & Broad, M. J. (2017). Governance Structures Voluntary Disclosures and Public Accountability: The Case of UK Higher Education Organisations. *Accounting, Auditing and Accountability Journal, 20*(1), 65–118.

Parker, L. (2011). University Corporatization: Driving Redefinition. *Critical Perspectives on Accounting, 22*(3), 434–450.

Ralph, M., & Stubbs, W. (2014). Integrating Environmental Sustainability into Universities. *Higher Education, 67*(1), 71–90.

Romolini, A., Fissi, S., & Gori, E. (2015). Quality Disclosure in Sustainability Reporting: Evidence from Universities. *Transylvanian Review of Administrative Science, 11*(44), 196–218.

Sassen, R., & Azizi, L. (2018a). Voluntary Disclosure of Sustainability Reports by Canadian Universities. *Journal of Business Economics, 88*(1), 97–137.

Sassen, R., & Azizi, L. (2018b). Assessing Sustainability Reports of US Universities. *International Journal of Sustainability in Higher Education, 19*(7), 1158–1184.

Sassen, R., Dienes, D., & Beth, C. (2014). Nachhaltigkeitsberichterstattung deutscher Hochschulen. *Zeitschrift für Umweltpolitik & Umweltrecht, 37*(3), 258–277.

Secundo, G., Dumay, J., Schiuma, G., & Passiante, G. (2016). Managing Intellectual Capital Through a Collective Intelligence Approach. *Journal of Intellectual Capital, 17*(2), 298–319.

Shabana, K. M., Buchholtz, A. K., & Carroll, A. B. (2017). The Institutionalization of Corporate Social Responsibility Reporting. *Business & Society, 56*(8), 107–1135.

Siboni, B., Del Sordo, C., & Pazzi, S. (2013). Sustainability Reporting in State Universities: An Investigation of Italian Pioneering Practices. *International Journal of Social Ecology and Sustainable Development, 4*(2), 1–15.

Veltri, S., & Silvestri, A. (2015). The Free State University Integrated Reporting: A Critical Consideration. *Journal of Intellectual Capital, 16*(2), 443–462.

Zorio-Grima, A., Sierra-Gracía, L., & Garcia-Benau, M. A. (2018). Sustainability Reporting Experience by Universities: A Causal Configuration Approach. *International Journal of Sustainability in Higher Education, 19*(2), 337–352.

Judith Frei is a researcher and senior lecturer at the Institute of Management Accounting at the Johannes Kepler University, Linz, Austria.

Melanie Lubinger is a researcher and university assistant at the Institute of Management Accounting at the Johannes Kepler University, Linz, Austria.

Dorothea Greiling is a full-professor and head of the Institute of Management Accounting at the Johannes Kepler University, Linz, Austria.

Public Sector Reporting: Lessons Learnt from Participatory Budgeting

Peter C. Lorson and Ellen Haustein

Introduction

In their model of public financial management paradigms, Xu and Chan (2016) describe a move to stronger citizen orientation: Whereas the new public management (NPM) model is focused on the public agency, the more recent stakeholder model relies on networks of public and business institutions and citizens. According to Beckett and King (2002, p. 470), contemporary administrative practices and perspectives can be discussed on a spectrum of two ends, between "'radical' movements like citizen-based governance and the more conservative movements like new public management (NPM) and reinvention". The NPM movement maintains a

Both authors were coordinators of the EU-funded project 'Developing and Implementing European Public Sector Accounting modules' (DiEPSAm) and currently lead the EU-project 'Empowering Participatory Budgeting in the Baltic Sea Region' (EmPaci).

P. C. Lorson • E. Haustein (✉)
Center for Accounting and Auditing, University of Rostock, Rostock, Germany
e-mail: peter.lorson@uni-rostock.de; ellen.haustein@uni-rostock.de

F. Manes-Rossi, R. Levy Orelli (eds.), *New Trends in Public Sector Reporting*, Public Sector Financial Management,
https://doi.org/10.1007/978-3-030-40056-9_4

managerial perspective, treating citizens as customers or consumers, in which performance or their satisfaction is measured. In this view, citizen participation is a way of production, with the citizen being the input. A refocus is needed here, as Beckett and King (2002) claim, with citizen participation producing a public or civic good, thereby leading to a larger outcome and a different way of public (more or less citizen-based) governance.

Thus, the view of citizens only helping the administrative process seems too narrow. Indeed, citizens are participating in fiscal or budgetary issues, in the least by their votes. However, usually, they do so poorly informed (Beckett and King 2002). More generally, it has been warned that "unengaged and uninformed citizens favour policies that appear to be in their immediate self-interest, and they believe in overly simplistic solutions" (Tanaka 2007, p. 149). Financial reporting can become relevant here to ensure well-informed decisions. In particular, in pluralistic societies, an increasing interest of citizens to engage in political issues is observed (Murphy and Moerman 2018). Still, citizen participation is restricted by reasons such as administrative barriers and a focus on old-fashioned and inadequate participation mechanisms (Timney 1998), key decisions taken by administrations and councils only (Berner 2001) and an exclusive reliance on professional expertise (Callahan 2002). In addition, the specialized accounting language and quantitative performance information do not attract citizens' interest or participation (Fountain et al. 2003). Thus, Kloby (2009, p. 373) summarizes that "translating financial information into language that the average citizen can understand may serve as a building block or initial step for changing professional norms, building citizen awareness and interest, and perhaps setting the stage for more complex methods of deliberation".

Therefore, participatory budgeting (PB) has evolved as a critical element of public management reforms in order to reshape the relationship between local governments and citizens and to increase transparency[1] of public sector finance (Justice and Dülger 2009; Bruns-Martos and Lapsley 2017). With PB, citizens are directly involved in the budgeting process of their public entity and the related budget allocation decisions (Allegretti

[1] Here, the elusive concept of transparency is understood as a process by which public authorities make understandable the process by which decisions have been taken, explain their decisions and make the information, on which the decisions were based, accessible (Södermann 1998; cited by Meijer 2014).

and Herzberg 2004; Pinnington et al. 2009). Thereby, Bruns-Martos and Lapsley (2017) argue that PB can become a mediating instrument between public administrations and the citizen domain. PB does also have potential to be used as a form of dialogic accounting (Aleksandrov et al. 2018). Still, in spite of a dialogic intent, new accounting tools are often implemented in a monologic way (Harun et al. 2015).

In order to stimulate the participation of citizens in PB and thus to make PB successful, ways to reduce barriers to participation by marginalized populations are needed (Pinnington et al. 2009). For instance, among the critical success factors of PB, Barbera et al. (2016, p. 1095) discuss responsiveness, in terms of "continuous attention to citizens' needs" and the capacity to address collective needs, as well as representation, that is, giving voice to different interests and views, by creative PB design. Flinders and Dommett (2013) draw on gap analysis, that is, the "gap that may emerge between what is promised and what is delivered when public expectations are inflamed through political statements", to reveal the ways in which citizens should be mobilized in particular PB schemes. More recent studies also take into consideration the role of non-human actors (e.g. PB manuals, project documents and meeting protocols) (Aleksandrov and Timoshenko 2018). Thus, practitioners had to develop and introduce a variety of pragmatic solutions (Bartocci et al. 2019), which represent a fruitful research endeavour. In particular US academics such as Justice and Dülger (2009) argue that "academics can learn from a contemporary international community of practice concerned with 'civil-society budget work'- a quasi-grassroots, quasi-pluralist movement" such as third-party involvement.

Still, PB is one only part of the overall reporting framework of public entities. According to the most recent reporting paradigm described by Xu and Chan (2016), the stakeholder model, key financial variables, such as revenues, expenditures, grants and loans, need to be communicated in order to demonstrate long-term-effectiveness and equity. To some extent, these figures are also communicated in PB projects, because citizens need to be well informed before taking their vote on how to spend the budget. As such, PB is seen as a suitable point of reference in order to elaborate how public sector reporting can be improved by learning from dialogic experiences made in PB projects worldwide in order to overcome institutionalized 'one-way' communication frames and technocratic approaches to accounting. Although two-way communication strategies are already discussed in literature to some extent (e.g. with respect to social, horizontal accountability, or democratic accountability[2]), the discussion can be enriched by learning from PB projects, as these are of high relevance due to their international application, with a high practical orientation.

Thus, the aim of this chapter is to present an overview of potential strategies for more citizen orientation in public sector reporting by drawing on PB research projects. The chapter is organized as follows: The links and spillover effects from PB to non-financial and financial reporting of public entities are highlighted in the next section. This is followed by drawing relevant conclusions for reporting of public entities with respect to implications for the actors involved (Section "Implications for Actors Involved in Reporting") and the reporting context (Section "Implications for Reporting Contents and Complexity"). We thereby review the extant literature on PB to summarize implications for reports better tailored to citizens' needs and expectations. Possibly, other ways of reporting for citizens are needed. Therefore, alternative ways of reporting are introduced in Section "Alternative Ways of Reporting". The chapter ends with a conclusion in Section "Conclusion" by presenting a table of the lessons learnt and implications that can serve as guidance for stronger citizen orientation in public sector reporting.

PB and Its Links to Financial Reporting

Budgeting is generally seen as the core function of public sector financial management, as it concerns the main financial decisions taken in public entities (Bergmann 2009). The budget is an annual or bi-annual financial plan that allocates the available financing and resources to each department, unit and activity inside the organization. The bindingness of the budget of public sector entities is a distinctive feature compared to the private sector: After the budget has been approved by the elected representatives of the public entity, only authorized transactions may be carried out by the public entity's administration.

Even though budgeting is the instrument for the implementation of reform objectives and achievement or enhancement of values Bearfield

[2] There is no commonly agreed definition of the term accountability. As a broad common understanding, it can be seen as a "positive quality in organisations or officials" in which an institution or individual is responsible for certain actions and required to explain about these actions (Bovens 2010, p. 946).

and Dubnick (2009), it is seen as "one of the last bastions of administrative expertise" (Beckett and King 2002, p. 464). Therefore, budgeting was found to be a closed process settled by experts and politicians, as in particular budgeting and finance officers are highly risk adverse and only focused on balancing the budget instead of opening the process (Miller and Evers 2002). Thus, Kloby (2009, p. 370) criticizes that "the budget process often excludes citizens from actively contributing to financial decisions. In addition, budget documents are more likely designed to comply with extensive financial reporting standards that result in lengthy and data-rich documents that deter citizens rather than inform them". Thus, Orosz (2002, p. 426) stresses that for participation in budgeting, "a re-focusing away from the pragmatic, legalistically-based, and expert-centric views" is needed. As a consequence of this and also in order to seek citizen engagement, at the end of the 1980s, the participatory budget of Porto Alegre, Brazil, also called Orçamento Participativo, was developed and implemented as the first of its kind.

In general, PB is a procedure that gives citizens the opportunity to participate in the planning of income and expenditure of public funds (Sintomer et al. 2012). PB serves multiple functions such as discussions of budgetary processes and public finance allocations, planning of strategic investments as well as control of expenditures (Célérier and Cuenca Botey 2015). Thereby, it opens up new ways of interaction of the public entity with the public and for public monitoring. It thus enables new ways of accountability.

In order to better frame the very broad definition, in an international review of PB, Sintomer et al. (2012) presented the following five criteria to be met for PB: (1) The procedure must explicitly concern financial matters. (2) Participation takes place at the local (i.e. municipal or city) or district level. (3) It is a permanent and repeated procedure. (4) The procedure includes a public discussion on budgetary issues, with the communication channel used not being decisive. However, a pure survey on finances, conventional councils or committee meetings with citizen participation is no PB. (5) The results of PB must be reported orally or in writing.

As not all PB procedures fulfil these criteria, for this chapter, a partial fulfilment is sufficient, for example, as research also covers PB projects that have been terminated. Accordingly, the criteria refer primarily to the applied procedural model and not to methods or effects of PB. Due to differences in the national legal settings, a wide variety of PB procedures have evolved over time. Depending on the national legal system, PB processes are either purely consultative (i.e. the politicians decide in the end) or really direct democratic, so that citizens decide. In addition, PB does not necessarily cover the entire budget of a public entity, but mostly, the budget available for PB is restricted to some unconditional government funds and (if applicable) self-generated revenues (Sintomer et al. 2012). As such the extent of PB is limited (Uddin et al. 2011).

Typically, the realization of the PB process consists of four sub-phases: (1) initiation and design, (2) preparation, (3) implementation and (4) accountability (Scherer and Wimmer 2012). The latter phase implies that accountability of the output of PB processes is to be given (Sintomer et al. 2012), which is a crucial step in order to make the PB process successful. In general, drawn from the US literature on PB, the intended outcomes of PB are as follows: "(1) informing decision making, (2) educating participants on the budget, (3) gaining support for budget proposals, (4) influencing decision making, and (5) enhancing trust and creating a sense of community" (Ebdon and Franklin 2006, p. 441). In an impact model of citizen participation in budgeting, these outcomes are linked to certain environmental and process design variables as well as to mechanisms and outputs (Ebdon and Franklin 2006). Part of trust and confidence also refers to accountability, disclosures and financial management of public entities (Kattelus et al. 2005).

But, as Orosz (2002, p. 428) stresses, valuing participation requires a shift from "viewing citizens-as-consumers-of-services to viewing citizens-as-community-members". This does not only apply to PB but also to financial reporting, which can be seen as the "mission of accounting", as it concerns the presentation of financial statements to external parties (Bergmann 2009, p. 78). Daniels and Daniels (1991) even claim that due to their voting power and resource provision, citizens are the most important addressees of (municipal) financial reports. This has however been contested by Jones (1992), who expects citizens to be not interested in financial reports. Still, as Tanaka (2007) highlights, even in a representative democracy, where citizens use their vote for others to take the decisions, it is a simple prerequisite that citizens are reasonably informed about public matters in order to be able to elect. This implies that public sector reporting information is also set up in a way to be open and "digestible" to citizens. Therefore, new or alternative ways of reporting for citizens of both financial and non-financial information need to be found as, for example, Cohen and Karatzimas (2015) argue. The following sections review lessons learnt from PB projects to draw conclusions for public sector reporting.

Implications for Actors Involved in Reporting

Building on PB research, this section reviews implications for the following actors with respect to public sector reporting: administrative staff, local councillors (i.e. politicians) and citizens, but also third parties such as the press.

One of the main hindrances of successful PB projects is that administrative staff and local councillors neglect the need for input by citizens, reject access to the budget or are unable to incorporate the PB outcome into the budget decisions (Ebdon and Franklin 2006). Thus, an interest inherent to public officials to share information about budgeting and financial matters is required, which would imply a turn away from public choice theory and Niskanen's (1971) theory of the self-interested, rational bureaucrat that strives for budget maximization. As, for example, Burke (2006, p. 206) observes, a responsive version of bureaucratic accountability is needed, that is, an "increasing emphasis on a shared and altruistic public interest, as well as increased information sharing and transparency of administrative information". Even for PB, it has been questioned whether its implementation leads to enhanced transparency and accountability (Uddin et al. 2011). This is especially the case if meetings in the PB process are dominated by councillors and technocrats. Therefore, in a situationist concept of the "spectacle", Uddin et al. (2011, p. 288) model PB as a type of integrated spectacle, that is, a way of explaining the "development of consumer society and the continuity of capitalism" to showcase that if public officials use citizen participation, they need to make sure that it allows for two-sided communication ways and is opened up for feedback by citizen. In a similar context, Bearfield and Dubnick (2009) show from a case of citizen participation on a large construction project that one-sided communication, that is, mere reporting of numbers and facts to the public, can result in single-loop learning of public officials, making them defensive. However, if the communication is interactive with the public and allows for reflection of different views, double-loop learning will arise, which helps to understand the underlying complexity of a certain problem. This, however, implies that sufficient time is given to the PB process in terms of citizens providing input, as Orosz (2002) highlights. She observed that administrative staff is often driven by timing pressures for budget adoption which harm "meaningful citizen input" (Orosz 2002, p. 424). But even if accounting reforms are targeted at strengthening democracy, such dialogic initiatives are weakened by the fact that the power is still held by the public entities, as shown in an Indonesian case study (Harun et al. 2015).

Also for PB, it has been argued that citizens lack the knowledge and expertise to engage in budgeting matters due to their highly complex and technical nature (Beckett and King 2002). As such, Ebdon (2002) reports that complexity of the budget and the underlying budget system was among the main barriers to participation by citizens. Since people do not know how to obtain information or do not understand the budget, they do not participate. Thereby, Beckett and King (2002, p. 464) indicate that there should be an effort for citizen involvement by administrative staff and politicians, "when it makes reasonable sense, when the issues are understandable, and when citizen involvement can be effective". In these cases, participation can inform "administrative expertise and legislative decisions" so that not only citizens benefit from their involvement. This does not only apply for municipal budgeting, but has even been claimed at OECD level for national budgeting: "Thus, public engagement creates mutual benefits: citizens become better educated about public policies and government activities; and by tapping into the experience and expertise of their constituents, officials can build more effective and responsive government" (Tanaka 2007, p. 140). However, as citizens are more locally bound and better understand the needs of their immediate surroundings (Guo and Neshkova 2012), PB is rather targeted towards local budgets.

In order to prevent from any frustrations or disappointments by citizens, educating the public about both the possibilities and the restrictions of PB is necessary. Thus, Ebdon (2002, p. 291) suggests that "one way to help citizens develop a more macro level view of budget trade-offs is to combine education and participation early in the process, at the budget development stage". As Célérier and Cuenca Botey (2015, p. 752) cite a local councillor commenting on a disappointed citizen: "PB is not demanding, it is participating". Thus, Tanaka (2007) stresses that citizens need to be informed about how their input will be used, in particular in case of consultative PB. Even if citizens have to be informed that PB is not necessarily representative, to the extent possible, PB actors should strive for representation, that is, try to include different citizens' interests, views and power positions (Barbera et al. 2016).

Justice and Dülger (2009, p. 255) stress that citizens are constrained in their "time, expertise and attention" resources and therefore highlight the importance of third-party budget intermediation, exemplified by international communities in terms of "civil-society budget work". Hence direct citizen involvement in budget formulation might not be the most feasible way to achieve high citizen involvement, but third parties are needed for a translation to citizens. Such role can also be played by press involvement (Ebdon 2002), that is, local newspapers that serve as intermediaries. Still, Miller and Evers (2002, p. 241) warn that the media also needs to be educated about budgeting and PB, showing that reporters with a lack of knowledge about budgeting and government can "increase cynicism by misreporting".

To sum up, the following conclusions can be drawn for public reporting with respect to the actors involved: Third parties such as the press or citizen initiatives can serve as support and must be sensitized for their important role, on the one hand, and, on the other hand, be educated and experienced in transporting financial data to their readership in an appropriate and understandable manner. Still, the main role is being played by administrative staff and politicians. In particular, when assigning roles of financial reporting for citizens, Kloby (2009, p. 367) shows that chief financial officers "play a leading role in determining the style and extent to which financial information is communicated to external audiences". In addition, public entities' departments in charge for certain services can be involved in reporting in order to increase transparency (Franzke and Kleger 2010). However, ordinary financial reporting does not increase citizen participation; thus, "citizen-based financial reporting" is required (Kloby 2009). In addition, in her study on the drivers for popular reporting, Kloby (2009) reveals the importance of elected officials for setting up and distributing such popular reports. The reports were even seen as a "learning tool for elected officials" (Kloby 2009, p. 382) and are explained in more detail in Section "Alternative Ways of Reporting".

Given the benefits of such alternative or new ways of reporting, both administrative staff and local councillors need to get engaged in developing ways of reporting for citizens which are both interesting and understandable. Particularly, municipalities should strive for more open processes, facilitated information collection of various stakeholders and transparency (Barbera et al. 2016). Thereby, co-creation of reports by preparers and users could be applied, which however so far has only been addressed for politicians as users (ter Bogt and van Helden 2011; ter Bogt et al. 2015). Resultantly, contents of public sector reports and their complexity are affected, which are addressed in the next section.

Implications for Reporting Contents and Complexity

Both for PB and for reporting in general, topics are decisive for interest by citizens. However, other topics need to be reported, which requires that citizens are sufficiently informed about why specific contents have been included. With respect to the topics of PB specifically, Miller and Evans (2002, p. 236) highlight that PB cannot cover all issues that are of relevance for citizens, but there are also what they list as "uncontrollable issues, budget knots, planning issues, and nonnegotiable issues". Uncontrollable issues lie beyond the immediate control of the administration and the council and are determined by, for example, law (specifically regarding taxes, expenditure controls and the budget process), obligations or commissions to deliver certain services or service levels or to include certain service recipients. For uncontrollable issues, understanding needs to be fostered by administrations, in order to reduce potential cynicism that is generated by budgeting (Miller and Evers 2002, p. 239). Budget knots refer to decisions that include trade-offs with foreseeable and unforeseeable consequences. Abilities of understanding and prediction of choices are needed in order to be prepared for interacting budget decisions. Here, citizen participation can even provide valuable insights about trade-offs and citizens' willingness to share risks. For planning issues, citizen participation is generally possible if the longer time horizon is respected. However, for nonnegotiable issues, administrations will try to keep these away from any influence by citizens, as their agenda has already been set. These issues concern, for example, questions about the sharing of tax burdens, spending of debt finance or deferred maintenance of infrastructure (Miller and Evers 2002). Nonnegotiable issues require more than mere citizen participation, but true citizen deliberation to engage in deeper inquiry into "theories and beliefs about government, particularly political representation and administrative delegation" (Miller and Evers 2002, p. 239). Here, PB is seen as one of the ways of participation to educate citizens and to seek their support (Ebdon 2002; Orosz 2002; Miller and Evers 2002). With respect to the topics reported and values presented, Orosz (2002) claims that a change in the value structures is needed. Here, administrative staff is required not to only see budgeting as a "technical product of accounting" and to report within its boundaries, but to place the same significance on citizens' views by respecting and weaving community values into the reports. According to such view, the budget becomes a tool for "community involvement". This implies, for example, a stronger reporting of specific micro projects of high public relevance and setting of different topics. Therefore, Barbera et al. (2016) call for extended responsiveness of PB projects in terms of identification of and responding to collective needs of citizens.

In addition, in order to foster citizen participation, Fountain et al. (2003) claim that the relevance of financial information and indicators of key performance should be explained by added narratives to citizens. Document length should be cut, and accomplishments and deficiencies of political and administrative efforts and financial management should be clearly explained. Thereby, financial officers need to detach from their "more is better mentality" (Kloby 2009, p. 381) by revealing the public entities' strategy so that citizens can get involved and can provide feedback. Thus, citizen-based reports shall be short and attractive and thereby present the "big picture" with visual displays and jargon-free language. However, none of the ten governments studied by Kloby (2009) had formalized processes or strategies for engaging citizens in planning or shaping the focus of the reports; instead, the reports were designed by the administrations only.

Financial information better shaped to citizens' needs can also support to achieve the overall goals of citizen participation, such as trust in the public entity's governments. For example, simplified budget presentations could help citizens to develop confidence in the fiscal and overall management capacities of the public entity and, as Orosz (2002) highlights, improve the image of its overall technical competence. In the same notion, Ebdon and Franklin (2006) point out that the nature and timing of data reported will influence citizens' view on the overall budgeting procedure, their perception of the budget office's professionalization and, in the end, their appreciation of participating.

A more critical view of accounting has been introduced by the term 'dialogic accounting'. In this context, monologic accounting is defined as "the production of traditional financial accounts and reports, and incorporates assumptions under which they are produced" and often claimed to produce neutral information, but even criticized as being a form of suppression of less powerful actors (Harun et al. 2015, p. 709). An alternative form of accounting is dialogic, which offers alternative views of what should be accounted for, in particular by including information on social, political, environmental, public, as well as economic matters. As such, accounting and reporting also incorporate non-financial information. There is an increasing stream of literature discussing dialogic accounting as a way of better reflecting and recognizing stakeholder voices and enhancing democratic aspirations (e.g. Bebbington et al. 2007; Christensen and Parker 2010; Brown 2009; Brown and Dillard 2013; Harun et al. 2015). In this notion, Aleksandrov et al. (2018) examined the extent to which PB serves as a way of dialogic accounting. However, in their analysis of a PB project in Russia, the extent of dialogic accounting was found to be limited, although it was the declared aim of the PB project to produce understandable budget information in the form of an "iBudget".[3] Relying on the concept of reflexivity, Aleksandrov et al. (2018) conclude that in the PB project, (1) only a limited orientation towards multiple ideological perspectives was apparent; (2) the representation of the budget process was simplified, but from a formal public perspective only; (3) the PB topics were mainly selected by internal choice, but avoided conflicts between the municipality and local council; (4) the possibilities for information use by non-experts were limited; (5) the dialogue was controlled by the iBudget simulation, instead of opening participatory processes; (6) PB was influenced by powerful elites, with (7) limited critical reflection and discourse; and (8) a communication concept of banking was imposed, thereby leading to further monologism. As a consequence, more efforts towards dialogic accounting are demanded.

To summarize, the findings for PB projects can also inspire public sector reporting. In particular, the topics reported and the understandability and length of the reports should be regarded. With respect to reporting content, at the simplest level, one requirement is that "good information is readily available"; therefore, all benefits of advanced media (e.g. budget simulations, internet forums; see Section "Alternative Ways of Reporting") should also be used (Tanaka 2007, p. 143) by still regarding its downsides (limited access for some citizen groups). Also, too complicated accounting standards are seen as detrimental for understandable reporting and the reports become lengthy and extensive in information (Kloby 2009). Alternative ways of reporting to citizens could provide a solution. Some of these are introduced in the next section.

[3] The iBudget is an institutional innovation that was set up as a PB experiment with the help of consultant researchers and allows for interactive dialogues between public officials and citizens (Aleksandrov et al. 2018).

Alternative Ways of Reporting

PB is particularly about engagement of different types of citizens (e.g. regarding age, gender, social status, education, etc.). Brown et al. (2015) present a review of research on how accounting and accountability need to be changed in order to address pluralistic societies and to take multiple perspectives seriously. They argue that specific groups (such as environmentalists, ethical investors, unionists, feminists, humanitarian agencies, new social movements within civil society and indigenous communities) are "marginalized by conventional accounting and accountability regimes", which requires other ways of incorporating their perspectives with the help of enhanced processes, different accounting regimes, other types of information or alternative media (Brown et al. 2015, p. 2). Therefore, they call for a future analysis of new demands for pluralistic reporting.

One alternative of reporting could be "integrated reporting", that is, representing clearly and concisely how a public entity creates and sustains public value (e.g. public welfare), taking into account economic, social and environmental factors (IIRC 2013) by reporting financial and non-financial information in an interconnected way. Reasons for incorporating integrated reporting in the public sector and how that can be realized are addressed by, for example, Oprisor et al. (2016) and Katsikas et al. (2017). As it is also the main topic of this book, integrated reporting is not addressed in details in this chapter.

In particular, in the US, a movement towards more citizen-based financial reporting can be observed in the form of popular reports (e.g. Cohen and Karatzimas 2015). Already in 1992, the US Governmental Accounting Standards Board (GASB) published a research report on popular reporting, and in 2019, in its potential standard-setting plans, it repeated calls to engage in research on popular reporting (GASB 2019). Popular reports are seen as important reporting instruments not only for citizens but also for elected officials (Kloby 2009). Besides past information, these reports can also include "narrative that describes new initiatives, future plans, and past accomplishments" (Kloby 2009, p. 382). In some administrations, parts of the popular reports are even included into annual plans or other reports to summarize activities, efforts and progress of public entities and are also included on their website in order to explain capital project expenditures of or revenues from recreational areas. Since 1991, the US Government Finance Officers Association (GFOA 2018) annually awards financial officers for preparing annual financial reports that seek an easy understanding by citizens and free accessibility for the general public. Nowadays, the award is open to US and Canadian general-purpose or special-purpose governments at state or local level. The criteria for the award are, for example, attractiveness and understandability of the report (for instance, by use of non-technical language) its ways of distribution, use of visual displays for quantitative information, appealing report design and use of narratives (GFOA 2018). Still, as Kloby (2009) finds, popular reports are rather published for reasons of information sharing and public relations than for enhancing citizen participation. However, Ebdon (2002) reports that some public entities make use of shortened budget reports, also to increase interest for PB. Thereby, Orosz (2002) reports about conferences and training programmes offered to administrative staff by professional organizations in the US about how to better approach citizens and how to enhance budget presentations.

Research in the PB context has shown that 'performance paradoxes' may occur, that is, situations in which "services may well improve but the public may not perceive or believe that this has occurred" (Flinders and Dommett 2013, p. 496). As a mitigation, McCall and Klay (2010, p. 85) suggest using service efforts and accomplishments (SEA) reporting, which they coin under the term "accountability reporting" for "linking performance reporting to financial reporting". Such reports include both information about performance achievements and the respective costs incurred. Thus, McCall and Klay (2010) criticize that financial reporting also provides information about financial stewardship, but lacks information about quantity and quality of a public entity's performance. In contrast, SEA reporting is directed towards citizens and particularly includes non-financial information. As a consequence, one of the cities studied by McCall and Klay (2010, p. 97) published four separate documents which reflect "a sophisticated consideration of different users' information needs". This leads to the question: Whether reports that are directed towards a general purpose are really the best choice for disclosures to citizens?

With respect to citizen participation at the national budgeting level, Tanaka (2007) particularly highlights the opportunities of online information and social media. Thereby, international examples are distinguished that split the steps of the typical PB process and seek public engagement either by (a) top-down information sharing, (b) interactive information, (c) consultation or (d) direct democracy. The following examples are a shortcut of the collection of public engagement, which Tanaka (2007) presents in her OECD cases: The first category, (a) top-down information sharing, is relatively widespread already and refers to the presentation of information through budget office websites. These websites need to be easily accessible and serve as verification of information. Countries such as Australia, Canada, France, Germany, Japan and the US have installed such websites,[4] at times even with additional content, such as podcasts in the case of Canada. A more complex way of educating citizens about how budgeting works is through (b) interactive information by designing online budget games and simulations. Thereby, game design is used in order to particularly attract younger generations. Still, the examples are relatively sparse so far because the games' design is relatively complex and the games can become outdated due to fast changes in the political agendas and budget issues. For example, in France, the Cyber-Budget[5] teaches budgeting terms and provides users with tasks to be resolved. In the UK or Canada, several cities and districts offer budget simulators.[6] By using (c) consultation, public entities can engage citizens in a bottom-up style by active listening in various ways, for example, by surveys, online or personal discussions, or online forums. The lower the proximity to citizens, the more online interaction with citizens takes place. Thereby, a larger audience can be reached, but representativeness is threatened. Again, the French government, some Canadian provinces and UK councils are examples for holding online forums also with respect to budget issues.[7] In preparation of the tax reform in Hong Kong, the government sought for the citizens' opinion through an online consultation.[8] Finally, Tanaka (2007) introduces ways of (d) direct democracy through PB, referenda and citizen memberships in the budget committee. These techniques are used already at local level, but cannot easily be installed at national level. At central or federal level, alternatives such as the block grant approach can be used, by which transfers of specific amounts of the national budget to lower government units are undertaken, which are subject to local priority setting.

[4] Corresponding websites: www.budget.gov.au, www.fin.gc.ca, www.performance-publique.budget.gouv.fr, www.bundeshaushalt.de, www.mof.go.jp, www.whitehouse.gov/omb/

[5] www.performance-publique.budget.gouv.fr

[6] www.delib.net/budget_simulator

[7] For example, www.forum-action-publique.gouv.fr, www.ontario.ca/page/budget-consultations

[8] www.taxreform.gov.hk

Still, all of these suggestions imply that the administrative staff and political decision makers are knowledgeable of accounting and the ways of how to display accounting figures. This also provides challenges for higher education. For instance, Kattelus et al. (2005) warn that most programmes for public administration are rather oriented towards non-accountants. Often, these programmes for preparing graduates for their jobs in government and not-for-profit organizations do not include teaching contents such as financial statement analysis or financial accounting, which leads to a separation of the budgeting and accounting functions. Therefore, vocational trainings and universities need to refocus on teaching accounting also in their public management courses.

This section has introduced alternatives ways of reporting and interacting with citizens. For public sector reporting, more citizen-focused approaches such as integrated reporting, popular reporting or SEA reporting could be applied. Also, public entities can seek multi-channel communication, including alternative media of reporting such as online tools. Thus, what Barbera et al. (2016) and Bartocci et al. (2019) demand for with respect to PB also applies to public sector reporting in general: creativity in design and, at times, more pragmatism is also needed.

Conclusion

This chapter focused on the question of how PB could inspire public sector reporting to better address citizens as potential users of reporting information. Table 1 shows a synopsis of the conclusions drawn by summarizing the main topics presented in sections 3–5. On the left-hand side, the table shows problems areas, whereas the middle column indicates lessons learnt or hindrances that occurred during the PB process. Although some of these problems can also occur in the case of public sector reporting in general, these have been specifically addressed in PB research. On the right-hand side of the table, possible implications for financial reporting are presented.

Research of PB projects worldwide showed that PB also addresses some problems related to inclusiveness of citizens. However, it became clear that the administrative staff and politicians need to become more open to the idea of citizens participating and being interested in public sector reporting. Thus, the reporting content and complexity need to be shaped accordingly by regarding, for example, the length of report, use of technical language, the topics presented, style and design of information as well

Table 1 Summary of implications for reporting

Section 3: Actors involved in reporting		
Actors	**Lessons learnt**	**Implications for reporting (simplified)**
Administrative staff and local councillors	PB input by citizens needs to be actively regarded Barriers to PB access for citizens are to be reduced, e.g. by active information sharing	Stronger orientation of administrative staff and elected officials towards accountability, i.e. increased information sharing Leading role by financial officers in reporting for citizens
	Dominance by technocrats and politicians in a one-sided PB process leads to a lack in transparency and accountability	Two-sided (interactive) communication ways needed
Administrative staff	Time pressures put by administrative staff or budget adoption harm citizens' input	Early citizen involvement needed in the budget and reporting process
Citizens	Citizens lack knowledge and expertise on how to engage in budgeting matters and how to cope with the information	Co-creation of reports by preparers and users
	PB processes and PB outcomes that are not appropriately reported and explained lead to frustrations or disappointments in citizens Marginalized citizen groups are excluded from typical PB processes	Information about how citizen input is used (e.g. consultative) Striving for representation
	Citizens have constraints in resources for engaging in PB	Use of third-party budget intermediation, i.e. by citizen initiatives or press

(*continued*)

Table 1 (continued)

Section 4: Reporting contents and complexity		
Problem area	**Lessons learnt**	**Implications for reporting (simplified)**
Topics	Not all topics are suitable for PB (because these are, e.g. uncontrollable or nonnegotiable), but topics not included might be decisive for citizens and absence of these topics can be irritating	Information about legal boundaries of issues/topics reported Extended responsiveness in terms of identification and towards collective needs of citizens required Reporting on (micro) projects instead of general-purpose information
	Budgeting seen as a "technical product of accounting" and does not reflect values of importance for citizens, leading to withdrawal of citizen support	Budget becomes a tool for "community involvement" (citizens as community members rather than service consumers)
Style of reporting	Technical accounting language in PB communication hinders citizen participation	Explanations by using narratives Simplified budget presentations
	Lengthiness and quantitative data richness of PB reports erode citizens' confidence in using financial data and their willingness to provide feedback	Creation of short, concise and attractive reports with visual displays and jargon-free language Strategies for engaging citizens in planning or shaping the reports' focus
Style of accounting	Monologic accounting only leads to 'cosmetic' implementation of PB without really regarding plural stakeholder voices and democratic aspirations, thereby downplaying the PB idea	More dialogic accounting style: • Feedback loops with citizens • Different ways of reporting (online, social media, face to face)
Access	Access to PB is crucial for participation	Use of advanced media and multi-channels
Expertise	Administrative staff and elected officials lack accounting knowledge, which hinders their ability to use PB	Education needed: • Seminars and awards for citizen-based reporting • Inclusion of accounting in public management courses

(*continued*)

Table 1 (continued)

Section 5: Alternative ways of reporting (Consequences?)	
Summary of problem areas	**Implications for reporting (simplified)**
PB report information is too quantitative and too technical	Integrated reporting/popular reporting
Lengthiness and detailedness of PB reports	Conciseness (e.g. popular reporting)
Performance paradoxes and missing links between financial and non-financial performance	Connectivity in reporting: • Integrated reporting • Service efforts and accomplishments (SEA) reporting
Limited citizen participation in PB	Multi-channel approach for citizen engagement, e.g.: (a) Top-down information sharing budget office websites (b) Interactive information: online budget games and simulations (c) Consultation: surveys, online or personal discussions, or online forums (d) Direct democracy: PB, referenda and citizen memberships in the budget committee

as accessibility. Parallels to the impact model of citizen participation in budgeting of Ebdon and Franklin (2006) can be detected here: The more the relevant actors (council and major) are involved by addressing large and heterogeneous groups of population through multiple channels, giving sufficient time for implementation, the better will be the long-term impacts of citizen involvement.

The chapter also highlighted that alternative ways of reporting seem to be more appropriate in contrast to general-purpose financial reports and may deserve even more attention. This calls for further research on integrated reports of public entities, popular reports or SEA reports, and their usability and use by citizens. The table presented in the chapter can be used by both practitioners and researchers: Local governments and councils receive input on citizen-based reporting in order to reflect on their status quo. For research, the collected implications can serve as a tool for designing studies to analyse and, later on, systemically test how outcome variables of citizen participation are affected. All these strands are fruitful research endeavours, as an "engaged public should lead to better public policy and budget outcomes, including more equitable and efficient allocation of resources and greater long-term fiscal stability" (Tanaka 2007, p. 144).

References

Aleksandrov, E., & Timoshenko, K. (2018). Translating Participatory Budgeting in Russia: The Roles of Inscriptions and Inscriptors. *Journal of Accounting in Emerging Economies, 8*(3), 302–326.

Aleksandrov, E., Bourmistrov, A., & Grossi, G. (2018). Participatory Budgeting as a Form of Dialogic Accounting in Russia. *Accounting, Auditing, and Accountability Journal, 31*(4), 1098–1123.

Allegretti, G., & Herzberg, C. (2004). *Participatory Budgets in Europe: Between Efficiency and Growing Local Democracy*, Amsterdam, NL: Transnational Institute and the Centre for Democratic Policy-Making.

Barbera, C., Sicilia, M., & Steccolini, I. (2016). What Mr Rossi Wants in Participatory Budgeting: Two R's (Responsiveness and Representation) and Two I's (Inclusiveness and Interaction). *International Journal of Public Administration, 39*(3), 1088–1100.

Bartocci, L., Grossi, G., & Mauro, S. G. (2019). Towards a Hybrid Logic of Participatory Budgeting. *International Journal of Public Sector Management, 32*(1), 65–79.

Bearfield, D. A., & Dubnick, M. J. (2009). All Mega-Projects Are Local? Citizen Participation Lessons from the Big Dig. *Journal of Public Budgeting, Accounting, and Financial Management, 21*(3), 392–425.

Bebbington, J., Brown, J., & Frame, B. (2007). Accounting Technologies and Sustainability Assessment Models. *Ecological Economics, 61*(2/3), 224–236.

Beckett, J., & King, C. S. (2002). The Challenge to Improve Citizen Participation in Public Budgeting: A Discussion. *Journal of Public Budgeting, Accounting, and Financial Management, 14*(3), 463–485.

Bergmann, A. (2009). *Public Sector Financial Management*, Harlow, UK, Pearson Education.

Berner, M. (2001). Citizen Participation in Local Government Budgeting. *Popular Government, 2001*, 23–30.

Bovens, M. (2010). Two Concepts of Accountability: Accountability as a Virtue and as a Mechanism. *West European Politics, 33*(5), 946–967.

Brown, J. (2009). Democracy, Sustainability and Dialogic Accounting Technologies: Taking Pluralism Seriously. *Critical Perspectives on Accounting, 20*(3), 313–342.

Brown, J., & Dillard, J. (2013). Agonizing Over Engagement: SEA and the Death of Environmentalism Debates. *Critical Perspectives on Accounting, 24*(1), 1–18.

Brown, J., Dillard, J., & Hopper, T. (2015). Accounting, Accountants and Accountability Regimes in Pluralistic Societies. *Accounting, Auditing, and Accountability Journal, 28*(5), 626–650.

Brun-Martos, M. I., & Lapsley, I. (2017). Democracy, Governmentality and Transparency: Participatory Budgeting in Action. *Public Management Review, 19*(7), 1006–1021.

Burke, B. F. (2006). Altruism, Accountability, and Transparency: Cooperative Aspirations in Contemporary State-Level Budgeting. *Journal of Public Budgeting, Accounting, and Financial Management, 18*(2), 198–223.

Callahan, K. (2002). The Utilization and Effectiveness of Citizen Advisory Committees in the Budget Process of Local Governments. *Journal of Public Budgeting, Accounting, and Financial Management, 14*(2), 296–317.

Célérier, L., & Cuenca Botey, L. E. (2015). Participatory Budgeting at a Community Level in Porto Alegre. *Accounting, Auditing, and Accountability Journal, 28*(5), 739–772.

Christensen, M., & Parker, L. D. (2010). Using New Ideals to Advance Professions. *Financial Accountability and Management, 26*(3), 246–266.

Cohen, S., & Karatzimas, S. (2015). Tracing the Future of Reporting in the Public Sector: Introducing Integrated Popular Reporting. *International Journal of Public Sector Management, 28*(6), 449–460.

Daniels, J. D., & Daniels, C. E. (1991). Municipal Financial Reports: What Users Want. *Journal of Accounting and Public Policy, 10*(1), 15–38.

Ebdon, C. (2002). Beyond the Public Hearing: Citizen Participation in the Local Government Budget Process. *Journal of Public Budgeting, Accounting, and Financial Management, 14*(2), 273–294.

Ebdon, C., & Franklin, A. L. (2006). Citizen Participation in Budgeting Theory. *Public Administration Review, 66*(3), 437–447.

Flinders, M., & Dommett, K. (2013). Gap Analysis: Participatory Democracy, Public Expectations and Community Assemblies in Sheffield. *Local Government Studies, 39*(4), 488–513.

Fountain, J., Campbell, W., Patton, T., & Cohn, M. (2003). *Reporting Performance Information: Suggested Criteria for Effective Communication.* www.seagov.org

Franzke, J., & Kleger, H. (2010). *Bürgerhaushalte: Chancen und Grenzen.* Berlin: Edition sigma.

GASB. (2019). *Technical Plan for the First Third of 2019: Potential Topics*. www.gasb.org

GFOA. (2018). *Popular Annual Financial Reporting Awards Program*. www.gfoa.org

Guo, H., & Neshkova, M. I. (2012). Citizen Input in the Budget Process: When Does It Matter Most? *The American Review of Public Administration, 43*, 331–346.

Harun, H., Van-Peursem, K., & Eggleton, I. R. C. (2015). Indonesian Public Sector Accounting Reforms: Dialogic Aspirations a Step Too Far? *Accounting, Auditing, and Accountability Journal, 28*(5), 706–738.

IIRC. (2013). *The International/IRS Framework*. The International Integrated Reporting Council.

Jones, R. (1992). The Development of Conceptual Frameworks of Accounting for the Public Sector. *Financial Accountability & Management, 8*(4), 249–64.

Justice, J. B., & Dülger, C. (2009). Fiscal Transparency and Authentic Citizen Participation in Public Budgeting. *Journal of Public Budgeting, Accounting, and Financial Management, 21*(2), 254–288.

Katsikas, E., Manes-Rossi, F., & Orelli, R. L. (2017). *Towards Integrated Reporting Accounting Change in the Public Sector*. Cham: Springer.

Kattelus, S. C., Cheng, R. H., & Engstrom, J. H. (2005). The Challenges of Cross-Disciplinary Work: Accounting and Financial Reporting for Governments and Nonprofits. *Journal of Public Budgeting, Accounting, and Financial Management, 17*(2), 152–165.

Kloby, K. (2009). Less Is More: Exploring Citizen-Based Financial Reporting in Local Government. *Journal of Public Budgeting, Accounting, and Financial Management, 21*(3), 368–392.

McCall, S. M., & Klay, W. E. (2010). The Uncertain Future of Accountability Reporting. *Journal of Public Budgeting, Accounting, and Financial Management, 22*(1), 84–111.

Meijer, A. (2014). Transparency. In M. Bovens, R. E. Goodin, & T. Schillemans (Eds.), *The Oxford Handbook of Public Accountability* (pp. 507–524). Oxford: Oxford University Press.

Miller, G. J., & Evers, L. (2002). Budgeting Structures and Citizen Participation. *Journal of Public Budgeting, Accounting, and Financial Management, 14*(2), 233–272.

Murphy, D., & Moerman, L. (2018). SLAPPing Accountability Out of the Public Sphere. *Accounting, Auditing, and Accountability Journal, 31*(6), 1774–1793.

Niskanen, W. A., Jr. (1971). *Bureaucracy and Representative Government*. Chicago: Aldine Press.

Oprisor, T., Tiron-Tudor, A., & Silvia, C. (2016). The Integrated Reporting System: A New Accountability Enhancement Tool for Public Sector Entities. *Audit Financiar, 14*(139), 749–762.

Orosz, J. F. (2002). Views from the Field: Creating a Place for Authentic Citizen Participation in Budgeting. *Journal of Public Budgeting, Accounting, and Financial Management, 14*(3), 423–444.

Pinnington, E., Lerner, J., & Schugurensky, D. (2009). Participatory Budgeting in North America: The Case of Guelph, Canada. *Journal of Public Budgeting, Accounting, and Financial Management, 21*(3), 454–483.

Scherer, S., & Wimmer, M. A. (2012). Reference Process Model for Participatory Budgeting in Germany. *ePart 2012: Electronic Participation*, pp. 97–111.

Sintomer, Y., Herzberg, C., Röcke, A., & Allegretti, G. (2012). Transnational Models of Citizen Participation: The Case of PB. *Journal of Public Deliberation, 8*, 2. Article 9.

Södermann, J. (1998). The Citizen, the Administration and Community Law. *General Report for the 1998 Fide Congress.* Stockholm, 3–6 June.

Tanaka, S. (2007). Engaging the Public in National Budgeting. *OECD Journal on Budgeting, 7*(2), 139–177.

Ter Bogt, H. J., & van Helden, G. J. (2011). The Role of Consultant-Researchers in the Design and Implementation Process of a Programme Budget in a Local Government Organization. *Management Accounting Research, 22*(1), 56–64.

Ter Bogt, H. J., van Helden, G. J., & van der Kolk, B. (2015). Challenging the NPM Ideas About Performance Management. *Financial Accountability and Management, 31*(3), 287–315.

Timney, M. (1998). Overcoming Administrative Barriers to Citizen Participation. In C. S. King & C. Stivers (Eds.), *Government Is Us, Public Administration in an Anti-Government Era* (pp. 88–99). London: Sage.

Uddin, S., Gumb, B., & Kasumba, S. (2011). Trying to Operationalise Typologies of the Spectacle: A Literature Review and a Case Study. *Accounting, Auditing, and Accountability Journal, 24*(3), 288–314.

Xu, Y., & Chan, J. L. (2016). Financial Management in Public Sector Organizations. In T. Bovaird & E. Loeffler (Eds.), *Public Management and Governance* (3rd ed., pp. 104–115). London: Routledge.

Peter C. Lorson is a full professor holding the Chair of Accounting, Management Control and Auditing; Executive Director of the Center for Accounting and Auditing at the University of Rostock, Germany; and member of the Working Group "Integrated Reporting" (Schmalenbach Association for Business Administration; Schmalenbach-Gesellschaft für Betriebswirtschaft e.V.).

Ellen Haustein is a post-doctoral researcher and lecturer at the same chair at the University of Rostock, Germany.

New Reporting Tools at the Central Government Level: Experiences in Light of a Budgeting and Accounting Reform in Austria

Iris Saliterer and Sanja Korac

Introduction

Following the book's overarching theme of how trends in public sector reporting contrast and compare to traditional tools, this chapter presents experiences with and effects of budgeting and accounting processes and reporting tools in the Austrian central government (i.e. federal government, comprising ministries and central government agencies). Set in the context of an extensive budgeting and accounting reform, it seeks to answer the question whether new tools of reporting may be better suited

I. Saliterer
University of Freiburg, Freiburg, Germany
e-mail: Iris.Saliterer@vwl.uni-freiburg.de; iris.saliterer@aau.at

S. Korac (✉)
German University of Administrative Sciences, Speyer, Germany
e-mail: korac@uni-speyer.de; sanja.korac@aau.at

F. Manes-Rossi, R. Levy Orelli (eds.), *New Trends in Public Sector Reporting*, Public Sector Financial Management,
https://doi.org/10.1007/978-3-030-40056-9_5

to provide a clearer picture of the financial situation (in terms of a fair presentation of the financial position, financial performance, and cash flow of the entity in question; see IFAC 2006) as well as of the non-financial performance (i.e. outcomes and outputs; see Van Dooren and Van de Walle 2008) of governmental entities compared to traditional systems of reporting. Along these lines, the chapter looks at (1) the *relative advantage* (see Davis 1989) of newly available reporting tools, that is, the degree to which those tools may be perceived as superior to the tools that they have replaced; and (2) their perceived *usefulness* from the perspective of *public managers* (directors general and heads of department in ministries and central government agencies) and *politicians* (federal legislators, i.e. members of parliament), that is, the extent to which users of those tools believe that the latter will help them to better perform their respective job (Davis 1989): in the case of public managers, for instance, internal management of public sector entities and demonstrating accountability (conveying to third parties how financial and non-financial resources are used; see Ricci 2019), and in the case of politicians, exerting control and oversight over the use of public financial resources. The aspects of relative advantage and usefulness are innovation attributes that have been widely studied in innovation literature (see Davis (1989) and studies that have built on his work), and the perceived usefulness of accounting systems, reporting tools, and accounting information from the perspective of both public managers and politicians has been a key element in prior public sector accounting research (e.g. Guthrie 1998; Nasi and Steccolini 2008; Kober et al. 2010; Montesinos et al. 2013).

The investigation of the relative advantage and the perceived usefulness of the new reporting tools that have been introduced at the central government level in Austria following the budgeting and accounting reform (2009–2013) builds on (1) a gap analysis between the standard on the presentation of financial statements, the old reporting tools, and the new ones; (2) a quantitative survey of heads of department in ministries and central government agencies; (3) interviews with directors general in ministries and central government agencies; as well as (4) interviews with federal legislators, that is, members of parliament. The chapter is structured as follows. The next section gives a short overview of prior empirical findings on the usefulness of accounting information and the systems and reports in which it is prepared and presented. Subsequently, the chapter briefly presents the budgeting and accounting reform at the Austrian central government level and the data that provided the basis for this study.

The results are organized around the assessment of the design and content of reporting tools and the perceptions of and experiences with newly available information in practice. In the last section, we blend the results with previous findings in this field and draw conclusions.

Relative Advantage and Perceived Usefulness of Accounting Information

A short glance at prior studies that have researched reporting tools in the public sector shows that the relative advantage and the perceived usefulness of reporting tools are inextricably linked to accounting systems and the accounting information presented in the latter. During the last decades, *accrual accounting* has been a linchpin of many public sector financial management reforms (see Guthrie et al. 1999), primarily due to its promise of providing users of accounting information (public managers, politicians, citizens) with 'better' information on the resources controlled by an entity and the cost of operations than traditional accounting systems (i.e. cash-based, obligation-/commitment-based) (see IFAC 2000). Many empirical studies, addressing different levels of government (federal, state, local) and thus including different groups of respondents, have attempted to answer the question of whether this is the case. Public managers (more specifically, chief financial officers) at the local level in Italy, for instance, did not perceive accrual accounting (and thus also the respective reporting tools) as useful (Nasi and Steccolini 2008), and politicians (Members of the Legislative Assembly) in Northern Ireland reported difficulties in understanding accrual-based information, expressing limited confidence in using the latter (Ezzamel et al. 2005; Ezzamel et al. 2014). Ezzamel et al. (2014) argued that the reasons behind the seemingly low perceived usefulness of accrual accounting by the surveyed legislators were information overload and the perception that their particular information interests were not represented. However, findings from other country contexts suggest that these issues may hollow out over more time. Early investigations of the usefulness of accrual-based information to decision-making in government departments and to their external users (legislators, citizens, creditors, donors, etc.) in Australia were rather sobering. Public managers (directors, managers, senior government officers, accountants, controllers, and analysts) perceived accrual-based information as not satisfying users' information needs, being only moderately relevant to internal decision-making, and not relevant to a wide range of users (see Jones and Puglisi

1997). However, studies that have been carried out at a point in time where with accrual accounting systems have matured and preparers (chief financial officers) as well as internal (i.e. heads of department, deputy heads, and general managers) and external users of financial reports (i.e. government officials in the Treasury and Finance departments and members of the public accounts committee) have gained familiarity and experience with the latter show that all these actors perceive accrual-based information as more useful than cash-based information (Andriani et al. 2010; Bergmann 2012; Kober et al. 2010). Similarly, investigations of Portuguese municipalities point to a shift in public managers' as well as politicians' stance toward accrual accounting. In contrast to prior findings (Jorge et al. 2008), a recent study shows that financial officials (public managers) as well as aldermen (politicians) perceived accrual-based information as useful (Nogueira and Jorge 2017).

Another element of new public financial management has been the approach of linking financial resources and policy goals (mirrored in non-financial *performance information*) (see Guthrie et al. 1999). Similar to the studies at the local level in the United States that present somewhat contrasting findings, for example, on the one hand reporting that performance information was barely important throughout the budget cycle (Melkers and Willoughby 2005) and on the other hand concluding that tools presenting performance information were useful in terms of enhancing public accountability and improving communications between the local government administration and citizens, but also between the local government administration and elected officials (Ho 2006), mixed findings prevail also in other country contexts. While some investigations point to a low perceived usefulness due to a lack of trust in the entities that present performance information (Bourdeaux 2008) or a merely symbolic adoption of performance information in general (Montesinos et al. 2013), Liguori et al. (2012) found that performance information was equally important for public managers (heads of department) as well as politicians (aldermen) at the Italian local level, and that both groups preferred non-financial measures over financial ones, thus indicating a high perceived usefulness of non-financial performance information. More recent findings on the Italian local level reported in a comparative study of local governments in Italy and Germany (Grossi et al. 2016) however suggest that politicians (councilors) were skeptical about the use of performance information in budgeting processes. Similar to the argument made in the context of introducing accrual accounting, the authors argue that an important driver of this skepticism was lack of knowledge, but some of the surveyed politicians also noted measurement difficulties with non-financial performance indicators. The latter seems to have negatively affected their perception of the appropriateness of presenting the non-financial alongside financial information. In this context, scholars have pointed at the (perceived) quality of performance information (e.g. cut-and-paste approaches) and opportunities to participate in the creation of measures (and thus influence the quality according to one's own expectations) as factors that affect performance information usefulness in a budgeting context (Joyce and Sieg 2000; Saliterer et al. 2019; Ter Bogt 2008; Ter Bogt et al. 2015). Further, it seems that the *purpose* that preparers of reporting tools have in mind influences the perceived usefulness of non-financial performance information by politicians. Presumptions that entities present such information merely in order to comply with reporting requirements that are set in legislation rather than for the purpose of improving decision-making (which has been reported to be the case in an earlier study; see Taylor 2009) fuel politicians' skepticism toward its usefulness (Grossi et al. 2016).

From a more general perspective, the literature addressing the usefulness of reporting tools provides mixed results. While those tools that present (non-financial) performance information are more likely to be perceived as useful if the presented information is trustworthy (mainly if measures are of high quality, if users could participate in the creation of measures, or if the purpose for presenting performance information goes beyond mere ceremonial efforts), for reporting tools that present accrual information, it is less the trustworthiness of the information but rather the complexity and understandability of accrual information that play a role in the perceived usefulness of the respective reports. However, there is some indication that with public managers and politicians becoming accustomed to accrual information, their perception of the respective reporting tools' usefulness will turn out more positively over time. Interestingly, only one of the above mentioned studies investigated the usefulness of (financial) reporting tools (Kober et al. 2010), and to the authors' best knowledge, no other empirical study has yet analyzed the usefulness of reports presenting performance information throughout the budget cycle at the central government level. However, the findings from the studies on state and local government levels are relevant to the questions investigated in the present chapter given that, first, they address the same developments in reporting tools, and second, the processes throughout the budget cycle as well as the actors involved are comparable.

The Budgeting and Accounting Reform in Austria

Between 2009 and 2013, Austria has implemented an extensive budgeting and accounting reform at the central government level (ministries and central government agencies) with the aim to base the federal budget system upon the principles of *outcome orientation*, *transparency*, and *efficiency*, and providing a *true and fair view* of the government's financial position. Applying these principles required extensive changes in the practices and processes both in the administrative and in the legislative realm. While in an initial phase, the reform focused on budget execution (budget flexibility in line ministries and central government agencies through carry-forward rules for unspent appropriations and virements) and budget planning (medium-term expenditure framework, MTEF), a second phase brought far-reaching changes to the budget structure (introduction of global budgets and streamlining of previously 1000 detailed appropriations) and the budget logic (performance budgeting and gender budgeting), as well as a shift toward an IPSAS (International Public Sector Accounting Standards)-oriented accrual-based budgeting and accounting system. The latter led to the introduction of new financial reporting tools (statement of financial position, operating statement, cash flow statement, and annexes) that present *cash-* as well as *accrual-based information*. This represents a substantial change to the preparation and reporting of budgeting and accounting information, given that before the reform, financial information was mainly presented on a cash or commitment basis. It has to be noted that, although the system is IPSAS oriented, the standards are not applied directly—rather, they are implemented through national law and respective regulations and directives, taking the Austrian legalistic tradition and national prerequisites and characteristics of public sector accounting into consideration (Steger 2012; Rauskala and Saliterer 2015; Saliterer and Korac 2018).

The newly introduced reporting tools have been designed with the aim to provide a clearer picture of the financial situation (fair presentation of the financial position, financial performance, and cash flow of the central government; see IFAC 2006) on the one hand, as well as of the non-financial performance (i.e. outcomes and outputs; see Van Dooren and Van de Walle 2008) on the other hand. Consequently, directors general and heads of department in ministries and central government agencies as well as federal legislators have access to different types of not only financial (*cash* and *accrual*) but also non-financial performance information (referred to as *performance information* in the following) throughout the budget cycle. The focus of this chapter is on year-end reports and therefore on the last stage of the budget cycle.

The central government in Austria is a particularly interesting case for analyses of the experiences with and effects of new reporting tools. First, the federal budgeting and accounting reform has been enacted by the Austrian parliament in a unanimous vote in 2007, indicating broad support by federal legislators. Second, sufficient time has elapsed since the full implementation of the federal budgeting and accounting reform (with the completion of the second phase in 2013), so that public managers (directors general and heads of department in ministries and central government agencies) as well as politicians (federal legislators, i.e. members of parliament) have experienced the new tools in their respective work routine (e.g. internal management of public sector entities and demonstrating accountability toward federal legislators and citizens in the case of public managers, and exerting control and oversight over the use of public financial resources in the case of politicians)[1] and therefore can report on the perceived relative advantage and usefulness of those tools.

Methods and Data Collection

The Austrian case presented in this chapter combines the results of (1) a gap analysis between the standard on the presentation of financial statements (IPSAS 1; see IFAC 2006), the 'old' cash- and commitment-based year-end reports, and the new accrual-based ones; (2) a quantitative survey of heads of department in ministries and central government agencies (n = 190); (3) interviews with directors general in ministries and central government agencies (n = 40); as well as (4) interviews with federal legislators (n = 17), more specifically, members of parliament who are members of the parliamentary budget committee. Given that before the budgeting and accounting reform, non-financial performance information was not included in the reporting tools, and in light of the lack of a

[1] For a more detailed discussion of public managers and politicians in budgeting at the central level, see chapters 8 and 9 in Shah (2007), and for a specific overview in Austria, see Downes et al. (2018, p. 21 ff).

commonly agreed-upon standard regarding the presentation of non-financial information, the gap analysis does not cover the comparison of the old and new reporting tools' relative advantage and usefulness in presenting such information. The relative advantage and the perceived usefulness of the new reporting tools in this respect are covered in the interviews with public managers and politicians.

The directors general and heads of department in ministries and central government agencies have been selected due to their budgeting responsibility (i.e. preparation of the budget and supplementary documents, including performance information, execution of the budget, budget controlling, and preparation of financial statements) for global budgets (directors general in ministries and central government agencies) or detail budgets (heads of department in ministries and central government agencies), and the interviewed federal legislators, more specifically, members of parliament who are members of the parliamentary budget committee, given their expertise in budgeting, public finance, or accounting (see Van Helden 2016). The survey included questions regarding the achievement of the reform goal to provide a clearer picture of the financial situation and the non-financial performance of the central government, as well as specific questions on the usefulness of the accrual-based accounting system and the integration of non-financial performance information, respective reports, and accounting information. The response rate of 54.7% yielded 104 questionnaires for further analysis. Interviews with directors general included multiple respondents and lasted about 80 minutes; interviews with federal legislators lasted 34 minutes on average. The questions covered the relevance and appropriateness, the perceived usefulness, and the relative advantage of reporting tools and the presented accounting information. The interviews were recorded, full transcriptions were produced, and a thematic analysis has been conducted, blending themes that emerged from the interviews with categories and findings in prior literature. All data have been collected during the evaluation of the federal budgeting and accounting reform in 2017, which has been coordinated by one of the authors of this chapter. Further assessments of specific aspects of fiscal transparency and budgeting that have been carried out by international organizations (International Monetary Fund [IMF], Organisation for Economic Co-operation and Development [OECD]) have contributed to the overall picture of the relative advantage and the usefulness of reporting tools at the Austrian central government level.[2]

Findings on the Relative Advantage and Usefulness of Year-End Financial Reporting Tools

The new financial reporting tools were expected to contribute to providing a true and fair view of the central government's financial position to citizens and their representatives, that is, federal legislators. In order to assess whether this is the case, and whether the new tools were better suited to do so than the traditional ones, this section first presents the findings from the gap analysis (see also Katsikas et al. 2016) between the standard on the presentation of financial statements, the 'old' cash- and commitment-based year-end reports, and the new accrual-based ones, and subsequently presents the results from the quantitative survey of heads of department in ministries and central government agencies, interviews with directors general in ministries and central government agencies, and interviews with federal legislators.

Gap Analysis Between the Standard, and the Old and New Tools in Financial Reporting

The gap analysis begins with a view of the compliance with/deviation from the relevant IPSAS 1 (that also refers to 2, 18, and 24), which describes the manner in which general-purpose financial statements (GPFS) are to be presented to ensure comparability both with an entity's financial statements of previous periods and with the financial statements of other entities (IFAC 2006). General-purpose financial statements should be designed to meet the general information needs of users who are not in a position to actively tailor financial reports that would meet their information needs (e.g. taxpayers, members of parliaments, creditors, suppliers, the media, and public sector employees). IPSAS 1 therefore addresses the presentation of financial statements, provides guidance for their structure, and sets minimum requirements for the content of financial statements prepared on an accrual basis. A complete set of

[2]The respective full reports are available via: https://www.bmf.gv.at/budget/haushaltsrechtsreform/externe-evaluierung-bundeshaushaltsrecht.html; last accessed: 10 May 2019.

financial statements in the sense of IPSAS 1 includes: a statement of financial position (balance sheet); a statement of financial performance (income statement); a statement of changes in net assets/equity; a cash flow statement; if the entity makes its budget publicly available: the approved budget, including a comparison of budget and actual amounts; and notes, comprising a summary of significant accounting policies and other explanatory notes.

Although the reporting tools that have been in place before the reform already comprised some of the components required by IPSAS 1, the provided information can be described as insufficient in providing a clearer picture of the central government's financial situation. The traditional Organic Budget Law (*Bundeshaushaltsgesetz, BHG*), which has been implemented in 1986, provided that the central government present an annual statement of income as well as a balance sheet. However, the underlying recognition and measurement rules could be described as inadequate from an IPSAS point of view. For example, traditional accounting provided a 50% depreciation rule (assets have been subject to a 50% depreciation in the year of acquisition and to a 50% depreciation in the year of their disposal), recognition and measurement rules for provisions were non-existent, disclosure of equity was insufficient, and the central government did not present a three-part cash flow statement.

In contrast, the new financial year-end reports appear relatively advantageous compared to the old ones. This is not only due to the definition of comprehensive accounting and valuation principles in the Organic Budget Law and respective regulations as well as directives, but also due to learning effects in preparing the financial reports. In sum, this has led to a steadily increasing quality in the presentation of information. Since 2013, the financial statements comprise a balance sheet, an income statement, a cash flow statement, a comparison of budgeted and actual figures, and notes, which comprise a summary of significant accounting policies (only in the first year of their adoption) as well as other explanatory notes (see Table 1). The changes in net assets/equity are not presented in a separate statement and, with regard to the content, can only be considered partly in line with the IPSAS requirements. While the formal requirements for general-purpose statements (in terms of available information) are largely met, the main area for improvement is seen in a more focused presentation of the required statements in one report. Currently, the necessary information—though available—is shown in different sub-reports. This fragmented presentation of information is not in line with the central

Table 1 Gap analysis between the standard, and the old and new tools in financial reporting

IPSAS requirements	*Old financial reporting tools (until 2012)*	*New financial reporting tools (from 2013)*
Statement of financial position (balance sheet)	~	+ (mostly IPSAS-compliant)
Statement of financial performance (income statement)	~	+ (mostly IPSAS-compliant)
Statement of changes in net assets/equity	–	~
Cash flow statement	–	+ (mostly IPSAS-compliant)
Approved budget, including a comparison of budget and actual amounts	+ (mostly IPSAS-compliant)	+ (mostly IPSAS-compliant)
Notes, comprising a summary of significant accounting policies and other explanatory notes	– (no explicit indication of notes, no statement on accounting policies)	~ (notes mostly IPSAS-compliant, but insufficient cross-referencing; statement on accounting policies, but no explanations)
One report comprising all necessary financial information (the complete set of financial statements)	–	– (financial information presented in different sub-reports)

Notes: + Existent and IPSAS-compliant; ~ Existent but non-IPSAS-compliant; – Nonexistent

Source: See Saliterer et al. (2018)

IPSAS requirement of presenting one report that is clearly distinguishable from other reports and comprises the complete set of the abovementioned financial statements (also showing the specified minimum of line items). On this note, the fragmented presentation may reduce the level of user-friendliness and decision-making relevance, and as such, may also be detrimental to the reports' perceived quality and usefulness from the perspective of stakeholders (Saliterer et al. 2018). The latter aspects were key issues in the empirical investigation with directors general and heads of department in ministries and central government agencies and the federal legislators, where the conducted surveys and interviews aimed at providing insights into the quality of presentation of information in the year-end financial reports as well as their usefulness (informative value). In this regard, it has to be noted that the statements above and the analysis of the newly introduced financial reports concern the reports for the years 2013–2016 (see the information on data collection in 2017).

Perceived Relative Advantage and Perceived Usefulness of the New Tools in Financial Reporting

The appendix of IPSAS 1 presents attributes that aim to ensure that users of financial statements are provided with useful financial information, not only from an accountability, but also from a decision-making perspective. The four attributes of understandability, reliability, relevance, and comparability in particular are considered as principal qualitative characteristics and hence also form the basis of the assessment of financial reports after the reform. While the assessment showed the need to provide further guidance for operationalizing the different attributes, it also revealed that the financial statements evidently meet the (observable) qualitative requirements (Saliterer et al. 2018). This is also supported by the empirical data. The quantitative survey of heads of department in ministries and central government agencies (endowed with budgeting responsibility for detail budgets) shows that, from their perspective (on average 59 responses), the introduction of the new financial reporting tools has *relative advantage* over the tools that have been in place before the reform. The respondents rate the new reports' contribution to providing a *true and fair view* (70% agree or fully agree), or a clearer picture, of the central government's financial situation, as higher compared to the traditional reports that have been in place before the reform. In particular, the presented information is perceived as more *complete/comprehensive* (referring to the extent of relevant information needed to assess the central government's financial position; 66% agree or fully agree), as of more *informational value* (referring to the meaningfulness of the presented information; 63% agree or fully agree), and as better *understandable* (referring to the time needed to obtain a view of the financial situation; 56% agree or fully agree). This impression of higher usefulness of the new tools in financial reporting was also confirmed in the interviews with federal legislators, who pointed to a relative advantage (in terms of *overall quality*) of the new (accrual-based) year-end financial reports in comparison to the old (cash- and commitment-based) ones. They also stressed that the new tools provided a *true and fair view*, or a clearer picture, of the central government's financial situation. Also in this respondent group, the newly implemented federal government financial statement (*Bundesrechnungsabschluss*, BRA) seems to have relative advantage over the traditional financial reporting tools.

In terms of *usefulness*, and in particular in providing a clearer presentation of information (clear structure, and providing a better decision-making basis), the view of heads of department was more critical (in both cases, only 46% agree or fully agree). This has also been shown in the interviews with directors general. In fact, the interviewees reported shortcomings in the clarity of presentation of the financial information and also perceived the presented information as overwhelming. The interviews with the federal legislators provided some support of the findings from the survey of heads of department and the interviews with directors general. The legislators' view of the usefulness of reported information, more specifically, gives insights into the suitability of reporting tools for external accountability purposes. Legislators, too, perceive that the introduction of the new financial reporting tools (particularly of the balance sheet and the income statement that as such have not existed before the reform) has led to an increased quality in the presentation of financial information. They also report that these tools contribute to obtaining a true and fair view of the central government's financial situation. However, the interviewees (being members of the budget committee, they have expertise in budgeting, public finance, or accounting) also pointed to some potential for improvement in the presentation of distinct financial information. While they acknowledged that the new budgeting and accounting system had its advantages, the interviewed legislators emphasized that for (political) stakeholders with no training or experience in accrual accounting, the old system was easier to grasp.

In the survey of heads of department, we also asked the respondents to indicate the *usefulness* of the (newly available) operating statement and the statement of financial position that presented accrual accounting information for different *purposes*. The usefulness of accrual information was rated highest when it came to the increased transparency of the consumption of resources (e.g. in form of depreciation; 73% (overall level)/61% (unit level) agree or fully agree) and future costs (e.g. liabilities, provisions; 59% (overall level)/61% (unit level) agree or fully agree). Nearly half of the respondents (46% agree or fully agree) acknowledge that the newly available information is relevant for managing their units and that it makes the consequences of decisions more transparent. Accrual information however neither changed the steering logic in their units (only 28% agree or fully agree) nor did it result in more objective and demand-oriented budget consultations (only 26% agree or fully agree). These results additionally supported the general picture gained during the interviews with directors general, who stressed that the operating statement and the statement of financial position were mainly useful for external accountability purposes, for example, the overall evaluation of the financial condition of the central government. However—similar to the results in the survey—they rated the importance of these information sources for internal management purposes in relation to administrative effort as rather low. This is partly due to implementation problems, that is, technical and conceptual challenges. More generally, directors general and heads of department in ministries and central government agencies emphasized the necessity of accrual accounting, but were more skeptical of accrual budgeting. In sum, they are somewhat reluctant to use accrual-based information (presented in the operating statement and the statement of financial position) for internal management purposes and still considered the cash (commitment)-based reports as most relevant in this regard.

Findings on the Relative Advantage and Usefulness of (Non-financial) Performance Reporting

Following the budgeting and accounting reform's principle of outcome orientation, new tools of non-financial reporting have been introduced to present different forms of performance information to stakeholders. Given that before the budgeting and accounting reform, non-financial performance information was not included in the reporting tools, the new tools of non-financial reporting appear to have a clear relative advantage over the tools in place before 2013. Performance information is now included in the budget documents that are presented to legislators for budget approval.

In Austria, requirements regarding the presentation of non-financial performance information in budget documents and in year-end reports on non-financial performance (reports on outcome orientation) are set in the Organic Budget Law (BHG 2013). For each of the 32 'budget chapters' (mirroring ministries, central government agencies), administrative decision-makers must present a brief *mission statement* and a maximum of five *outcome targets* (one of which needs to refer to *gender equality*). At the subsequent level (70 global budgets), a maximum of five *activity objectives* per outcome target are defined. There is only a *loose link* between the allocated *resources* and the *performance information* provided in the budget documents; thus, the Austrian system can be described as performance-informed rather than performance-based, or direct performance budgeting (see OECD 2007; Robinson 2007; Moynihan and Beazley 2016). Performance information that refers to 'detail budgets' (operational units), and thus comprises more specific information that is required for the internal management of operational units within ministries and central government agencies, is not part of the budget documents and therefore not presented to federal legislators or the public.

As part of the budget documents that form the basis for the Annual Budgeting Act, the defined mission statements, outcome targets, and activity objectives however are—in principle—subject to legislative approval in the parliament. This information however is only *indicative*, and thus not legally binding. Yet, the national audit office evaluates the performance information's validity and reliability *ex post* and publishes the results in publicly accessible reports. In addition to including outcome targets and activity objectives in budget documents, and to disclosing their achievement in a non-financial year-end report (report on outcome orientation), performance information is included in ex-ante (planning) as well as ex-post *impact assessments* (reporting), which are mandatory for all new laws and policy initiatives. However, these are stand-alone assessments conducted by ministries and central government agencies and are not integrated in the budget documents or the report on outcome orientation. Given this chapter's focus on year-end reports, the tool of impact assessments will not be discussed further in the following.

Ensuring transparency in the new budgeting and accounting system requires not only the presentation of targets and objectives, but also the preparation of reports where an ex-post view of the achievement or the progress in the achievement of the latter are disclosed. However, financial and non-financial (performance) year-end reporting are decoupled: performance information is *not integrated* in the *financial statement of the federal government*. Information on the achievement of or progress toward achieving outcome targets and activity objectives is presented in a separate report (*report on outcome orientation*) and published on a *website* ('outcome monitoring': www.wirkungsmonitoring.gv.at). This is in line with IPSAS 1.18, which recommends either including non-financial information directly in the year-end report or presenting it in a separate statement (note that IPSAS 1 does not provide standards on the nature or quality of non-financial performance indicators). Both reporting tools are publicly accessible. The report on outcome orientation is compiled by the Federal Chancellary, which is responsible for the framework and the methodologies for performance management in the central government in general, as well as for the quality assurance in the selection, presentation, and disclosure of performance information in central government entities. For this purpose, the Federal Chancellary monitors the performance indicators and provides training to staff across the entities. On the website, users can access *all* performance information provided by the ministries and central government agencies. While this may result in information overload to non-professional users, the presentation of performance information lends from approaches of *popular reporting*, or *citizen-centered reporting* (e.g. use of graphs, charts, and tables to convey the information), which may alleviate this potential overload.

Perceived Relative Advantage and Perceived Usefulness of the New Tools in Non-financial Reporting

The presentation and disclosure of performance information were expected to contribute to increasing transparency, that is, providing a clearer picture of the central government's non-financial performance to the parliament and the public. A considerable number of heads of department reported (40% agreed or fully agreed to the statement) that the introduction of performance information contributed to achieving this goal, supporting the view of the new tools' relative advantage compared to the situation before the reform. Moreover, 48% of the respondents (fully) agreed that the outcome-oriented structure of the budget documents increased the understandability and the informational value of the budget, thus indicating *usefulness* of these tools. This was also confirmed in the interviews with directors general, who were generally welcoming of the respective tools, but mainly saw them as a means for meeting external accountability requirements. Several interviewees perceived the performance information to be useful in informing the public, as well as their own employees, about the aims and objectives of their units, and explicitly reported about the strong efforts in setting targets. Nevertheless, some of them questioned the 'translation' of highly specialized tasks into only three to five outcome targets, the 'exercise' of defining targets where they were predetermined by their legally provided tasks and duties anyway, cut-and-paste approaches, and the selection of low-conflict outcome targets.

Legislators expressed a similar view: while they acknowledged that performance information, in principle, was considered *useful*, they sometimes criticized that the quality of the presented information (the defined outcome targets) varied across the central government entities. Further, legislators reported a cut-and-paste approach, easy-to-reach targets, and a misalignment between the outcome targets and the activities to achieve those targets (see also Saliterer et al. 2019), while at the same time recognizing the general difficulty of measuring outcomes in the public sector. This group explicitly established a link between the (perceived) quality of the reported performance information and its usefulness. However, legislators also pointed to a significant shortcoming in the reporting. By design (of the practices and procedures in reporting), there is a time lag between the presentation of the financial statement and that of the report on outcome orientation. For example, the financial statement for the year 2017 was presented to the parliament in June 2018, but the report on outcome orientation was prepared and published by the Federal Chancellary in October 2018. As a consequence, financial and non-financial reports are presented separately, but in addition, also with a time lag. Thus stakeholders are given little opportunity to obtain an integrated view of the central government's financial and non-financial performance. The results are also reflected in the recent assessments by the OECD and the IMF (Downes et al. 2018; Alves et al. 2017). While the system of performance-informed budgeting was described as well-structured and successfully implemented, the coherence and relevance of the targets and objectives, the alignment of indicators, and the only loose connection between the government program and the selected outcome targets in line ministries were the main points of critique.

Discussion and Conclusion

The present chapter set out to explore whether new tools of reporting may be better suited to provide a clearer picture of the financial situation (i.e. present fairly the financial position, financial performance, and cash flow) as well as of the non-financial performance of the Austrian central government compared to traditional ones that have been in place before the extensive federal budgeting and accounting reform. Along these lines, both a qualitative assessment/content analysis and quantitative and qualitative empirical evidence showed that the recently implemented *accrual-based reporting tools* hold the promise of providing a true and fair view (clear picture) of the government's financial situation (and performance) from the perspective of both public managers and politicians, and thus are *relatively advantageous* over traditional reporting tools.

Our results show that, despite its promised and largely achieved *usefulness*, implementing accrual accounting and reporting in the public sector remains a challenging endeavor. While the introduction of the new accrual-based accounting system and the respective reports provides a more comprehensive view of the central government's financial situation, cash-based information is still pivotal in budget negotiations. In this regard, our results support earlier findings in different European countries (Sterck and Scheers 2006; Nasi and Steccolini 2008). Given the findings in contexts where public managers have gained more experience with the new accounting systems and reporting tools (Andriani et al., Kober et al. 2010), a possible explanation for the (still) dominant role of cash-based information in the Austrian context is the relatively limited experience with the new reporting tools. However, measures like the definition of fiscal targets on an accrual basis (see Bergmann 2012, p. 20; Downes et al. 2018), which are likely be implemented in the Austrian budgeting and accounting system only in the medium to long term, may enhance the usefulness of the respective new reports.

The legislators' view included in the present chapter suggests a high perceived usefulness of accrual-based financial year-end reports, but only limited use of accrual-based information. Along these lines, some legislators felt that for some addressees of financial information, the cash-/commitment-based budgeting and accounting system was easier to grasp. The question of whether and to what extent this is true for legislators with no particular expertise in budgeting, public finance, or accounting and for other addressees of financial reports (e.g. citizens, interest groups) was however beyond the scope of the applied analyses. As these tools have been introduced relatively recently (2013), again, the mentioned challenges may be overcome as the tools and systems mature over time: addressees of financial reports will become more accustomed with the latter. Reports may however also be further developed and intermediaries (e.g. Budget Office) may help in 'translating' the rich information in summaries of financial statements to the parliament and the public, and thus increase the reports' usefulness (see also Posner and Park 2007).

The Austrian case shows that public managers (directors general and heads of department in ministries and central government agencies) perceived *non-financial reports* as relatively advantageous over the situation before the reform (lack of non-financial performance information). In several terms, the Austrian case shows however that the outcome targets and indicators presented throughout the budget cycle (used for external accountability) and the more detailed, operational targets and indicators used in management control systems in ministries and agencies (used for internal steering and organizational learning) are only loosely coupled (see Laegreid et al. 2008). While this finding indicates a comparatively low perceived usefulness of non-financial reporting tools for internal management, it may not be understood as an indicator for line ministries rejecting performance information. Rather, it may simply suggest that public managers see more value in more nuanced targets and objectives when it comes to the purpose of internal management.

Interviews with federal legislators also indicated a perceived *relative advantage* of performance-informed budgeting and respective reports, but at the same time, this group perceived the *usefulness* of the presented non-financial information in a more nuanced way. Their points of criticism of the presented and reported performance information are consistent with the issues raised by public managers, and also with findings in earlier studies, for example, the quality of performance information (e.g. Joyce and Sieg 2000; Grossi et al. 2016). To influence the latter, federal legislators established a designated committee (particularly focusing on outcome targets) that scrutinizes the provided information and is a crucial intermediary as well as a platform for participation in the topic of performance-informed budgeting and the performance information reported throughout the budget cycle (see also Saliterer et al. 2019).

Focusing on public managers (directors general, heads of department), the present chapter offers insights into the perceived usefulness of the new available information for internal management and for external accountability, while the perspective of politicians (federal legislators) offers insights into the respective tools' usefulness in exerting control and oversight over the use of public financial resources by initiating or enhancing a dialogue with primary addressees of reporting tools. The limitation of the study lies with the focus on federal legislators, thus largely leaving other addressees (e.g. citizens, interest groups) out of the picture. Finally, our findings point to the need of considering the completeness/consistency of reports less from a perspective of structure, and more from a perspective of time. While the separate disclosure of the financial reports and the report on outcome orientation (performance information) may negatively affect their usefulness, it turned out that it is rather the time lag in the presentation of the reports that was detrimental to particularly the legislators' possibility of gaining an integrated view of the central government's financial as well as non-financial performance. This issue may be addressed by integrating ex-post performance information at a chapter level into year-end financial statements.

References

Alves, M., Sayegh, A., Renteria, C., et al. (2017, November). Austria. Fiscal Transparency Evaluation. International Monetary Fund. Technical Assistance Report.

Andriani, Y., Kober, R., & Ng, J. (2010). Decision Usefulness of Cash and Accrual Information: Public Sector Managers' Perceptions. *Australian Accounting Review, 20*(2), 144–153.

Bergmann, A. (2012). The Influence of the Nature of Government Accounting and Reporting in Decision-Making: Evidence from Switzerland. *Public Money & Management, 32*(1), 15–20.

BHG. (2013). Bundesgesetz über die Führung des Bundeshaushaltes (Bundeshaushaltsgesetz 2013 – BHG 2013) StF: BGBl. I Nr. 139/2009 (NR: GP XXIV RV 480 AB 578 S. 51.)

Bourdeaux, C. (2008). Integrating Performance Information into Legislative Budget Processes. *Public Performance & Management Review, 31*(4), 547–569.

Davis, F. D. (1989). Perceived Usefulness, Perceived Ease of Use, and User Acceptance of Information Technology. *MIS Quarterly, 13*(3), 319–340.

Downes, R., Von Trapp, L., & Jansen, J. (2018). *Budgeting in Austria*. Paris: OECD.

Ezzamel, M., Hyndman, N., Johnsen, A., Lapsley, I., & Pallot, J. (2005). Accounting, Accountability and Devolution: A Study of the Use of Accounting Information by Politicians in the Northern Ireland Assembly's First Term. *The Irish Accounting Review, 12*(1), 39–62.

Ezzamel, M., Hyndman, N., Johnsen, A., & Lapsley, I. (2014). Reforming Central Government: An Evaluation of an Accounting Innovation. *Critical Perspectives on Accounting, 25*(4–5), 409–422.

Grossi, G., Reichard, C., & Ruggiero, P. (2016). Appropriateness and Use of Performance Information in the Budgeting Process: Some Experiences from German and Italian Municipalities. *Public Performance & Management Review, 39*(3), 581–606.

Guthrie, J. (1998). Application of Accrual Accounting in the Australian Public Sector–Rhetoric or Reality. *Financial Accountability & Management, 14*(1), 1–19.

Guthrie, J., Olson, O., & Humphrey, C. (1999). Debating Developments in New Public Financial Management: The Limits of Global Theorising and Some New Ways Forward. *Financial Accountability & Management, 15*(3–4), 209–228.

Ho, A. T.-K. (2006). Accounting for the Value of Performance Measurement from the Perspective of Midwestern Mayors. *Journal of Public Administration Research and Theory, 16*(2), 217–237.

IFAC. (2000). *Government Financial Reporting. Accounting Issues and Practices.* Study 11. New York: International Federation of Accountants. http://www.ifac.org

IFAC. (2006). *IPSAS 1 – Presentation of Financial Statements.* http://www.ifac.org

Jones, S., & Puglisi, N. (1997). The Relevance of AAS 29 to Australian Public Sector: A Cause for Doubt? *Abacus, 33*(1), 1–18.

Joyce, P. G., & Sieg, S. (2000). *Using Performance Information for Budgeting: Clarifying the Framework and Investigating Recent State Experience.* Prepared for the 2000 Symposium of the Center for Accountability and Performance of the American Society for Public Administration.

Jorge, S. M., da Costa Carvalho, J. B., & Fernandes, M. J. (2008). From Cash to Accruals In Portuguese Local Government Accounting: What Has Truly Changed. *Revista de Estudos Politécnicos/Polytechnical Studies Review, VI*(10), 239–261.

Katsikas, E., Manes-Rossi, F., & Orelli, R. L. (2016). *Towards Integrated Reporting: Accounting Change in the Public Sector.* Cham: Springer.

Kober, R., Lee, J., & Ng, J. (2010). Mind Your Accruals: Perceived Usefulness of Financial Information in the Australian Public Sector Under Different Accounting Systems. *Financial Accountability & Management, 26*(3), 267–298.

Lægreid, P., Roness, P. G., & Rubecksen, K. (2008). Performance Information and Performance Steering: Integrated System or Loose Coupling? In V. Dooren & V. de Walle (Eds.), *Performance Information in the Public Sector* (Governance and Public Management Series). London: Palgrave Macmillan.

Liguori, M., Sicilia, M., & Steccolini, I. (2012). Some Like it Non-Financial... *Public Management Review, 14*(7), 903–922.

Melkers, J., & Willoughby, K. (2005). Models of Performance-Measurement Use in Local Governments: Understanding Budgeting, Communication, and Lasting Effects. *Public Administration Review, 65*(2), 180–190.

Montesinos, V., Brusca, I., Rossi, F. M., & Aversano, N. (2013). The Usefulness of Performance Reporting in Local Government: Comparing Italy and Spain. *Public Money & Management, 33*(3), 171–176.

Moynihan, D., & Beazley, I. (2016). *Toward Next-Generation Performance Budgeting: Lessons from the Experiences of Seven Reforming Countries.* Washington, DC: The World Bank.

Nasi, G., & Steccolini, I. (2008). Implementation of Accounting Reforms. An Empirical Investigation into Italian Local Governments. *Public Management Review, 10*(2), 175–196.

Nogueira, S. P. S., & Jorge, S. M. F. (2017). The Perceived Usefulness of Financial Information for Decision Making in Portuguese Municipalities the Importance of Internal Control. *Journal of Applied Accounting Research, 18*(1), 116–136.

OECD. (2007). *Performance Budgeting in OECD Countries.* http://siteresources.worldbank.org/

Posner, P., & Park, C.-K. (2007). Role of the Legislatur in the Budget Process: Recent Trends and Innovations. *OECD Journal on Budgeting, 7*(3), 1–26.

Rauskala, I., & Saliterer, I. (2015). Public Sector Accounting and Auditing in Austria. In I. Brusca et al. (Eds.), *Public Sector Accounting and Auditing in Europe – The Challenge of Harmonization* (pp. 12–22). Basingstoke: Palgrave Macmillan.

Ricci, P. (2019). Accountability. In A. Farazmand (Ed.), *Global Encyclopedia of Public Administration, Public Policy, and Governance.* New York: Springer.

Robinson, M. (Ed.). (2007). *Performance Budgeting: Linking Funding and Results.* New York: Springer.

Saliterer, I., & Korac, S. (2018). *Externe Evaluierung der Haushaltsrechtsreform des Bundes im Jahr 2017.* Endbericht. Available via: https://www.bmf.gv.at/

Saliterer, I., Korac, S., Bergmann, A., & Fuchs, S. (2018). *Evaluierung der Haushaltsrechtsreform des Bundes im Jahr 2017.* Arbeitspaket 3 – Doppisches Haushaltswesen. Available via: https://www.bmf.gv.at/

Saliterer, I., Korac, S., Moser, B., & Rondo-Brovetto, P. (2019). How Politicians Use Performance Information in a Budgetary Context – New Insights from the Central Government Level. *Public Administration* online first.

Shah, A. (Ed.). (2007). *Budgeting and Budgetary Institutions.* Washington, DC: The World Bank.

Steger, G. (2012). Budget Reform in Austria: From Traditional to Modern Budgeting. *Presupuesto y Gasto Público, 69*, 147–162.

Sterck, M., & Scheers, B. (2006). Trends in Performance Budgeting in Seven OECD Countries. *Public Performance & Management Review, 30*(1), 47–72.

Taylor, J. (2009). Strengthening the Link Between Performance Measurement and Decision Making. *Public Administration, 87*(4), 853–871.

Ter Bogt, H. J. (2008). Management Accounting Change and New Public Management in Local Government: A Reassessment of Ambitions and Results – An Institutionalist Approach to Accounting Change in the Dutch Public Sector. *Financial Accountability & Management, 24*(3), 209–241.

Ter Bogt, H. J., Van Helden, G., & Van Der Kolk, B. (2015). Challenging the NPM Ideas About Performance Management: Selectivity and Differentiation in Outcome-Oriented Performance Budgeting. *Financial Accountability & Management, 31*(3), 287–315.

Van Dooren, W., & Van de Walle, S. (Eds.). (2008). *Performance Information in the Public Sector: How It Is Used*. New York: Palgrave Macmillan.
Van Helden, J. (2016). Literature Review and Challenging Research Agenda on Politicians' Use of Accounting Information. *Public Money & Management, 36*(7), 531–538.

Iris Saliterer is Professor of Public and Non-profit Management at the University of Freiburg, Germany, and an associate professor at the Alpen-Adria-Universitaet Klagenfurt, Austria. She was coordinator of the external evaluation of the Austrian federal budgeting and accounting reform in 2017 and the leading researcher for the work package on accrual accounting. Her research focuses on public sector budgeting and accounting, performance management, financial resilience, and delivery of public services.

Sanja Korac is Professor of Public Management at the German University of Administrative Sciences Speyer, Germany, and an associate professor at the Alpen-Adria-Universitaet Klagenfurt, Austria. Her main research areas include public sector accounting, performance management, financial resilience, and motivation in the public sector. She has been part of the research team in the external evaluation of the Austrian federal budgeting and accounting reform in 2017.

No Longer Only Numbers: An Exploratory Analysis of the Visual Turn in Reporting of Public Sector Organisations

Pasquale Ruggiero

Introduction

Organisations' communication takes place in different ways, either written or oral. Among the former, accounting documents have been one of the most used tools by organisations and their different stakeholders to provide information for their decision-making processes. The increasing organisational and environmental complexity in which organisations operate has led them to develop reporting models based on a multidimensional concept of performance (Bourguignon et al. 2004) in order to pursue communication objectives hardly achievable through traditional accounting reports (Inkinen et al. 2017). Organisations have developed various reports for communicating their information, especially that information which is difficult to translate in financial figures (e.g. intangible

P. Ruggiero (✉)
University of Siena, Siena, Italy

Brighton Business School, Brighton, UK
e-mail: ruggiero@unisi.it

F. Manes-Rossi, R. Levy Orelli (eds.), *New Trends in Public Sector Reporting*, Public Sector Financial Management,
https://doi.org/10.1007/978-3-030-40056-9_6

resources/performance). The development of these reports has, on the one hand, constituted an element through which companies can take on board non-financial aspects with greater awareness; on the other, these reports have made it possible for companies to enhance their communication relationship with stakeholders and be more compliant with the increasing demand for accountability.

Any organisation is an entity participating in a network of relationships within which it implements communicative and exchange processes. This is the case also for public sector organisations (hereafter PSOs), especially after recent decades, during which they have experienced a wide and deep reform process—the so-called New Public Management (NPM) (Barzelay and Armajani 1992; Hyndman and Lapsley 2016). Public administrations have tried to translate and implement in their sector the logics and tools of private sector management for providing public services more efficiently and effectively. This translation has been carried out directly by innovating public administrations or indirectly by an increasing involvement of private sector organisations in the production and provision of public services (Denis et al. 2015; English and Guthrie 2003). Unlike private organisations, PSOs use public resources, and because of the impact produced through their activities at the social level, the larger is their audience and the greater the typology of stakeholders and their interests in accountability processes (Brennan and Solomon 2008; Brown et al. 2015; Piotrowski and Steccolini 2014). Accountability and its related tools are an issue not only for *accounters* but also for *accountees*. PSOs are interested in developing appropriate reporting tools mainly for two reasons: to communicate and manage internally their performance in a continually improved manner and to legitimate their existence at the social level.

Despite this growing demand for accountability, PSOs have adopted new reporting systems containing no longer only numbers, especially financial figures, such as social reporting (Contrafatto 2014; Monfardini et al. 2013), intellectual capital statements (Dumay et al. 2015) and integrated reporting (Eccles and Krzus 2015).

The drawing-up of a reporting document raises problems not only related to the definition of its content but also for transferring the information it contains in the most effective and efficient way. Both aspects need to be managed to comply with the increasing request of accountability for PSOs. According to Davison (2008), corporate annual reports are an exercise in communication to be managed and studied from different perspectives. Even though the quantity of material published by PSOs is steadily increasing, the analysis conducted by most research rarely focuses on understanding and analysing the words, images, music and visuals in general that complement the information on financial performance. This is especially true for PSOs, for whom the visual dimension of reporting is particularly important, as they need to communicate to their stakeholders performance that is difficult to translate into financial figures. This contribution aims at filling this gap by analysing the visual dimension of the annual reports of PSOs in order to understand their capacity for contributing to an increase in accountability processes. In particular, the chapter focuses on the images used in PSOs' sustainability/integrated reports.[1]

To meet the aforementioned objective, an exploratory analysis of a case was carried out (Yin 2003). In particular, the sustainability/integrated reports published by a public sector organisation (Hera) operating in the Italian multi-utility sector was analysed using a longitudinal approach. Since 2003, Hera has developed reporting documents different from classical and compulsory financial accounting documents, that is, sustainability reports. These reports, especially those published recently, contain most of the information required by the IIRC to classify a report as integrated (Katsikas et al. 2017). To develop the case study, the official reports issued by Hera during the period 2003–2017 were analysed.

The structure of the chapter is as follows. Section "The Visual Turn in Accounting: A Brief Literature Review" provides a literature review on the visual turn in accounting. Looking at Barthes' theory on the rhetoric of image, section "Images, Text and Messages in Reporting: A Theoretical Framework" develops the theoretical framework adopted for the analysis. Section "Case Study" is dedicated to presenting the case study. The last section offers a discussion and some final remarks.

[1] In this chapter, we refer interchangeably to sustainability or integrated reporting, since the underlying principles, respectively the Global Reporting Initiative (GRI) and the integrated reporting (IR) model, are from some points of view similar or even overlapping. For example, it is possible to recall that both the GRI and the IR speak about materiality, meaning that the information provided has to be relevant for receivers. Additionally, according to the GRI and the International Integrated Reporting Council (IIRC), both financial and non-financial performance must be reported.

The Visual Turn in Accounting: A Brief Literature Review

The drawing-up of reporting documents is a communication practice of fundamental importance for managing organisations' relationships. Over the years, reporting practices of non-financial information have become increasingly important and have supplemented traditional reporting tools (Busco et al. 2018; Modell 2004). These reports differ from traditional ones not only in their content but also in the lower number of rules that regulate their drawing-up and issuing. Therefore, "an increasing proportion of that communication is carried out by the discretionary use of words and pictures that surround the financial statements and other regulated discourses" (Davison 2008: 792). Furthermore, non-financial reports communicate aspects that are mainly immaterial and difficult to be translated into numbers. As a consequence, the *paratext* used in reporting companies' performance is increasingly important (Davison 2011b). Practitioners also recognise the importance of the non-technical aspects of organisational reports. According to the Accounting Standard Board (ABS 2000), increasingly greater attention should be directed to the use of graphs, especially if related to financial information, because of their potential in contributing to impression management.

Although modern society is defined as the society of image, accounting scholars have shown little interest in analysing the visual dimension in organisations, especially in their accounting reports (Davison 2010). While there is a mass of research on its accounting content, the changing form of the report as a whole has been subject to relatively little systematic investigation. Rather, attention has focused on the factors impinging on the choice of accounting methods, the increasing extent of regulatory influences and, more recently, the creative design of the accounting methods mobilised in the reports. All such topics are important and remain in need of further investigation.

Research on the visual dimension of accounting has been mainly linked to the memorisation aspects that images allow (Carruthers 2008) and therefore to the resulting cognitive impacts. According to Carruthers (2008: II), "merely running one's eyes over the written pages is not reading at all, for the writing must be transferred into memory, from graphemes on parchment or papyrus or paper to images written in one's brain by emotion and sense". Therefore, images are the way of perceiving and memorising the message coming from what a reader is looking at, either written words or pictures or photographs or paintings (Quattrone 2009).

One of the main reasons why the study of images in accounting has scarcely attracted the interest of scholars could be related to the ambiguity of the object to investigate because of the multiplicity of messages that could derive from its analysis (Davison 2010). This aside, the visual dimension of reporting documents is an important issue in the accounting field of study mainly for two reasons. First, images convey messages that could be differently interpreted by their viewers. Therefore, in order to increase the probability that the desired message is conveyed correctly, the decision on the images to report should be the result of a well-defined strategy. Second, although accountants are responsible for the definition and preparation of the information to be communicated, the final reporting document issued by an organisation is also the result of the activity of other subjects, who, because of their different knowledge and sensitivity, could insert additional contrasting messages in the report. Both these reasons lead accounting scholars and accountants to consider the study of visual dimension an issue as important as any other aspect related to the reporting documents of organisations. "The discretionary material unconsciously places an organisation within much broader historical, geographical, social, political and cultural vistas; it is words and pictures which are silently revelatory, often through style alone, of the context in which a business operates" (Davison 2008: 793). The need to pay more attention to the structuring of the non-financial part of corporate reports also derives from the decreasing attention that general readers lend to financial statements (balance sheet and profit-and-loss account) compared with the narrative parts contained in reporting documents (Bartlett and Chandler 1997; Loughran 2018; Yekini et al. 2016).

The visual aspects of reporting and their importance were identified towards the end of the 1990s by Hopwood (1996: 56), who published an introduction to a special issue in Accounting, Organizations and Society (AOS), where he states that "creating corporate annual reports has become an activity in its own right". This change is also witnessed by the different meaning attributed to the word publicity when referred to an annual report. Compared with the initial meaning of publicity as the way of making corporations "visible to a wider community, today, in a world of multi-coloured and even multi-media corporate reporting, 'publicity' implies something very different. Rather than being associated with a rhetoric of visibility, representation and openness, 'publicity' now implies a more active management of the corporate image. [...] A more proactive construction of a quite particular visibility and meaning often appears to have replaced a seemingly more passive rhetoric of revealing what was there" (Hopwood 1996: 55–56). Three articles were published in this special issue of AOS.

In recognising the important role played by the visual in the annual corporate reports of US companies, Graves, Flesher and Jordan (1996) have discussed two important aspects: (a) the impact played by the institutional environment, that is, the television-based culture of the US during the 1960s, on the development of the visual structures of organisational reports and (b) the participation of images in defining messages to accounts readers apart from those mainly financial. According to the scholars, "the aesthetic moment that inheres in the idea of balanced accounts does not constitute the only, remnant meaning in accounts for contemporary (postmodern) report readers and, consequently, that the 'complementary' aestheticism that inheres in visual design does not, in itself, fully explain its inclusion in those reports. [...] accounts have not lost their claim to truth among the American public, but constitute, for Americans in general, a meaningful – and thus authentic – social construct" (Graves et al. 1996: 59). McKinstry (1996) focused his interest on development of the visual dimension in a single organisation, Burton plc, over the period 1930–1994. This longitudinal case study made clear a change in the nature of the organisational report. After 1984, Burton plc had started to use their annual reports as a communication tool, especially after the experiencing of a period of crisis. This change was mainly due to the different relationships of the design industry with large entities and the adoption of reports as a tool for persuading readers. McKinstry (1996) highlights an important drawback coming from this change in the role of organisational reports. The new relationship between organisations and the design industry was considered as able to change the statutory environment within which organisational reports were produced, with a negative effect on their readers. "The requirement for audited accounting statements was originally intended as a protection for shareholders and creditors, achieved through independent third-party check. [...] *Correspondingly* this seems an ill-advised development, if the non-statutory material is capable of overriding in the minds of readers the numerical and other statutory messages now relegated to the rear of annual reports" (McKinstry 1996: 110, emphasis added by the author). In the last paper included in the special issue, the visual dimension of organisational reports is analysed to make clear its modern and postmodern interpretation. In particular,

Preston, Wright and Young (1996) highlight the importance of considering images not only as a representative tool of reality, but as a constitutive tool "at the disposal" of any reader in order to build a reality through establishing a relationship with the producer. "Recognizing this potential in turn creates an opportunity either to challenge the realities and identities that corporations seek to represent and constitute, or [...] to utilise images to rethink our bodily roots and view subjectively not as natural or historical (or even corporate) given, but rather, as an open-ended project to be continually constructed" (Preston et al. 1996: 133).

Even after the publication of the aforementioned papers in 1996, there has still been scarce interest in the visual dimension of organisational reports, apart from Davison's contributions. Aware of the important role played in studying accounting from a communication perspective, Davison has looked at the visual dimension of organisational reporting mainly through the lens of Barthes' theory (Davison 2011a). She has analysed both financial and non-financial reports, but her attention has been attracted mainly by the use of images for communicating performance characterised by an immaterial dimension, such as intangible resources. At the same time, Davison has given a solid contribution to the literature by importing from other disciplines and framing theoretical frameworks able to provide accounting scholars with a tool for analysing systematically and critically the visual dimension of organisational reports. Looking at the *Oxfam Annual Review 2003/2004* front cover, Davison (2007) has pointed out the possibility of the same image communicating two types of "message" which presuppose a different role of the viewer. One message come from the intention of the photographer, and a second one, more emotional and not strictly depending on the photographer's will, stemming from the interaction between the spectator and the photograph he/she is looking at. Therefore, images could be an important way of conveying messages to the spectator, especially for public organisations compared with private ones. PSOs are characterised by a wider and differentiated audience of stakeholders interested in dimensions other than financial and with even potentially contrasting interests. This is even more important for that kind of organisation which has a hybrid nature, where public and public values merge together (Thomasson 2009). Images could be a way of giving relevance to aspects that are difficult to translate into financial figures. Davison (2008, 2010, 2011a) has stressed the idea that images are a tool for conveying to readers of organisational reports messages regarding intangibles aspects of an organisation such as its identity or its leadership. As an example, Davison (2010) focused her attention on the portraits of organisational leaders in annual reports. Leadership is an intangible value that could be better represented through top managers' portraits in addition to or more than a narrative about their role and actions within companies. Another important contribution from Davison is related to the understanding and use of visual rhetoric in accounting. In particular, Davison (2014) stresses the concept of repetition to highlight how images could be a tool for encouraging readers to make a comparative analysis on a given issue.

Some other papers have used/studied images to define and give meanings to concepts such as globalisation (Preston and Young 2000), to define the identity of an NGO (Dhanani 2018) or to understand a gender issue in a specific society (Kuasirikun 2011).

Scholars are increasingly interested in analysing the role, messages and meanings conveyed through images in organisational reports. To this end, images are no more considered a simple representational tool able to complement financial information provided through numbers, graphs and narratives. Images contribute to building a reality within which the spectator will make decisions and take actions. For this reason, analysis of the images used in organisational reports is a topic that can no longer be ignored by accounting scholars.

Images, Text and Messages in Reporting: A Theoretical Framework

The visual part of a report has some interpretative difficulties that other forms of communication, such as words and numbers/graphs, do not have. While words can be quantified and analysed through coding mechanisms and graphs can be evaluated according to their accuracy, images cannot be easily submitted to such evaluative forms. (Davison 2010).

Most of the analyses of the visual dimension of organisational reports have used Roland Barthes' frameworks (Davison 2008). Barthes has dedicated most of his research to study of the literary dimension of social relations (Barthes 1972, 1974), but much of his late work has focused on the understanding of visual images and how they influence social relationships (Barthes 1977). In evaluating the message coming from an image, he highlighted his composite structure as the result of contributions from the different people and environments (source and channel of transmission) that are involved in the production of a given object, the image, which has to be viewed by another subject (the point of reception). Therefore, the communicative result of this object depends on the interaction that is established between the object and its viewer, even regardless of its author (Barthes 1977). In addition, the communicative result that will be realised depends not only on the vision of the image but also on its surrounding elements. In fact, the image could be presented together with texts and titles, all organised in a specific layout (Davison 2011b). Both aspects presented deserve further study for being better used in analysing the visual dimension of organisational reporting.

The message coming from an image can be of two types: a denoted (first-order) and a connoted (second-order) message (Barthes 1977). An image, especially if photographic, is "evaluated" by the viewer primarily for the reality represented. It is generally believed there is a close link or overlap between what the image shows and the reality (if there is one) represented. This implies that the message conveyed by an image is without a code and is continuous. The lack of a code means that the viewer is simply looking at the object represented without making any reasoning about it. "The denotative level of analysis describes the signifier and responds to the question 'what is it?'" (Greenwood et al. 2018: 8). This implies that the viewer does not interrupt fruition of the message conveyed by an image. This continuity is interrupted when the viewer wishes to describe the image. In this case, the conveying of the so-called connoted message comes from the use of a code belonging to the knowledge available at a social level and owned by the viewer of an image, for example, the language. "To describe is thus not simply to be imprecise or incomplete, it is to change structure, to signify something, different to what is shown" (Barthes 1977: 18–19). The emergence and acceptance of the concept of connoted message was made possible above all thanks to the contributions provided by cultural theory. "The code of connotation was in all likelihood neither 'natural' nor 'artificial' but historical, or, if it be preferred, 'cultural'" (Barthes 1977: 27). According to Davison (2010), cultural theory has made it possible to overcome the idea that there is a single correct way of interpreting the visual dimension of an image, of understanding the role played by the receiver of a message in identifying the unconscious conveyed by any image. Although it is possible to study them separately, the two types of messages coming from an image are to be considered in their joint existence. The second-order message requires the existence of the analogical dimension of the image in order to allow the viewer to develop a meaning using a code. Similarly, regarding the concept of sign, Williamson (1978: 16) states: "A sign is quite simply a thing – whether object, word, or picture – which has a particular meaning to a person or group of people. It is neither the thing nor the meaning alone, but the two together. The sign consists of the Signifier, the material object and the Signified, which is its meaning. These are only divided for analytical processes: in practice a sign is always thing-plus-meaning". Therefore, the effectiveness of an image depends on the author in combining text and image as a whole object and the availability for the viewer of the recalled knowledge.

Even if an image is often shown along with some text, it is important to analyse the role played by this last in building what the viewer sees. It exists as a role that is different from what is normally believed to be the relationship between images and text. The former are usually regarded as tools to support the latter for making the message conveyed more easily perceivable by a reader. Images are supposed to implement a process of reduction of the meaning conveyed by a text. In analysis of the visual dimension, it is possible to identify a reversed role between text and images. The text that accompanies an image has a connotative role, especially when the text is a caption more than headlines or accompanying articles. This text has the role of speeding up conveyance of the second-order message channelled to a viewer. This is possible because the text ought to allow delimitation of the meaning that the author of the message intended to convey to a viewer. The reductionist role played by the text is implemented by selecting from the knowledge available for the viewer. More precisely, the text inserted in an image recalls the knowledge that a viewer has to use to grasp the second-order message coming from the image. This role of the text is carried out in a more effective way the closer the text is to the image so as to become almost part of the denotative message conveyed by the image itself.

Case Study

Methodology and Research Question

In this section, the theoretical framework developed in the previous section is used to analyse the visual dimension of organisational reports of a public sector organisation. This analysis was focused on non-compulsory reports, for example, sustainability reports, because of their objective to communicate information on different dimensions of performance of an organisation which could interest a wider audience of stakeholders potentially characterised by contrasting interests. In particular, the chapter aims at understanding the potential contribution of images in communicating non-financial aspects and integrating more messages at the same time. To this end, Hera was chosen as a case study because of its private legal status (a joint-stock company) and its field of activity (public services). Compared with private sector organisations not providing public services, Hera is required to be compliant with the requests coming from stakeholders who have different or even potentially contrasting interests, that is, investors, local public administrations and citizens. This implies communicating with them and persuading each of them through the same report or with different reports aiming to account for different purposes (Behn 2003). Therefore, accountability has become an increasingly important issue to manage. Organisations, especially those operating in the public sector, have tried to govern their accountability duties by providing different reports focused on specific performance, for example, financial statements for their financial performance (Guthrie et al. 1999; Hyndman and Liguori 2016) and social reporting (Monfardini et al. 2013), sustainability reporting (Busco et al. 2018), environmental reporting (Contrafatto 2014) and integrated reporting (Eccles and Krzus 2010; Katsikas et al. 2017; Ruggiero and Monfardini 2013) for their non-financial performance. Because of this multidimensionality, variety of audience and increasing number of reporting practices, images could play an important role in channelling additional messages in a way that is quicker and simpler than providing different and long reports difficult to be "received" by their readers.

Among the different reporting practices adopted by PSOs, this chapter focuses on analysis of the images in sustainability/integrated reports. This reporting practice has gained ever wider adoption in the private and public sectors (Dumay et al. 2016), moving from its environmental perspective to an integrated one (Adams 2015; Flower 2015). It reports different dimensions of an organisation that are of interest for various stakeholders, therefore fitting the characteristics and accountability needs of organisations operating in the public sector (CIPFA 2016; Katsikas et al. 2017).

The Research Site

Hera was created in 2002 out of the aggregation of 11 municipal companies operating in the Emilia-Romagna region of Italy. Over time, Hera has embarked on a journey of consistent and balanced growth, incorporating other companies operating in the same areas of activity. Hera, publicly listed since 2003, turned 15 on 1 November 2017 and is now among the nation's largest multi-utilities, working mainly in the environment (waste management), water (aqueduct, sewerage and purification) and energy (electricity, gas distribution and sales, energy services) sectors. Because of its field of activity and its status as listed company owned by both private and public sector organisations, Hera has to be accountable to different stakeholders and therefore provide useful information for all of them. To this end, a sustainability reporting practice has been implemented since 2003, and over the years, its content and underlying organisational practice has increasingly covered all the dimensions settled by the GRI and the IIRC (Katsikas et al. 2017; Ruggiero and Monfardini 2013).

Result of the Study

Focusing on the visual dimension of Hera's sustainability reports (available on the organisation's website), it is possible to highlight a disappearance of images in its reports apart from the first one published in 2003. In the reports published from 2006 onwards, images are used only on the front cover of the report.

In the 2003 report, images are differently used according to the topic discussed. The front and back covers of the report convey a fundamental message about the organisation's objective. The connoted message of the image is related to the legs of children while they are walking or chatting in a square. While the children's legs are in focus, the square is not. This image gives a clear evidence about the reality it is going to recall to the viewer (Greenwood et al. 2018)

This highlights the second-order message conveyed by the image because of the knowledge code it recalls (Barthes 1977). Despite who they are, where they are and what they are doing, one of the main objectives of current society is to look after children and to guarantee them a future: Hera is involved in reaching this objective (Fig. 1a) to guarantee intergenerational equity. It is the combination of the reality represented

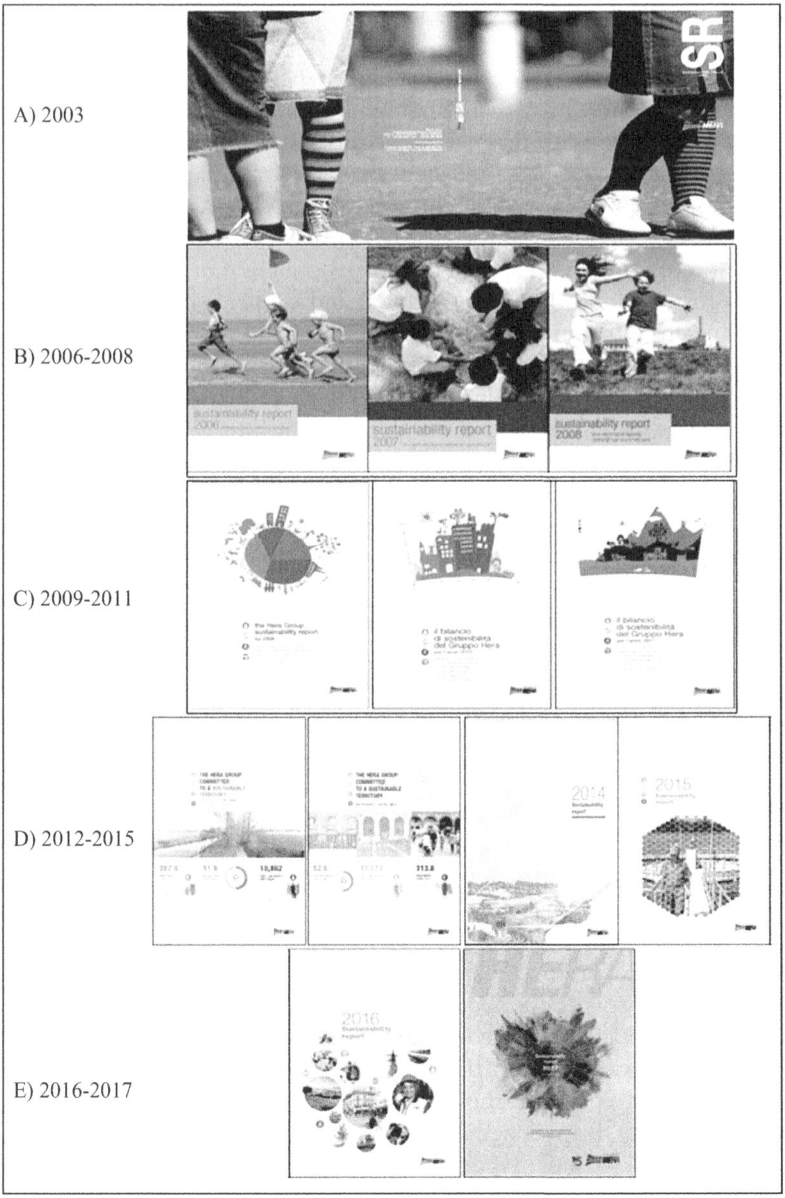

Fig. 1 The covers of the 2003–2017 Hera Sustainability Reports

and the underlying code recalled that makes the image communicative for the viewer (Williamson 1978).

In the rest of the 2003 Sustainability Report, many other images are used. Most of these images are photographs of social and historical places. These images are both denotative, because they report the places where the organisation operates, and connotative (Barthes 1977). The use of these images could have different objectives to be reached. First, one of the messages coming from the picture of places is about the organisation's interest more for what happens outside its organisational borders than its internal issues and problems. A second and deeper message comes from the interaction of some text, that is, captions, and the images used in the report. In particular, for every photograph the name of the place shown in the image was reported. Almost all of them are places belonging to the area within which the organisation operates. The interdependence between the images and their text potentially gives the viewer a twofold message related to the concept of identity—a sense of identification of the "local" viewer with the organisation, since both of them are part of the same environment, and the idea that the organisation is doing something to her/his advantage by looking after the places where she/he lives. Furthermore, the identity of the organisation itself is strictly linked to the places shown in the photographs; therefore, the organisation itself is part of that environment, not only physically but also from a cultural perspective.

Most of the other images in the Hera 2003 Sustainability Report show landscapes or part of a natural environment not strictly related to the places where the company operates. This is the denoted message of these images (Barthes 1977). But for this kind of image, there is a strict message conveyed to the viewer almost overlapping the denotative message, that is, the values and the efforts of the organisation are aimed at guaranteeing a sustainable natural environment in the future. Few images are related to the personnel of the organisation or to its structures. With reference to employees, there are five images in the report and one of these is related to the leisure activities provided to the organisation's personnel. Another important message contained in the 2003 report regards the concept of leadership (Davison 2010). In particular, this message is conveyed to the viewer using two pictures: those of the chairman of the Board of Directors and of the CEO. Both images focus on the upper part of their bodies. The choice of using passport-type photos implies the will to focus the message exclusively on the person and not on the spatial code of the image, that is, the "environment" within which the photo is taken. This choice is supported by the emphasis attributed to their facial expression and dress code. These are aspects that are mainly emotional, therefore soliciting a face-to-face interaction with the viewer to elicit specific reaction from her/him and consequently construct the desired message (Campbell et al. 2009). The smiling of the two persons is considered as a contagious feature able to create an idea of involvement and sharing of ideas and action, typical characteristics of a leader (Cherulnik et al. 2001). The formal dress worn by the two persons shown in the photographs recalls, especially in the Italian culture, a status of power in the organisation (Rafaeli and Pratt 1993).

The use of images in the Hera sustainability reports has totally changed since publication of the 2006 report. Since then, images are used only on the cover page while the rest of the report is composed of text and graphs. This change could be explained with the listing on the Italian Stock exchange since 2003. After this date, publication of the sustainability report was suspended until 2006. This suspension of the publication and the use of images only on the front cover of the subsequent sustainability report could be justified with a deeper focus of the company on its financial performance and at the same time the will to concentrate in the front cover as many important messages as possible—messages designed to ingrain a certain perspective in the reader of the reports from their initial reading. It seems that the reader should have in mind a well-defined sign and message, that contained in the front cover, while reading the report. It seems much more that using the image only on the front cover, the company would recall a myth able to inform all the reading (Barthes 1972).

By focusing on the Hera reports' cover pages, it is possible to note four different messages conveyed to the viewer. Consistent with the 2003 report, all the cover pages of the 2006–2008 reports show the same subjects, children, and the images convey messages related to concepts such as future (given by the sense of movement), well-being (given by the happiness of the children) and environmental sustainability (given by the natural spaces where the children are photographed) (Fig. 1b).

The cover pages of the 2009–2011 reports have a very different content and structure. First, the images are no longer photographs but coloured drawings. The subjects shown are no longer only children. Drawn in the same image are buildings, factories, trees, animals and human beings (adults and children). Therefore, the connotative message becomes more complex because the reality represented is made up of different objects and subjects (Fig. 1c).

Moving to the connoted message coming from the images (Barthes 1977), these latter make clear to the viewer that Hera's activities and objectives are multidimensional because the objects affected by the organisation and who it cares for are different. Apart from this multidimensionality, what also comes from the images is the idea of the unity of all that has been represented on the cover pages. This unity comes primarily from the use of some math codes such as a circle graph and a quadrant of the Cartesian plane (Carruthers 2008; Quattrone 2009). In both cases, all the dimensions surrounding Hera are represented because a circle graph and a Cartesian plane provide a classification of 100% of the phenomenon analysed.

From the visual dimension standpoint, the next four Hera Sustainability Reports (2012–2015) are less effective in conveying messages (Fig. 1d). The images, which are photographs of natural environment and places respectively in 2012 and 2013, are shown along with financial figures, but the two objects are physically separated in the page layout, apart from a weak linkage made by using colours (Davison 2011b). This makes it more difficult for the visual dimension of the cover pages to convey messages to viewers. In 2012 and 2013, the focus is more on economic figures than on images and the text used in the cover pages is more explicative of the financial figures than the images. On the front cover it is explicitly written that the report "contains figures for the three areas of responsibility: economic, social and environmental". The reason for the predominance given to figures rather than images can be identified in the will of the organisation to highlight the results reached after ten years of activity since the first issue of its sustainability report. In the 2014–2015 reports, the images regain predominance, even if the concept of unity conveyed in the 2009–2011 reports disappears. The images used in these reports show an employee of the organisation doing her/his job. In both cases, employees' activity is linked to the natural environment, conveying the message that safeguard and sustainability are the main objectives of the organisation's activities.

The last two Sustainability Reports (2016–2017) issued by Hera take an important step forward in conveying a message coherent with the main ideas underlying integrated reporting: the existence of different capitals to be managed and the idea that capitals are interdependent and therefore business activities could affect more capitals at the same time (Fig. 1e). The denoted message is less important than the connoted one (Barthes 1977). The cover page of the 2016 report contains images referring to the natural environment, the workforce, the manufactured and the community. What is much more important from an integrated reporting perspective is the idea of interdependence among the different capitals conveyed through the lines linking all the images to each other and the idea that these interdependencies are affected by the activities carried out by the organisation—activities that are represented by five different symbols being part of the network shown and which represent the different fields of activities in which the organisation operates.

Similar ideas are conveyed through the cover page of the 2017 report even if the message regarding the existence of different dimensions/capitals, represented through the image of a fragmented wheel, is less evident. Nevertheless, the message of interdependence given by the mixture of colours underlying the image of the fragmented wheel is still conveyed.

Discussion and Final Remarks

The proliferation of the types of reports published by companies is testimony that, for various reasons, accountability pressure and, in turn, the messages to be communicated both inside and outside organisations have significantly increased and are no longer confined to the financial information that companies are required to publish (Dumay et al. 2010). In this context, sustainability/integrated reporting could become increasingly important given its potential capacity for being a tool able to convey information not on individual aspects of an organisation but on all its different components, defined as capitals or dimensions of performance respectively in the IR model and the GRI, and their interdependencies. However, many difficulties could be encountered in drawing up this kind of report especially because of the immateriality of much of the information it contains (Davison 2010). Visual communication is an important tool through which reporting could better achieve its communicative objectives. However, this would imply a fundamental starting point: companies should increase their awareness of the importance of governing the visual dimension of their reports, similar to the effort they already put into governing their financial reports (Katsikas et al. 2017). Furthermore, to counteract some of the problems coming from the implementation of the NPM reform in PSOs (Dunleavy et al. 2005), use of the visual dimension in organisational reports could overcome the problem of an excessive focus of accountability processes on financial figures and short-termism (Gray and Jenkins 1993).

In the case of Hera there was a rather abrupt retreat in use of the visual in the sustainability reports published by the organisation. However, at least with reference to the cover pages of the reports, there was a continuous improvement in the visual arrangement of the message conveyed through images, with a clearer use of the denoted and connoted messages coming from the images (Barthes 1977). During the last two years, the message conveyed was more consistent with the aspects characterising a sustainability/integrated report. Through the images on the reports' front covers, the connoted messages conveyed to readers have increased over the years (Barthes 1977), together with the space for an emotional interpretation of those images (Davison 2007). Hera moved from an initial focus on the organisation's mission, which is safeguard of a sustainable environment, especially for the younger generation, to the presentation of images capable of recalling an additional concept characterising sustainability/integrated reporting: the existence of different interdependent capitals or dimensions of performance. In this way, it seems that along the time the company has tried to recall myths widespread in the actual historical period (Barthes 1972).

The images on the cover pages of the 2012 and 2013 reports are of interest because financial figures were shown together with other images in an attempt to create a composite image. This could be an important starting point for improving the construction of images functional to the conveying of messages coherent with another feature of integrated reports: explanation of the relationship between financial and non-financial performance in an organisation. Numbers represented within a non-accounting "context" lose their metric value in order to acquire a greater reporting value. "The image no longer illustrates the words; it is now the words which, structurally, are parasitic on the image" (Barthes 1977: 25). As part of an accounting document, the number exists as it relates to the others surrounding it, allowing the construction and representation of an order of magnitude. Instead, when the number becomes part of a visual representation, its role and meaning may also change. The number no longer wants to represent in quantitative terms the phenomenon to which it refers, but only intends to highlight and give importance to the underlying phenomenon that it would represent. The number becomes an image and therefore changes its nature: from a measure of size, it becomes a visual element that must be combined with other images to produce a non-quantitative message. In this case, according to Barthes (1977: 21), in the report the company utilises the special credibility of the accounting figures "in order to pass off as merely denoted a message which is in reality heavily connoted". This way of reporting images is even more evident in the last two reports, where connotation assumes "so completely the 'objective' mask of denotation". Images are no more functioning as supporting the meaning contained in a text made of letters or figures. Reversely, it is the figure "which comes to sublimate, patheticize or rationalize the image" (Barthes 1977: 25). Moving from the distinction between denoted and connoted message, another important aspect to highlight are the connotation procedures used by the company. It is possible to observe an increasing awareness/capacity of the company in exploiting the six procedures of connotation, which are trick effects, pose, objects, photogenia, aestheticism and syntax (Barthes 1977: 20–25). In the first 11 front covers, the connoted message has been produced almost exclusively by showing objects—predominantly, children, people and places of the environment that together constitute the connoted message linked to codes of sustainability and intergenerational equity. The use of objects is easier or could be perceived as such because "they are discontinuous and complete in themselves [...] and refer to clear, familiar signifieds" (Barthes 1977: 21–22). Because of these features, objects "produce" a stable and veritable lexicon able to travel meanings that are readable by their viewers. In the last reports, objects have been coupled with other procedures. In particular, in the front cover of the 2014 report, a trick effect has been used to emphasise the idea that the company looks over and takes care of the environment. In the report 2016, a syntax procedure has been used by putting together and therefore concatenating different images regarding different objects. Each object individually would have not been able to produce the connoted message. The syntax used aims at providing the idea of the interrelationships and interdependencies among the different activities carried out and the different capitals (natural, intellectual, human, manufactured, relational) used and produced by the company.

This chapter highlights the role that images could play in organisations' reports in conveying messages to their readers especially if these messages contain information that is difficult to translate into numbers or text. The integration between accounting figures and images could offer the opportunity of overcoming some of the potential deficiencies in the accountability process of PSOs after implementation of the NPM reforms: focus on financial performance and short-term orientation. PSOs are called on to pursue different and often potentially contrasting objectives for which they are accountable. The "strategic" use of the visual dimension in reporting practices could represent one of the ways for solving the complexity of their managerial and accountability issues. This implies the need for accounting scholars to devote more effort to analyse the visual dimension of reporting, first, by preparing theoretical approaches that are able to provide a scientific analysis of the visual dimension of accounting (Greenwood et al. 2018). This chapter is an exploratory analysis on a PSO that should be broadened through analysis of other experiences and cases. Following on from the analysis carried out in this work, future research could focus on the use of the visual dimension in other typologies of organisational reports and the linking of the visual dimension of the reporting with the other visual communication tools used by companies, such as their websites.

References

ABS (Accounting Standard Board). (2000). *Year-End Financial Reports: Improving Communication.* Discussion paper: Accounting Standard Board Publications, Milton Keynes.

Adams, C. A. (2015). The International Integrated Reporting Council: A Call to Action. *Critical Perspectives on Accounting, 27*, 23.

Barthes, R. (1972). *Mythologies.* New York: The Noonday Press.

Barthes, R. (1974). *S/Z.* Oxford: Blackwell.

Barthes, R. (1977). *Image, Music, Text.* London: Fontana Press.

Bartlett, S. A., & Chandler, R. A. (1997). The Corporate Report and the Private Shareholder: Lee and Tweedie Twenty Years on. *British Accounting Review, 29*, 245.

Barzelay, M., & Armajani, B. J. (1992). *Breaking Through Bureaucracy: A New Vision for Managing in Government.* Berkeley: University of California Press.

Behn, R. D. (2003). Why Measure Performance? Different Purposes Require Different Mesures. *Public Administration Review, 63*(5), 586.

Bourguignon, A., Malleret, V., & Nørreklit, H. (2004). The American Balanced Scorecard Versus the French Tableau de Bord: The Ideological Dimension. *Management Accounting Research, 15*(2), 107.

Brennan, N. M., & Solomon, J. (2008). Corporate Governance, Accountability and Mechanisms of Accountability: An Overview. *Accounting, Auditing & Accountability Journal, 21*(7), 885.

Brown, J., Dillard, J., & Hopper, T. (2015). Accounting, Accountants and Accountability Regimes in Pluralistic Societies. *Accounting, Auditing & Accountability Journal, 28*(5), 626.

Busco, C., Giovannoni, E., Granà, F., & Izzo, M. F. (2018). Making Sustainability Meaningful: Aspirations, Discourses and Reporting Practices. *Accounting, Auditing & Accountability Journal, 31*(8), 2218.

Campbell, D., McPhail, K., & Slack, R. (2009). Face Work in Annual Reports: A Study of the Management of Encounter Through Annual Reports, Informed by Levinas and Bauman. *Accounting, Auditing & Accountability Journal, 22*(6), 907.

Carruthers, M. (2008). *The Art of Memory* (A Study of Memory in Medieval Culture) (2nd ed.). Cambridge/New York: Cambridge University Press.

Cherulnik, P. D., Donley, A., & Miller, R. (2001). Charisma Is Contagious: The Effect of Leaders Charisma on Observers' Affect. *Journal of Applied Social Psychology, 31*(10), 2149.

CIPFA. (2016). *Focusing on Value Creation in the Public Sector. An Introduction for Leaders*. London. www.cipfa.org

Contrafatto, M. (2014). The Institutionalization of Social and Environmental Reporting: An Italian Narrative. *Accounting, Organizations and Society, 39*, 414.

Davison, J. (2007). Photographs and Accountability: Cracking the Codes of an NGO. *Accounting, Auditing & Accountability Journal, 20*(1), 133.

Davison, J. (2008). Rhetoric, Repetition, Reporting and the "dot.com" Era: Words, Pictures, Intangibles. *Accounting, Auditing and Accountability Journal, 21*(6), 791.

Davison, J. (2010). [In]Visible [In]Tangibles: Visual Portraits of the Business Élite. *Accounting, Organizations and Society, 35*(2), 165.

Davison, J. (2011a). Barthesian Perspectives on Accounting Communication and Visual Images of Professional Accountancy. *Accounting, Auditing & Accountability Journal, 24*(2), 250.

Davison, J. (2011b). Paratextual Framing of the Annual Report: Liminal Literary Conventions and Visual Devices. *Critical Perspectives on Accounting, 22*(2), 118.

Davison, J. (2014). Visual Rhetoric and the Case of Intellectual Capital. *Accounting, Organizations and Society, 39*(1), 20.

Denis, J. L., Ferlie, E., & Van Gestel, N. (2015). Understanding Hybridity in Public Organizations. *Public Administration, 93*(2), 273.

Dhanani, A. (2018). Identity Constructions in the Annual Reports of International Development NGOs: Preserving Institutional Interests? *Critical Perspectives on Accounting, 59*, 1.

Dumay, J., Guthrie, J., & Farneti, F. (2010). GRI Sustainability Reporting Guidelines for Public and Third Sector Organizations. *Public Management Review, 12*(4), 531.

Dumay, J., Guthrie, J., & Puntillo, P. (2015). IC and Public Sector: A Structured Literature Review. *Journal of Intellectual Capital, 16*(2), 267.

Dumay, J., Bernardi, C., Guthrie, J., & Demartini, P. (2016). Integrated Reporting: A Structured Literature Review. *Accounting Forum, 40*(3), 166.

Dunleavy, P., Margetts, H., Bastow, S., & Tinkler, J. (2005). New Public Management Is Dead-Long Live Digital-Era Governance. *Journal of Public Administration Research & Theory, 16*, 467.
Eccles, R. G., & Krzus, M. P. (2010). *One Report: Integrated Reporting for a Sustainable Strategy*. Chichester: Wiley.
Eccles, R. G., & Krzus, M. P. (2015). *The Integrated Reporting Movement. Meaning, Momentum, Motives, and Materiality*. Hoboken: Wiley.
English, L. M., & Guthrie, J. (2003). Driving Privately Financed Projects in Australia: What Makes them Tick? *Accounting, Auditing & Accountability Journal, 16*(3), 493.
Flower, J. (2015). The International Integrated Reporting Council: A Story of Failure. *Critical Perspectives on Accounting, 27*, 1.
Graves, O. F., Flesher, D. L., & Jordan, R. E. (1996). Pictures and the Bottom Line: The Television Epistemology of U.S. Annual Reports. *Accounting, Organizations and Society, 21*(1), 57.
Gray, A., & Jenkins, B. (1993). Codes of Accountability in the New Public Sector. *Accounting, Auditing & Accountability Journal, 6*(3), 52.
Greenwood, M., Jack, G., & Haylock, B. (2018). Toward a Methodology for Analyzing Visual Rhetoric in Corporate Reports. *Organizational Research Methods, 22*(3), 798.
Guthrie, J., Olson, O., & Humphrey, C. (1999). Debating Developments in New Public Financial Management: The Limits of Global Theorising and Some New Ways Forward. *Financial Accountability & Management, 15*(3), 209.
Hopwood, A. G. (1996). Introduction. *Accounting, Organizations and Society, 21*(1), 55–56.
Hyndman, N., & Lapsley, I. (2016). New Public Management: The Story Continues. *Financial Accountability and Management, 32*(4), 385.
Hyndman, N., & Liguori, M. (2016). Public Sector Reforms: Changing Contours on an NPM Landscape Public Sector Reforms. *Financial Accountability & Management, 32*(1), 5.
Inkinen, H., Kianto, A., Vanhala, M., & Ritala, P. (2017). Structure of Intellectual Capital – An International Comparison. *Accounting, Auditing & Accountability Journal, 30*(5), 1160.
Katsikas, E., Manes-Rossi, F., & Orelli, R. L. (2017). *Towards Integrated Reporting: Accounting Change in the Public Sector*. Cham: Springer.
Kuasirikun, N. (2011). The Portrayal of Gender in Annual Reports in Thailand. *Critical Perspectives on Accounting, 22*(1), 53.
Loughran, T. (2018). Linguistic Tone and the Small Trader: Measurement Issues, Regulatory Implications, and Directions for Future Research. *Accounting, Organizations and Society, 68–69*, 38.
McKinstry, S. (1996). Designing the Annual Reports of Burton PLC from 1930 to 1994. *Accounting, Organizations and Society, 21*(1), 89.

Modell, S. (2004). Performance Measurement Myths in the Public Sector: A Research Note. *Financial Accountability and Management, 20*(1), 39.
Monfardini, P., Barretta, A. D., & Ruggiero, P. (2013). Seeking Legitimacy: Social Reporting in the Healthcare Sector. *Accounting Forum, 37*(1), 54.
Piotrowski, S. J., & Steccolini, I. (2014). Introduction: Accountability Processes in Modern Day Government. *International Review of Public Administration, 19*(2), 160.
Preston, A. M., & Young, J. J. (2000). Constructing the Global Corporation and Corporate Constructions of the Global: A Picture Essay. *Accounting, Organizations and Society, 25*(4–5), 427.
Preston, A. M., Wright, C., & Young, J. J. (1996). Imag[in]ing Annual Reports. *Accounting, Organizations and Society, 21*(1), 113.
Quattrone, P. (2009). Books to Be Practiced: Memory, the Power of the Visual, and the Success of Accounting. *Accounting, Organizations and Society, 34*(1), 85.
Rafaeli, A., & Pratt, M. G. (1993). Tailored Meanings: On the Meaning and Impact of Organizational Dress. *The Academy of Management Review, 18*(1), 32.
Ruggiero, P., & Monfardini, P. (2013). The Case of HERA. In C. Busco, M. L. Frigo, A. Riccaboni, & P. Quattrone (Eds.), *Integrated Reporting: Concepts and Cases that Redefine Corporate Accountability* (p. 313). New York: Springer.
Thomasson, A. (2009). Exploring the Ambiguity of Hybrid Organisations: A Stakeholder Approach. *Financial Accountability & Management, 25*(3), 353.
Williamson, J. (1978). *Decoding Advertisements. Ideology and Meaning in Advertising*. London: Marion Boyars.
Yekini, L. S., Wisniewski, P. T., & Millo, Y. (2016). Market Reaction to the Positiveness of Annual Report Narratives. *The British Accounting Review, 48*, 415.
Yin, R. K. (2003). *Case Study Research Design and Methods* (3rd ed.). London: Sage.

Pasquale Ruggiero is Associate Professor of Business Administration and Public Management at the University of Siena (Italy) and Senior Lecturer in Management Control System at the Brighton Business School (UK). His research is focused mainly on management accounting and management control systems, especially in public sector organisations.

Are Romanian Higher Education Institutions Prepared for an Integrated Reporting? The Case of Babeş-Bolyai University

Adriana Tiron-Tudor, Gianluca Zanellato, Tudor Oprisor, and Teodora Viorica Farcas

Introduction

The present research focuses on changes that occurred in recent years in organisations reporting, grounded on the shift towards a more balanced presentation of both financial and non-financial information. The most recent form of holistic reporting is integrated reporting (IR), which evolved from a refined prototype of sustainability reporting, but with slightly different drafting: a more compact structure and an increased set of governing principles. Initially developed for private sector entities, recent developments show a more prominent intention to introduce this reporting system in the public and not-for-profit sectors (Adams and Simnett 2011). During the last decades, public entities have undergone substantial changes in their reporting practices, inspired by the New Public

A. Tiron-Tudor (✉) • G. Zanellato • T. Oprisor • T. V. Farcas
Babeş-Bolyai University of Cluj-Napoca, Cluj-Napoca, Romania

F. Manes-Rossi, R. Levy Orelli (eds.), *New Trends in Public Sector Reporting*, Public Sector Financial Management,
https://doi.org/10.1007/978-3-030-40056-9_7

Financial Management (Parker 2011; Siboni et al. 2013; Manes-Rossi et al. 2018a, b) paradigm, with the aim to enhance trust and improve communication with citizens and other stakeholders.

Within this context, one field of public services which offers implementation perspectives is higher education institutions (HEIs) (Romolini et al. 2015; BUFDG 2016). The myriad of interactions with stakeholders, the diversity of resources employed and the prospective impact on society give IR available incentives for adoption within public sector HEIs (Guthrie et al. 2015).

Recent studies (Veltri and Silvestri 2015; Bartocci and Picciaia 2013) highlight the key developments, examples and implementation perspectives for the IR in the public sector and even synthesise hybrid forms of reporting (such as "integrated popular reporting"), as a means for safeguarding accountability and transparency (Cohen and Karatzimas 2015). Consequently, IR might help one consider the organisation as a whole and unitary functional system, mainly designed for creating value for a broad range of stakeholders (Vermiglio 2012).

Unfortunately, despite their diversity and complexity, universities have tended to be weak in communicating the roles they play and the value they add to people's lives. HEIs have not always been outstanding in capturing and explaining this complexity or telling stories that matter memorably to people who need to hear them. In this sense, the relationships between HEIs and the environment they operate in, as well as their stakeholders, should be increased (Ramirez et al. 2016; p. 178). For these issues, IR can be the answer, as it can help universities tell their story better (BUFDG 2016). This study contributes to the international debate, in line with Adams' call (2015) for a debate concerning IR adoption in HEIs, since few studies have been carried out in this context (Brusca et al. 2018).

Drawn on the previously stated literature gaps, the present contribution aims to analyse how the fundamental concepts of IR are addressed within the boundaries of public higher education institutions, in the context of a regulation-compliance-oriented setting such as Romania. To achieve this aim, the present contribution focuses on one of the most prestigious public HEIs, Babeş-Bolyai University (BBU), which has a significant impact on society. By the employment of content analysis on the university's current reporting set, the extents to which the fundamental concepts of IR are already a part of its disclosure pattern have been investigated.

The affinity for international standards exhibited by Romanian organisations (Albu et al. 2011) (even in the public sector) constitutes a key driver in the context of adopting and applying a new reporting system, such as IR.

The main findings show that, although the official regulation reference does not expressly delineate the fundamental concepts of IR, the existing reporting set includes significant parts of fundamental concepts of IR, based on other frameworks linked to systems which take into account (or have evolved from) a sustainability set.

Results confirm the existence of a prototype of new reporting trends in Romanian public sector HEIs. Aligned to an evolutionary phase towards IR, the current reporting set of public sector entities is indeed close to IR (in terms of fundamental elements), and the pool of data needed to issue an integrated report is already encompassed and accessible in the current reporting set. The remainder of the chapter is composed as follow: the literature review presents the existent studies regarding integrated reporting and the HEIs as well as the presentation of the case study; the methodology section presents the checklist for the analysis. Moreover, the results and discussion section summarises the outcomes of the analysis, and the conclusion section presents the main contribution of the present study as well as the limitations and lines for further studies.

Literature Review

Integrated reporting (IR) has attracted attention due to its ability to combine in one document financial and non-financial disclosures and to provide information on future trends and directions. Environmental, social, sustainability and governance information previously kept separate from financial information is united by IR through the publication of a single report highlighting, from a stakeholder's perspective, the organisation in society and sustainable development (Reimsbach et al. 2018). Based on the aforementioned motivations, IR can be considered as a rebranded synthesis of existing reporting components. Since most of the reporting components are embedded in a current reporting set, the instances of its fundamental concepts should also be presented (in various forms).

The IR Framework is driven by integrated thinking, which should lead to integrated decision-making and execution towards the creation of value. "Through integrated thinking, organisations are stimulated to focus on the connectivity and interdependencies among a range of factors that have a material effect on their ability to create value over time" (Busco et al. 2013, p. 13). To this scope, scholars investigated whether the adoption of IR leads to internal mechanisms of change, outlining that in the case of five Italian state-owned enterprises. The authors outline that the presence of cross-functional teams, inside each organisation, has been fundamental in driving the change towards integrated thinking (Guthrie et al. 2017).

Moreover, the International Integrated Reporting Committee (IIRC) introduces the capitals useful for an organisation when implementing an integrated report. The capitals are the resources and relationships used and affected by an organisation. They are stocks of value that are increased, decreased or transformed through the activities and outputs of the organisation. The capitals are categorised as financial, manufactured, intellectual, human, social and relationship, and natural capital (IIRC 2013, p. 4). Organisations are not required to adopt these categories, but they can be used as a guideline to ensure no capital that the organisation uses or affects is overlooked (IIRC 2013, p. 12). The IIRC aims that reporting entities take these capitals seriously, as an integrated report should explain the increases and decreases in the pool of capitals (Adams et al. 2016) even if there is a limited disclosure requirement concerning movements of the capitals in the IR Framework (Flower 2015).

Each organisation should identify the capitals (or resources) that are material to it, consider and quantify the capital inputs, and note that not all capitals will necessarily be equally relevant or applicable. Only those considered sufficiently important or material should be included. There is a considerable variety in how universities report the capitals, and even if the financial review, financial statements and notes explain financial capital, other capitals are not reported as explicitly. In general, universities also report the intellectual and human capitals using different frameworks. Studies investigating how intellectual capital disclosure occur are focused on different areas such as New Zealand, Australia and the UK (Low et al. 2015), the UK, Spain (Sánchez et al. 2009), Italy (Sangiorgi and Siboni 2017), social responsibility disclosure in Canada (Maingot and Zeghal 2008), Spain (Jorge and Peña 2014) and sustainability reporting (Lozano 2011; Adams 2013; del Mar Alonso-Almeida et al. 2015).

The most debatable capitals of HEIs in the literature are intellectual and human capitals. The HEIs are an ideal epicentre for the request of these concepts, mainly because they make rigorous use of intangible assets such as human resources, skills, abilities and knowledge (Manes-Rossi et al. 2016). Also, regulators and scholars have developed guidelines and frameworks to support the correct identification of the intellectual and human capital components and stimulate the diffusion of standard practices of managing and reporting them within universities (Ramirez et al. 2016; Sangiorgi and Siboni 2017).

Nevertheless, some universities started considering IR as a valuable tool for understanding the value of people, knowledge, and relationships and the financials of universities. In this vein, some good practices emerged in South Africa, Stellenbosh University, and eight UK universities producing IR annual reports (BUFDG 2017). HEIs have a significant role in society and economy (Tiron-Tudor et al. 2018), and it is essential for all stakeholders to be informed about universities' contribution to society in an integrated manner. IR offers an opportunity for universities to develop their annual reports into engaging information for their stakeholders (BUFDG 2016). In the same vein, the Charted Institute of Public Finance & Accounting (CIPFA), in cooperation with the IIRC, proposes a study on how public sector organisations can benefit from the adoption of International Integrated Reporting Framework (IIRF). Accordingly, the study demonstrates how IR can help public sector organisations and be a driver of integrated thinking and decision-making. To this extent, the study presents interesting statistics on how IR can help in understanding the value creation process inside an organisation. In particular, the study outlines the task of public sector organisations which "are in charge of with delivering high-quality services in an economically, socially and environmentally sustainable manner" (CIFPA 2016; p. 10).

Academia also started to become interested in IR in the university's environments. Bringing IR on the 'turf' of HEIs involves some initial endeavours, using a case study approach (Veltri and Silvestri 2015), but the benefits of IR model are not fully understood and not all elements are correctly addressed. This consideration could be attributed to the early phase of implementing IR, and changes, as well as improvements, are expected to occur in the following years. For example, Veltri and Silvestri (2015) investigated the integrated report issued by the Free State University in South Africa. The authors suggest that IR has been, instead, used as a communication tool, which is issued to enhance university reputation, and, on another side, they found no evidence of enhanced university stakeholder engagement. Other studies were conducted in France (Chatelain-Ponroy and Morin-Delerm 2016) Japan (Nomura and Abe 2010), the UK (Lozano 2011) and the US (Krizek et al. 2012).

Two recent research mark the strategic focus of driving higher education institutions from the UK towards IR (BUFDG 2016, 2017). This initiative is a landmark on the path of IR implementation in HEIs and points out how this new reporting system would contribute to 'better storytelling'. Also, it places great emphasis on the transition from a historical perspective to future orientation and reveals the importance of principles, content elements and the intelligibility of such a report.

A number of studies have examined disclosure in the HEI sector from different points of view (Gallego-Alvarez et al. 2011; Lozano 2011), some of them being focused on voluntary reporting of intellectual capital (IC) (Low et al. 2015; Sangiorgi and Siboni 2017) or sustainability disclosure (Lozano 2011). In this vein, the present study contributes to the literature by investigating whether, for the selected case study, the information required for the implementation of integrated reporting is already present or not.

Romanian Universities' Mandatory Requirements

The mission of the universities is to generate knowledge and transfer it to society. Universities generate knowledge by basic and continuous academic training in order to satisfy the need for the competency of the socio-economic environment and by scientific research and innovation. The results of research are transferred to the society. Knowledge created by universities is in the field of science and engineering, arts, literature and languages. (Romanian Education Law 2011, art 117).

Romanian HEIs' annual report, called "Rector Report", includes mandatory disclosure regulated by law and voluntary disclosure of other relevant supplementary issues. The annual report is a component of public responsibility and a fundamental condition in order to access funding from the state budget.

The HEIs' Rector has the obligation to present a report on the universities' status, on an annual basis, no later than the first working day of April of each year. The report must be published on the website of each university and is sent to all stakeholders. Such report includes at least the following mandatory elements (Romanian Education Law 2011, art. 130, pp. 2 and 3):

(a) the financial situation of the universities, financing sources and types of expenses;
(b) the situation of each study programme;
(c) the situation of the university's staff;

(d) the results of the research activities;
(e) the situation of the quality of the activities performed in the universities;
(f) the situation of the observance of the academic ethics and the ethics of the research activity;
(g) the situation of the vacancies; and
(h) the situation of the professional insertion of the graduates from previous promotions.

If a university belongs to the public sector, according to Law no. 544/2001—referring to free access to information, public sector entities are compelled to disclose in visible places or on the Internet the following financial reports: draft budget, approval of the budget, budget execution, execution of the development budget, budget correction, as well as the budgetary execution account.

Case Study: Babeş-Bolyai University

Babeş-Bolyai University (BBU) is a comprehensive public university, one of the largest and most relevant Romanian universities concerning its sustainability orientation (Dabija et al. 2017). With an academic tradition starting in 1581, in Cluj-Napoca, Transylvania, Romania, BBU is today the largest university in the country (with over 42,000 students in 2018) and one of the best and most representative Romanian universities. Indeed, at the national level, BBU has been awarded the title of "University of Advanced Research and Teaching" (i.e., an intensive-research university) and was ranked the best Romanian university in the national meta-ranking of the Ministry of Education and Research (2016). At the international level, BBU is a constant presence in the international ranking of universities as one of the best and most representative universities in Romania and Eastern/Central Europe.

BBU has officially been ranked a four-star university, after a QS Stars evaluation at the beginning of 2018. This distinction offers the status corresponding to a highly acclaimed international university, demonstrating excellence in both research and teaching. BBU provides a stimulating academic environment, through excellent opportunities for academic development and by ensuring employability for its graduates. The university also contributes to a knowledge-based society through advanced innovations. The QS Stars evaluation has applied criteria covering the following academic components: teaching (4 indicators), research, innovation, internationalisation, employability (3 indicators), learning environment (6 indicators) and inclusiveness (4 indicators). One additional indicator (specialist criteria) targeted the evaluation of one academic programme. BBU is also the first of the seven Romanian universities included in the 2019 Times Higher Education's Emerging Economies University Rankings, according to the performance indicators grouped into five areas: teaching (the learning environment), research (volume, income and reputation), citations (research influence), international outlook (staff, students and research) and industry income (knowledge transfer).

The university shows also an orientation towards civil society using specific actions and programmes. The university supports and takes part in the organisation of cultural and artistic events in cooperation with local authorities and other cultural and social institutions and organisations.

In 2019, BBU joined the UN Sustainable Development Solutions Network (SDSN), being the first university in Romania to be part of the network, which has been operating since 2012 under the auspices of the UN Secretary-General. The network promotes practical solutions for sustainable development, including the implementation of Sustainable Development Goals (SDGs) and the Paris Climate Agreement.

The affiliation also comes as recognition of BBU's strategy in the area of sustainable development. "It is an important step in two directions: the international recognition of the research results in the area of sustainable development, as well as the recognition and continuation of the projects already included in the 'BBU, Goes Green strategy'". Moreover, BBU publishes annually the "BBU sustainable development report". For 2017, the 22-page report included elements like international context, BBU context, types of academic programmes, research directions and programmes, grants for students, accommodation and food facilities, study facilities, social, medical, transportation and cultural services, and the BBU botanical garden and green spaces.

In the case of BBU, Dabija et al. (2017) demonstrate that students and university staff have a positive perception concerning BBU's orientation towards sustainability and the measures taken in this respect. All stakeholders expressed highly favourable opinions of the university's dealings with different sustainability aspects, such as its attitude towards its employees, its performance within the higher education market and its establishment of an attractive and innovative educational programme, in compliance with sustainability principles, environmental protection and new attitudes towards society.

Methodology

IR is not a brand-new territory, but a rebranded synthesis in the context of a holistic mix of existing reporting components, it is a tool for measuring the amount of information concerning the six capitals of an IR which already exist in the current reporting setting has been designed. In this vein, the present contribution deeply investigates the quality of the contents (Yin 2017). The disclosure index (DI) has extensive use in the literature, to measure the extent, but not necessarily the quality, of the disclosure (see Marston and Shrives 1991). Also, it sets the ground for delineating a benchmark for each group/type of entities when performing testing (allowing us to theorise different or intermediary levels of closeness between current reporting sets and IR), according to their specificity (Pina and Torres 2003). Noteworthy to mention is the discussion held with key-role people inside the university, both staff and academics. Even if each one of the interviewed people were aware of the environmental, social and economic disclosure issues, these people were outlining to authors specify disclosure parts of the report they were responsible for, suggesting, also, to verify the institution's website.

The aim of the DI based on the IR Conceptual Framework is to capture the closeness of current university reports to the IR six-capital model. The index comprises nine items, based on the IR Framework (Table 1).

The checklist in Table 1 shows that for some items, there are multiple paragraph references. The corresponding selection is explained by the decision to compress the disclosure proxy using multiple references, as guidelines were overlapping between them (referring to the same aspects) and we intended to avoid measuring the same thing with two separate items. Hence, in the same paragraph (2.15) there are six individual disclosure proxies, mainly since the mentioned paragraph is quite extensive and offers keywords, explanations, definitions, examples and tables (in our case, markers) for each of the six capitals. The markers can be identical in phrasing to the disclosure identifier (which is easily found using the search function) or derived (using schematics, images or thesaurus—for example, synonyms, idioms or similar expressions—which are more challenging to find and require extensive reading and interpretation of the report).

For each one of the capitals, markers have been identified, as paragraph 2.15 is considered to be comprehensive (with a vast extension) enough to

Table 1 Disclosure index checklist design based on IR Framework

Index	*Item*	*References from the IR Framework*
The Capitals	1. Disclosure of the financial capital	Paragraph 2.15
	2. Disclosure of the manufactured capital	Paragraph 2.15
	3. Disclosure of the intellectual capital	Paragraph 2.15
	4. Disclosure of the human capital	Paragraph 2.15
	5. Disclosure of the social and relationship capital	Paragraph 2.15
	6. Disclosure of the natural capital	Paragraph 2.15
	7. Disclosure of the links and relationships between capitals	Paragraph 2.3
	8. Disclosure of the dynamics of the capitals	Paragraphs 2.11, 2.13, 2.14
	9. Disclosure of trade-offs between the capitals	Paragraph 2.12

Source: IIRC (2013)

provide the identification needed to reveal disclosures. The first six disclosure items, from the proposed checklist, represent static presentations of each type of capital within the reporting sets. Examples of markers for the six capitals (individually) are as follows (IIRC 2013; ACCA & NBA 2013):

- Financial capital: numerical key performance indicators (KPIs) and text data concerning 'funds', 'investments', 'financing', 'debt', 'equity', 'grants', 'revenues', 'costs', and so on; this type of capital exhibits extensive disclosure outlets (such as financial statements and reports, including notes, as well as crucial figures published through e-disclosure).
- Manufactured capital: numerical KPIs and text data concerning 'physical objects', 'goods and services', 'buildings', 'equipment', as well as other elements of 'infrastructure' used to manufacture the formerly mentioned goods and services.
- Human capital: numerical KPIs and text data concerning the labour force from the organisations, including 'a number of employees', 'diversity', 'average age', 'training and learning', 'workplace injuries', 'absenteeism' and 'wage information'.
- Intellectual capital: numerical KPIs and text data concerning intangibles that provide a competitive advantage, including: 'patents', 'research projects', 'research deliverables', 'new technologies', 'brand

awareness', 'development of new products', 'process development' and 'software development'.

- Social and relationship capital: numerical KPIs and text data concerning the institutions and relationships established within and between each community, group of stakeholders and other networks (and an ability to share information) to enhance individual and collective well-being, including 'workplace satisfaction ranking', 'lawsuits', 'involvement in social actions and cultural projects', 'customer [or in the case of HEIs—student] satisfaction index', 'development of social inclusion projects', 'philanthropy' and so on.
- Natural capital: numerical KPIs and text data concerning renewable and non-renewable environmental stocks that provide goods and services that support the current and future prosperity of an organisation, including 'air', 'water', 'land', 'forests', 'minerals', 'biodiversity', 'ecosystem health', 'CO_2 emissions', 'energy consumption', 'amount of waste', 'recycling', 'environmental accidents', 'environmental and animal protection' and so on.

The links and relationships between capitals are marked only in the case disclosure evidence was available for two (or more) capitals (or components of capitals) presented in a unidirectional or bidirectional connection with other capitals (or components of capitals), without one impacting the other's dynamic (i.e. increase or decrease). Examples of markers are 'employees as an active contributor to intellectual capital' or 'material effects on natural capital manifested by products and services sold' (a full range of markers can be found in ACCA&NBA 2013, p. 24).

In itself, the dynamic is to be disclosed (and implicitly marked) only when the data source presents information over the increase or decrease individually (per capita). Examples of markers are tables from reporting sets which emphasise the evolution of KPIs in consecutive years.

Ultimately, the trade-off is a result of alternative decision-making (usually, in a cost–benefit analysis) and discloses the dynamic of a capital at the expense of another, with different evolutions concerning value. According to IIRC (2013), trade-offs occur (ACCA&NBA 2013, p. 22)

- between capitals or between components of capital (e.g., creating employment, which increases human capital, through an activity that negatively affects the environment and therefore decreases natural capital),

- overtime (e.g., choosing a course of action when it is likely that a different course would result in a more significant capital increment but not until a later period), and
- between capitals owned by the organisation and those owned by others or not owned at all.

Each item was developed in categories, subcategories and markers based on the IR Framework and literature. Markers are predefined keywords used to identify the existence of the foreseen elements (Coy 1995; cited by Guthrie and Abeysekera 2006). For example, human capital (Leitner 2004; Ramirez and Gordillo 2014; Ramirez et al. 2016; Secundo et al. 2017) is composed in our case of 26 markers that include both the explicit and tacit knowledge of the university staff (teachers, researchers, PhD students, managers, administration and service staff), developed through formal and non-formal education and learning processes embedded in their activities. It is also identifiable in the knowledge that stands behind their expertness, which individuals take with them when they leave the institution, such as the expertise, knowledge and experience of researchers, professors, administrative and technical staff, as well as PhD students' competencies (Table 1).

Similarly, markers for each of the six capitals have been developed. The other three elements, links and relationships between capitals, dynamics of the capitals and trade-offs between the capitals, were not considered as markers themselves. In this vein, the established 147 markers for each capital are human capital (26), intellectual capital (22), social and relational capital (38), financial capital (31), natural capital (15) and manufactured capital (15). A binary coding system has been used—whereby a score of 1 signifies the existence of one of the markers within the set of reports being analysed, and a score of zero otherwise. The index is based on the IR fundamental concept of the capitals and is at the basis for identifying the extent to which the pool of data is available for this synthesis process to be carried out.

Results and Discussions

(a) *General remarks about the BBU website*

The university website is very well structured, offering the possibility to search keywords and also having predefined buttons that enable user navigation. A confirmation of this reality is represented by the university being ranked as the most transparent by a national study done by Alianța Națională a Organizațiilor Studențești din România (ANOSR—National Alliance of Student Organization in Romania) (2016) regarding universities' transparency based on a disclosure index composed of 125 elements. The ANOSR (2016) outlines that in the case of the majority of Romanian universities, there is no transparency, universities are not disclosing on their website information, documents and management decisions, or if information is disclosed, it is hard to understand, as it is hidden in various corners/places on the website.

(b) *Matching the set of reports (Rector's annual report, financial reports and sustainable development reports) with IR six capitals*

The BBU Rector's annual report for 2017 is presented in 70 pages plus 68 pages of annexes and includes mandatory elements: (a) the financial situation of the universities, financing sources and types of expenses; (b) the situation of each study programme; (c) the situation of the university's staff; (d) the results of the research activities; (e) the situation of the quality of the activities performed in universities; (f) the situation of the observance of the academic ethics and the ethics of the research activity; (g) the situation of the vacancies; and (h) the situation of the professional insertion of the graduates from previous promotions. Moreover, the annual report includes voluntarily the following elements related to (i) non-traditional education; (j) Cluj University Press (the BBU printing house); (k) university branches; (l) BBU's relation with the business environment, fundraising, students' practices and alumni; (m) international cooperation; (n) IT and data communication; (o) public relations and communication; (p) BBU's relation with the students; and (q) administration and assets.

Comparing the IR framework capitals with the mandatory disclosure requirements of Romanian universities, there are some similarities. Accordingly, resemblances are presented as follows: financial capital: (a) the financial situation of the university, financing sources and types of expenses; human capital: (c) "the situation of the university's staff" and (g) the situation of the vacancies; and intellectual capital: (d) the results of the research activities, (h) the situation of the professional insertion of the graduates from previous promotions and (f) the situation of the observance of the academic ethics and of the ethics of the research activity.

No elements related to the social, natural and manufactured capitals are requested by the Romanian regulation, but analysing the second part of the Rector's annual report, there are related elements like the following: manufactured capital: (j) Cluj University Press (the BBU printing house), (k) university branches and (q) administration and assets; the social capital: (l) BBU's relation with the business environment, fundraising, students' practices and alumni; (m) international cooperation; (n) IT and data communication; (o) public relations and communication; and (p) BBU's relation with the students.

Moreover, in the sustainable development report, there are additional elements concerning all the capitals and especially the natural capital, like BBU's botanical garden and green spaces. The report also includes strategies and activities for sustainable development, the 'BBU Goes Green' strategy, the biodiversity and sustainable development committee, sustainable development strategy implementation, strategic directions for actions, with estimated results and indicators, long-term objectives and action plan.

(c) *BBU capitals disclosure in the 2017 set of reports*

The markers established for the six IR capitals are disclosed in BBU's 2017 set of reports in a significant percentage (Table 2).

In the following sections, results for each capital are explained in detail regarding the components.

Table 2 Analysis results

Capital	*Total markers*	*Existing markers*	*Percentage of existing markers*	*Absent markers*	*Percentage of absent markers*
Financial	31	27	87.10%	4	12.90%
Human	26	19	73.08%	7	26.92%
Social and relations	38	25	65.79%	13	34.21%
Intellectual	22	14	63.64%	8	36.36%
Manufactured	15	9	60.00%	6	40.00%
Natural	15	8	53.33%	7	46.67%
Total	147	102	69.39%	45	30.61%

Financial Capital

For universities, financial capital is mainly represented by the funds at their disposal to carry out their activities. These funds can be obtained externally or internally. The university's financial capital is sophisticated, with diversified revenue and expenditure categories. Nevertheless, BBU manages to provide consistent, transparent and structured information about obtaining and managing money resources. The markers elected within this capital included some of mandatory nature (required to be reported by law), but the most important ones are non-binding ones. Although national regulation requires a relatively wide range of financial data, the university voluntarily provides additional information. The percentage of markers present is high because parts of them are mandatory to be disclosed. The additional disclosure from the institution provides an orientation towards transparency, which can be considered as the beginning of a pathway towards IR.

Manufactured Capital

Less obvious but existing within universities is manufactured capital, which includes current activity resources available to the university to carry out its activity: buildings, lands, vehicles, equipment and furniture. Here are also included the goods manufactured by universities for sale or internal use, even if the manufacturing capital is often created by another type of organisations.

Although manufactured capital is more challenging to outline within the university context, the BBU reporting set provides information about it in a significant percentage (60%) of the markers established. Infrastructure data, generally fixed and current assets, are provided about university libraries. The information about inventory is disclosed just as a value in the financial statements. Moreover, the structure of inventories and the number of offices and their status are not disclosed.

Intellectual Capital

In the universities' case, intellectual capital represents one of the most important values and is composed of intangible assets, including intellectual property, that is, patents, copyright, software, and other rights and licences. In particular, here are also included databases, research projects, research infrastructures, organisational culture, research and education processes, the existence of study/research centres and the use of information technologies.

Intellectual capital is seen as a dynamic system of intangible resources and activities, underpinning the sustainable competitive advantage of the university. For studying this capital, markers have been selected for intellectual infrastructure—patents, licences, copyrights, research projects and so on. The result is almost satisfactory, as this capital is specific to universities. However, several steps are required in order to respond to the IR framework, as intellectual capital represents the forefront for HEIs and there is a current need for greater disclosure (Ramirez et al. 2016; Manes-Rossi et al. 2018a, b).

Human Capital

For higher education institutions, human capital translates into skills, skills, staff experience and motivation to innovate, expertise, know-how, teacher knowledge and experience, administrative and technical staff, and student skills, ability to innovate, learning ability and teamwork.

To study information on human capital, we have chosen to look for markers that refer to hired personnel, their qualifications and other data related to them, staff mobility. BBU counts a high percentage of markers, meaning that consistent information was found about them, either directly on the university website or in various published reports.

In general, the university reveals information about the state of its human capital. Noteworthy to mention are the missing markers, which are statistical indices/data, whose absence is not surprising, for example, the absenteeism rate, the withdrawal rate, the number of accidents per million hours worked. The most disclosed category analysed in human capital is related to university employees. The markers of this category include essential and relevant data for the interested parties. The university offers relevant information about its staff, as results reached 87.5% consistent information about research employees in the Employees category. In terms of human capital, more statistics should be included in the reporting set in terms of the average age, the evolution of the number of employees and the number of graduates. It goes without saying that in the reporting set of BBU, we find other essential information that has not entered the area of the chosen markers. Similar results have been observed in previous studies on intellectual capital, regarding human capital.

Social and Relational Capital

The current capital represents relationships between stakeholders, communities and networks, and the ability to share information to enhance individual and collective welfare. Social and relational capital also includes standard rules, shared values and behaviours, relations with public and private partners, notoriety, position and image on social networks, involvement in training activities, collaborations with international research centres, teacher and researcher networks, international exchanges of students and staff, participation in university consortia and university's international recognition. The specific markers, for this capital, generally refer to the university's relationship with stakeholders and its actions to measure and maintain these relationships, and how the university is involved in cultural and social activities. The result obtained in the study of this capital reveals a high percentage of reported information, which proves that the university values its relations with society, its former students and its staff, choosing to share its actions to increase the elements of this capital—through various reports, Rector's report, strategic plans or the website.

Natural Capital

This capital is not of limited relevance to universities, taking into consideration the trend towards sustainable development, which translates into all renewable and non-renewable resources and process environments that offer goods or services that support the past, current or future prosperity of the university. Universities are recognised for the promotion of environmental protection, and in turn, BBU takes action in this respect. BBU provides information concerning the natural capital in its sustainable development report, information concerning water consumption, paper consumption, waste management and others. Moreover, a particular page of the university's green policy was created: green.BBUcluj.ro. As far as the reporting of the natural capital information is concerned, the percentage of markers present is given by markers about BBU's environmental sustainability actions. A cynical part is represented by the lack of information on the impact of the university on the environment (water, paper, energy), these issues being crucial to the IR model.

In conclusion, with an average of 69.39% of the information sought, BBU generally reports significant aspects at the level of each capital. The highest value is recorded in the area of financial capital, 87.1%, and the lowest score is for natural capital—this score is explained by the lack of information related to the impact of the university on the environment, however, reporting much information related to its actions to support it. Another higher level was recorded for social and relational capital, with value for the remaining three human, intellectual, production capitals being over 60%.

This study's aim is to analyse whether the BBU reporting set presents consistent information about the capital items—in particular, whether BBU presents information for all capitals and if the quantity of information is significant. The positive results confirm that BBU generally reveals the majority of the information needed for an integrated report, but that information is dispersed, unconnected and presented rigidly.

From a critical point of view, the lack of a cross-functional team (Guthrie et al. 2017) does not consent BBU to implement an IR, as reports are presented separately. In this vein, the institution shall take into consideration existing studies, even if they are built on another type of organisations (Guthrie et al. 2017).

The point is that the information requested for an integrated report needs to change the approach, and an effort has to be made to reveal a few more compelling contents required by the IR. In practice, BBU has to shape information to obtain an integrated report, because most of the content information is present, can be interpreted and can be seen in dynamics.

When talking about IR, it is possible to state that IR proposes a concise communication of the entity's activity model by which it generates value and reveals information about the six capitals, but not at all taking into account the principles and the constituent elements. It is important to note that integrated thinking must also be approached to explain the link between the above.

This study revealed that the BBU reporting set is at a good starting point towards a possible integrated approach. It is important to note that, at the time of the study, there was still no talk of integrated reporting in Romanian higher education institutions; the study only examined whether it is an appropriate approach.

Conclusions

Universities are social trendsetters, so the idea of studying sustainability, social responsibility and economic aspects in an integrated manner in a university could be regarded as a novelty approach.

IR guidelines given by the International Integrated Reporting Council (IIRC) and the adoption of content analysis have provided the opportunity to examine the trend and extent of IR content elements associated in universities reports, using the case of BBU.

The results indicate a significantly high number of IR capitals embedded in the university's annual reporting set. By analysing the variety of content in annual reports, this research examines to what extent BBU is disclosing financial and non-financial information under the IR's six-capital lens.

The findings allow policymakers to evaluate the extent to which integrated thinking is taking place and influencing universities in the selection and presentation of information.

The research has implications for society within and beyond the different universities' context. Universities are places of advanced thinking and can lead the way for other sectors by demonstrating the potential of integrated thinking to create a cohesive wide-ranging discourse. Moreover, IR may generate better visibility and knowledge of the values of exploiting capitals (financial, intellectual, human, manufactured, social and natural) and offer a multifaceted approach to reassess universities' performance in various sectors that supports the growth of integrated thinking.

By investigating the level of disclosure on IR capitals in the case of BBU, this study contributes to the academic debate exploring the IR implications in universities in the context of the research of prior scholars (De Villiers et al. 2014; Cheng et al. 2014; Veltri and Silvestri 2015; BUFDG 2016).

To reach the IR standard, BBU does not necessarily need to work much further behind the scenes. Much of the information already exists, proven by the results of the study. It takes new, critical analysis and creativity to get the narrative out of figures and tell the story of the university with the clarity and energy the university and its stakeholders deserve. The existence of an adapted IR framework, the example of British universities, studies in this field and the small recommendations of this study provide the university with ideas not only about where to go, but about the steps it needs to follow to get there.

Babeş-Bolyai University is, according to this study's results, prepared to issue its first integrated report, aligning, in this manner, the university with the best-performing reporting system currently in place. IR will bring many benefits, including international competitiveness, a better understanding of the university's purpose, its plans for the future, and how to respond to the needs of stakeholders. Being one of the best-performing Romanian universities, BBU can give the tone to accomplishing performance, being one step ahead of the others universities, also becoming an excellent example in this area, and last but not least, making its voice heard abroad.

Moreover, this contribution presents some limitations. First, it focuses only on one HEI. Emphasising the construction of an IR only through available data can represent a limitation, as it does not take into consideration further efforts, required by BBU to develop an IR, developing integrated thinking, which is a crucial aspect when approaching or navigating in the IR journey. Second, it does not compare to similar cases from similar environments. In this vein, further studies should stress the lack of integrated thinking in the case of the current investigated HEI as well as compare the results with similar HEIs, in order to observe similar behavioural reporting patterns.

References

ACCA and NBA. (2013). *Capitals Background Paper for/IRS, International Integrated Reporting Council.* Available at: www.theiirc.org. Retrieved 4 May 2019.

Adams, C. A. (2013). Sustainability Reporting and Performance Management in Universities: Challenges and Benefits. *Sustainability Accounting, Management and Policy Journal, 4*(3), 384–392.

Adams, C. A. (2015). The International Integrated Reporting Council: A Call to Action. *Critical Perspectives on Accounting, 27*, 23–28.

Adams, S., & Simnett, R. (2011). Integrated Reporting: An Opportunity for Australia's Not-for-Profit Sector. *Australian Accounting Review, 21*(3), 292–301.

Adams, C. A., Potter, B., Singh, P. J., & York, J. (2016). Exploring the Implications of Integrated Reporting for Social Investment (Disclosures). *The British Accounting Review, 48*(3), 283–296.

Albu, N., Nicolae Albu, C., Bunea, Ş., Artemisa Calu, D., & Mădălina Girbina, M. (2011). A Story about IAS/IFRS Implementation in Romania. *Journal of Accounting in Emerging Economies, 1*(1), 76–100.

Andronesi, M., Banabic, D., Buzea, C., & David, D. (2016, Decembrie). Report on the National Exercise about the University Metaranking-2016 of the Romanian Ministry of Education and Research. *Revista De Politica Ştiintei Si Scientometrie – Serie Noua, 5*(4), 267–277.

ANOSR. (2016). *Priorităţile studenţilor pentru anul 2016*. Available at: www.anosr.ro. Retrieved 4 May 2019.

Bartocci, L., & Picciaia, F. (2013). Towards Integrated Reporting in the Public Sector. In *Integrated Reporting* (pp. 191–204). Cham: Springer.

Brusca, I., Labrador, M., & Larran, M. (2018). The Challenge of Sustainability and Integrated Reporting at Universities: A Case Study. *Journal of Cleaner Production, 188*, 347–354.

BUFDG. (2016). *Integrated Reporting (IR) in Higher Education. Helping Universities Tell Their Stories Better*. Available online: www.efficiencyexchange.ac.uk. Retrieved 4 May 2019.

BUFDG. (2017). Annual Report 2017. Available at: www.bufdg.ac.uk. Retrieved 4 May 2019.

Busco, C., Frigo, M. L., Quattrone, P., & Riccaboni, A. (2013). Towards Integrated Reporting: Concepts, Elements and Principles. In *Integrated Reporting* (pp. 3–18). Cham: Springer.

Charted Institute of Public Finance & Accounting. (2016). *Integrated Thinking and Reporting: Focusing on Value Creation in the Public Sector*. Available online: www.cipfa.org. Retrieved 4 May 2019.

Chatelain-Ponroy, S., & Morin-Delerm, S. (2016). Adoption of Sustainable Development Reporting by Universities: An Analysis of French First-Time Reporters. *Accounting, Auditing & Accountability Journal, 29*(5), 887–918.

Cheng, M., Green, W., Conradie, P., Konishi, N., & Romi, A. (2014). The International Integrated Reporting Framework: Key Issues and Future Research Opportunities. *Journal of International Financial Management & Accounting, 25*(1), 90–119.

Cohen, S., & Karatzimas, S. (2015). Tracing the Future of Reporting in the Public Sector: Introducing Integrated Popular Reporting. *International Journal of Public Sector Management, 28*(6), 449–460.

Dabija, D. C., Postelnicu, C., Dinu, V., & Mihăilă, A. (2017). Stakeholders' Perception of Sustainability Orientation within a Major Romanian University. *International Journal of Sustainability in Higher Education, 18*(4), 533–553.

De Villiers, C., Unerman, J., & Rinaldi, L. (2014). Integrated Reporting: Insights, Gaps and an Agenda for Future Research. *Accounting, Auditing & Accountability Journal, 27*(7), 1042–1067.

del Mar Alonso-Almeida, M., Marimon, F., Casani, F., & Rodriguez-Pomeda, J. (2015). Diffusion of Sustainability Reporting in Universities: Current Situation and Future Perspectives. *Journal of Cleaner Production, 106*, 144–154.

Flower, J. (2015). The International Integrated Reporting Council: A Story of Failure. *Critical Perspectives on Accounting, 27*, 1–17.

Gallego-Alvarez, I., Rodríguez-Domínguez, L., & García-Sánchez, I. M. (2011). Information Disclosed Online by Spanish Universities: Content and Explanatory Factors. *Online Information Review, 35*(3), 360–385.

Guthrie, J., & Abeysekera, I. (2006). Content Analysis of Social, Environmental Reporting: What Is New? *Journal of Human Resource Costing & Accounting, 10*(2), 114–126.

Guthrie, J., Veltri, S., & Silvestri, A. (2015). The Free State University Integrated Reporting: A Critical Consideration. *Journal of Intellectual Capital, 16*(2), 443–462.

Guthrie, J., Manes-Rossi, F., & Orelli, R. L. (2017). Integrated Reporting and Integrated Thinking in Italian Public Sector Organisations. *Meditari Accountancy Research, 25*(4), 553–573.

International Integrated Reporting Council. (2013). *The International (IR) Framework*. Available at: www.integratedreporting.org. Retrieved 4 May 2019.

Jorge, M. L., & Peña, F. J. A. (2014). Determinants of Corporate Social Responsibility and Business Ethics Education in Spanish Universities. *Business Ethics: A European Review, 23*(2), 139–153.

Krizek, K. J., Newport, D., White, J., & Townsend, A. R. (2012). Higher Education's Sustainability Imperative: How to Practically Respond? *International Journal of Sustainability in Higher Education, 13*(1), 19–33.

Leitner, K. H. (2004). Intellectual Capital Reporting for Universities: Conceptual Background and Application for Austrian Universities. *Research Evaluation, 13*(2), 129–140.

Low, M., Samkin, G., & Li, Y. (2015). Voluntary Reporting of Intellectual Capital: Comparing the Quality of Disclosures from New Zealand, Australian and United Kingdom Universities. *Journal of Intellectual Capital, 16*(4), 779–808.

Lozano, R. (2011). The State of Sustainability Reporting in Universities. *International Journal of Sustainability in Higher Education, 12*(1), 67–78.

Maingot, M., & Zeghal, D. (2008). An Analysis of Voluntary Disclosure of Performance Indicators by Canadian Universities. *Tertiary Education and Management, 14*(4), 269–283.

Manes-Rossi, F., Citro, F., & Bisogno, M. (2016). Intellectual Capital in Action: Evidence from Italian Local Governments. *Journal of Intellectual Capital, 17*(4), 696–713.

Manes-Rossi, F., Nicolò, G., & Tartaglia Polcini, P. (2018a). New Trends in Intellectual Capital Reporting: Exploring Online Intellectual Capital Disclosure in Italian Universities. *Journal of Intellectual Capital, 19*(4), 814–835.

Manes-Rossi, F., Tiron-Tudor, A., Nicolò, G., & Zanellato, G. (2018b). Ensuring more Sustainable Reporting in Europe Using Non-financial Disclosure—De Facto and de Jure Evidence. *Sustainability, 10*(4), 1162.

Marston, C. L., & Shrives, P. J. (1991). The Use of Disclosure Indices in Accounting Research: A Review Article. *The British Accounting Review, 23*(3), 195–210.

Nomura, K., & Abe, O. (2010). Higher Education for Sustainable Development in Japan: Policy and Progress. *International Journal of Sustainability in Higher Education, 11*(2), 120–129.

Sánchez, M. P., Elena, S., & Castrillo, R. (2009). Intellectual Capital Dynamics in Universities: A Reporting Model. *Journal of Intellectual Capital, 10*(2), 307–324.

Parker, L. (2011). University Corporatisation: Driving Redefinition. *Critical Perspectives on Accounting, 22*(4), 434–450.

Pina, V., & Torres, L. (2003). Reshaping Public Sector Accounting: An International Comparative View. *Canadian Journal of Administrative Sciences/ Revue Canadienne des Sciences de l'Administration, 20*(4), 334–350.

Ramirez, Y., & Gordillo, S. (2014). Recognition and Measurement of Intellectual Capital in Spanish Universities. *Journal of Intellectual Capital, 15*(1), 173–188.

Ramirez, Y., Tejada, A., & Manzaneque, M. (2016). The Value of Disclosing Intellectual Capital in Spanish Universities: A New Challenge of our Days. *Journal of Organizational Change Management, 29*(2), 176–198.

Reimsbach, D., Hahn, R., & Gürtürk, A. (2018). Integrated Reporting and Assurance of Sustainability Information: An Experimental Study on Professional Investors' Information Processing. *European Accounting Review, 27*(3), 559–581.

Romanian Education Law. (2011). Art 117.

Romolini, A., Fissi, S., & Elena, G. O. R. I. (2015). Quality Disclosure in Sustainability Reporting: Evidence from Universities. *Transylvanian Review of Administrative Sciences, 11*(44), 196–218.

Sangiorgi, D., & Siboni, B. (2017). The Disclosure of Intellectual Capital in Italian Universities: What Has Been Done and What Should Be Done. *Journal of Intellectual Capital, 18*(2), 354–372.

Secundo, G., Perez, S. E., Martinaitis, Ž., & Leitner, K. H. (2017). An Intellectual Capital Framework to Measure Universities' Third Mission Activities. *Technological Forecasting and Social Change, 123*, 229–239.

Siboni, B., del Sordo, C., & Pazzi, S. (2013). Sustainability Reporting in State Universities: An Investigation of Italian Pioneering Practices. *International Journal of Social Ecology and Sustainable Development (IJSESD), 4*(2), 1–15.

Tiron-Tudor, A., Nistor, C. S., & Ştefănescu, C. A. (2018). The Role of Universities in Consolidating Intellectual Capital and Generating New Knowledge for a Sustainable Bio-Economy. *Amfiteatru Economic, 20*(49), 599–615.

Veltri. S., & Silvestri, A. (2015). The Free State University Integrated Reporting: A Critical Consideration. *Journal of Intellectual Capital, 16*(2), 443–462.

Vermiglio, C. (2012). Integrated Reporting for Italian Local Governments. In *Background for Debate, Financial Reporting Workshop, Naples, [pdf]*. Available at: http://www.frworkshop.com/napoli/eng/papers/Vermiglio.pdf. Accessed 13 June 2016.

Yin, R. K. (2017). *Case Study Research and Applications: Design and Methods*. Los Angeles: Sage.

Adriana Tiron-Tudor is a full professor and PhD supervisor in Accounting and Audit Department, Faculty of Economics and Business Administration, Babeş-Bolyai University in Cluj-Napoca (Romania). Her research interest is in corporate and public sector entities' reporting, including integrated, financial and non-financial reporting.

Zanellato Gianluca is a PhD candidate in Accounting and Audit Department, Faculty of Economics and Business Administration, Babeş-Bolyai University. His research interest covers accountability in state-owned enterprises and sustainable development.

Tudor Oprisor is a PhD research assistant at Accounting and Audit Department, Faculty of Economics and Business Administration, Babeş-Bolyai University. His main research interest is in implementation perspectives for integrated reporting in public sector entities.

Teodora Viorica Farcas is an associate lecturer at Babeş-Bolyai University, holding a PhD in Accounting from the University of Nantes, France, and Babeş-Bolyai University. Her research interest is in corporate reporting, with a specific focus on integrated and non-financial reporting.

Determinants of Environmental, Social, and Governance Reporting of Rail Companies: Does State Ownership Matter?

İsmail Çağrı Özcan

Introduction

Government ownership used to characterize the rail industry. Apart from several exceptions concentrated mostly in North America, governments owned and operated rail companies, the majority of which were unprofitable. The main reason for the governments in sustaining these rail operations was achieving social goals. But the privatization waves started in the eighties spread to the rail industry. As parts of this tendency, governments tended to commercialize their state-owned rail companies to make them follow a more profit-oriented path, liberalized the once monopolistic rail activities to allow private parties to operate, and privatized their rail-related enterprises to reduce their burden on the public budget and improve their efficiency. All such efforts created a more competitive environment in the rail industry and increased the number of private rail companies.

İ. Ç. Özcan (✉)
Department of Aviation Management, Ankara Yıldırım Beyazıt University, Ankara, Turkey
e-mail: icozcan@ybu.edu.tr

F. Manes-Rossi, R. Levy Orelli (eds.), *New Trends in Public Sector Reporting*, Public Sector Financial Management,
https://doi.org/10.1007/978-3-030-40056-9_8

Contrary to the government-owned rail enterprise, private rail companies now have to operate in a relatively different playing field. They have private shareholders, whose expectation is to maximize their wealth. Unlike public rail companies, which are backed by the governments when they require necessary funds, private rail companies need to borrow from creditors. Moreover, in a world of financial scandals like Enron, Tyco, and Arthur Andersen, private companies should meet the transparency expectations of their shareholders and creditors. In such a business environment, corporate governance mechanisms serve to ensure a win-win situation for all parties involved in the equation. The shareholders are benefiting from corporate governance by monitoring the company management to behave at their interest. Corporate governance helps lenders to reduce the likelihood of not receiving their loans back. In turn, corporate governance enables companies to borrow with lower interest rates (Bhojraj and Sengupta 2003) and decrease their cost of equity (Chen et al. 2009).

In addition to corporate governance, the social and environmental actions of companies have been attracting growing interest. Consumers and individual investors are demanding companies to be socially and environmentally responsible in any decision and action they make, ranging from labor relations to production technologies. Therefore, like in the case of corporate governance, companies with better social and environmental responsibility practices can attain a lower cost of equity [(El Ghoul et al. 2011) and (Dhaliwal et al. 2014)] or they can reach higher market valuations (Plumlee et al. 2015).

For all these reasons, environmental, social, and governance (ESG) disclosure activities became a powerful tool for companies to improve their financial competence, enhance their relationships with stakeholders, and improve their public image. In parallel, the literature is growing on the ESG reporting performance of companies. However, despite this growing literature, the disclosure performance of rail companies remained almost totally untouched. This aim of this chapter is to fill this gap by examining the determinants of the ESG reporting performance of publicly traded rail companies. Our particular focus will be on the association between government ownership and ESG disclosure performance—because, against the privatization waves in the rail industry, many governments maintain their partial stakes in privatized rail companies (because of the strategic importance of the sector). We believe that the findings of this chapter can contribute to both ESG reporting and privatization literature. Our analyses, based on a sample of 33 rail companies from 9 countries over the

2010–2017 period, suggest that government ownership, board size, percentage of independent directors, company size, and financial leverage have a positive association with ESG disclosure scores, whereas higher profitability and tangibility ratios tend to reduce ESG disclosure performance. In addition, we document that rail companies founded in common law countries are likely to have lower ESG disclosure scores than those established in civil law countries. Section "Literature Review" of this chapter outlines the relevant literature. Section "Methodology and Data" explains both methodology adopted and data used. Section "Empirical Results" discusses the findings of the econometric models, and the last section presents the conclusions and policy implications.

Literature Review

A quick review of the literature reveals that the ESG reporting performance of transport companies is not vast. The relevant research on the transport industry mostly concentrates on airlines and airports because of the availability of larger samples to examine. However, these studies examine a single dimension of ESG activities. For example, Skouloudis et al. (2012), Seo et al. (2015), Wang et al. (2015), Kuo et al. (2016), Ilkhanizadeh and Karatepe (2017), Karaman and Akman (2018), and Karaman et al. (2018) analyze either sustainability reporting or social responsibility of the airlines. The only study we are able to identify regarding the rail industry is the paper examining the determinants of governance disclosure of rail companies (Özcan 2018).

Despite the limited scope of research focusing on ESG activities of the transport industry, the literature abounds in the studies examining the various aspects of ESG performance. An in-depth analysis of these groups of research reveals a list of major determinants of ESG reporting.

Corporate Governance

Corporate governance is obviously a strong determinant of ESG reporting performance. Ownership structure, board size, and representation of independent/outside directors on the board are the most frequently used corporate governance variables in the literature.

Larger and more evidence-based groups of relevant research indicate the positive effect of government ownership on the disclosure performance of companies. Using a Canadian sample, Cormier and Gordon (2001) document that public ownership has a statistically significant positive effect on the social disclosure performance of companies. Similarly, Ferguson et al. (2002) indicate that H-share firms (owned by the government) traded on the Hong Kong Stock Exchange tend to disclose more information when compared with other firms listed on the same stock exchange. This finding is noteworthy because H-share firms have relatively higher uncertainties. Eng and Mak (2003) show that there is a positive association between the proportion of ordinary shares owned by the government and the disclosure score of companies after analyzing a sample of 158 Singaporean companies. Amran and Devi (2008) report a similar finding for the Malaysian case. Their analyses indicate that higher ratios of government shareholding tend to increase corporate social responsibility disclosure performance. Wang et al. (2008) reveal that the percentage of state-owned shares of a company has a positive effect on the voluntary disclosure performance of Chinese companies. Using a sample of 50 listed companies in the Stock Exchange of Thailand, Sukcharoensin (2012) documents that companies with majority government ownership tend to perform better in terms of corporate social responsibility. Based on a sample of 446 publicly traded companies, Wang et al. (2012) report that listed Chinese companies controlled by government are more likely to have superior performance in terms of both non-environmental social responsibility information and environmental information disclosure. Hsu et al. (2017) document a positive linkage between state ownership and environmental engagement using a dataset covering 3624 companies around the world. Hsu et al. (2017) underline that this association is significant in developing countries, whereas they fail to depict a similar linkage in developed countries. Hsu et al. (2017) also assert that government ownership serves to handle the difficulty to implement regulations in developing economies. Examining a dataset consisting of 203 companies from China, Malaysia, India and the United Kingdom, Adnan et al. (2018) document that government ownership, which is measured by a dummy variable equal to 1 for companies where the government owns more than 50% of the stake, has a positive effect on the quality of corporate social responsibility reporting.

On the other hand, anecdotal evidence provides counter-arguments regarding the social and environmental responsibility of state companies. Feigenbaum (1982) points out how state-owned oil companies in France engaged in currency speculations against French Franc and set a greedy pricing strategy in the domestic market. Stiglitz (1996) underlines that the competition and commercialization in the global oil industry forced state companies to abandon their social responsibility activities. Stiglitz (1996) also highlights the greater reaction of state enterprises (when compared with their private counterparts) to the new pollution regulations in the United States.

Board size is another widely used corporate governance variable. After analyzing samples from Indonesia, Said et al. (2009) and Siregar and Bachtia (2010) report that larger boards tend to increase social disclosure performance. Likewise, Giannarakis (2014b) underlines a positive association between board size and ESG disclosure scores after examining a sample of 366 Fortune 500 firms.

The last major corporate governance variable is the percentage of independent/outside directors on the board. From the agency theory point of view, we may argue that corporate governance (disclosure) performance can be improved by employing more independent directors who will deal with monitoring and control functions.[1] Likewise, since outside linkages can be strengthened by independent directors according to dependence theory, we can expect higher disclosure performance by recruiting more independent directors. Using a Hong Kong sample, Chen and Jaggi (2000) show that financial disclosure is positively affected by the higher shares of independent board members. Samaha et al. (2012) point out the positive association between higher ratios of non-executive directors on the board and corporate governance disclosure based on a sample of 100 Egyptian firms. Contrary to these findings, Eng and Mak (2003) report a negative association between the share of independent directors on the board and voluntary public disclosure after analyzing a Singaporean sample of listed companies. When discussing their findings, Eng and Mak (2003) underline that independent board directors might be a substitute for voluntary public disclosure.

Financial Parameters

Profitability is a commonly used financial variable in comparable studies. Following the footsteps of the agency theory, managers of financially well companies will presumably disclose more to benefit from the good performance according to Inchausti (1997). The findings of Cormier and

[1] We should note both Lipton and Lorsch (1992) and Jensen (1993) maintain that board size should not exceed a threshold value to prevent possible communication and coordination problems.

Magnan (1999) reveal a positive association between profitability and environmental disclosure of Canadian firms. Likewise, Collett and Hrasky (2005) show that more profitable firms tend to perform better regarding voluntary corporate governance disclosure in Australia. Giannarakis (2014a) indicates a positive linkage between profitability and ESG disclosure scores. Based on a similar rationale, Barako et al. (2006) point out how bad-performing firms tend to disclose less to shield their low performance from stakeholders. Unlike the studies documenting how higher profitability leads to more disclosure, Baldini et al. (2018) reveal that higher profitability has a negative effect on ESG disclosure scores.

The size of companies is also widely employed in the literature. The great majority of the relevant literature show that larger firms tend to perform better in terms of reporting [(Wallace et al. 1994), (Meek et al. 1995), (Zarzeski 1996), (Ahmed and Courtis 1999), (Cormier and Magnan 1999), (Klapper and Love 2004), (Barako et al. 2006), (Khanchel 2007), (Reverte 2009), (da Silva Monteiro and Aibar-Guzmán 2010), (Bokpin 2013), (Giannarakis 2014b), (Branco and Rodrigues 2008), (Samaha et al. 2012), (Giannarakis 2014a), (Chiu and Wang 2015), and (Velte 2016)]. The resource availability of large companies, which enables them to assign necessary funding and labor to manage reporting activities, can be one explanation for this positive linkage. Another possible underlying reason might be the more frequent actions of larger firms to be disclosed.

Financial leverage has also been very frequently used in comparable studies as a determinant of ESG reporting performance. One can argue that, because of their riskier financial status, disclosing more should be to the advantage of highly leveraged firms to better communicate with their major stakeholders. The findings of a group of studies confirm this theoretical expectation [(Ahmed and Courtis 1999), (Jaggi and Low 2000), (Barako et al. 2006), (Khanchel 2007), and (Baldini et al. 2018)]. Contrarily, (Meek et al. 1995), (Cormier and Magnan 1999), (Zarzeski 1996), (Giannarakis 2014a), and (Velte 2016) document the negative association between financial leverage and various reporting performance measures such as sustainability reporting quality, voluntary annual report disclosure index, environmental disclosure, and ESG disclosure. A possible explanation of this negative linkage might be that highly leveraged firms may already be sharing their private information with their creditors (Zarzeski 1996).

The linkage between tangibility and ESG reporting performance is relatively more straightforward. Since intangible assets might be more easily manipulated by managers of companies, companies with higher ratios of intangible assets can be expected to have a better disclosure performance to reduce their risks. The relevant literature supports this expectation. For example, since it is more challenging to audit intangible assets against stealing and misuse, Himmelberg et al. (1999) indicate that it is to the advantage of firms with higher proportions of intangible assets to employ better corporate governance practices, which will signal their good intention and behavior. Following a similar logic, Klapper and Love (2004) document a negative impact of higher tangibility ratios on the corporate governance performance of companies. Likewise, Khanchel (2007) reports the negative association between the tangibility of companies and their governance scores.

Legal System

Apart from corporate governance and financial variables, legal systems of countries can also affect ESG reporting performance. Among the two dominant legal systems, common law dominates the United Kingdom and former colonies of the British Empire, whereas civil law system is widely adopted in continental Europe and many non-British countries. Sarkar (2011) underlines the superiority of the common law system regarding the protection of the rights of creditors with respect to bankruptcy and credit contracts, whereas the civil law system is more powerful in terms of control rights of small investors and creditors of firms.

Methodology and Data

As underlined earlier, the scope of the research on the ESG aspect of the transport industry is limited. This study aims at filling this gap for the rail industry. Our study is superior to Özcan (2018) in several aspects. First, we use a weighted measure for environmental, social, and governance disclosure rather than focusing on only the governance dimension. Second, this chapter incorporates the ownership variable into the analyses and tests whether government ownership affects ESG reporting performance. We employ the following specification to examine the factors affecting the ESG disclosure performance of publicly traded rail companies:

$$Y = \alpha + \beta X + '\varepsilon$$

where Y is the measure for ESG disclosure performance, X is a vector of explanatory variables, and $\acute{\varepsilon}$ is the error term.

For Y, we adopt the ESG disclosure scores, published by Bloomberg, of publicly traded rail companies. These scores, compiled by Bloomberg, are an aggregate measure and rely on the environmental, social, and governance disclosure performance of companies.

Our policy variable in X is government ownership. As discussed in the introduction, companies are engaging in corporate governance and social and environmental responsibility activities for many reasons. Especially from the social and environmental responsibility perspective, what state-owned enterprises (SOEs) have been doing is more understandable when compared with totally private companies. Apart from profitability, SOEs have been aiming at fulfilling various social goals such as creating jobs, attaining geographic equity, and providing subsidized goods/services. Such actions, in fact, can be considered as a means of addressing social responsibility issues. In addition, the relevant literature suggests that SOEs can be a tool for handling environmental problems especially in the emerging countries, where the institutional framework is far from adequate (Hsu et al. 2017). Therefore, we may argue that state ownership can be a promoting factor for social and environmental responsibility activities. In addition, SOEs have been placing a growing interest in corporate governance issues. To respond to this trend, for example, the OECD and the World Bank published guidelines and toolkits.

In this chapter, we adopt three government ownership variables. The first one, government share, is a continuous variable and corresponds to the percentage share of government ownership in the rail company. Unlike government share, the second and third policy variables we use are dummy variables. The government minority stake is equal to 1 if the government retains less than 50% of the ownership, whereas government majority stake is equal to 1 when the government is the majority shareholder (have >50% of the ownership). Following the relevant literature discussed in Sec. 2, we expect that all three government ownership variables will get positive coefficients.

Following the comparable studies, we include a set of control variables in X. These control variables stand for major characteristics of corporate governance, companies' financial features, and a nationwide macro parameter. We use two very frequently adopted board-structure variables as regards corporate governance. The first one is board size. Following the literature, we expect to document the positive effect of board size, which is equal to the number of board members, on ESG disclosure performance. The second board-structure variable we use in X is the representation of independent members on the board. Based on the arguments of agency and dependence theories, we can expect a higher disclosure performance by recruiting more independent directors. In our analyses, we anticipate that the independent board member variable, which we measure by the ratio of the number of independent directors to the total number of board members, will get a positive coefficient.

X also includes four explanatory variables coming from financial statements of rail companies. The first one is profitability. We believe that profitable companies tend to perform better in terms of ESG disclosure. The logic behind this expectation is that top managers of more profitable companies can use disclosure activities as a way of making their own promotion. In our study, we employ return on assets (ROA) to measure the profitability of rail companies. We anticipate that the ROA variable, which is equal to the ratio of pretax income to the total assets, will get a positive coefficient.

The second financial variable we employ is the size of rail companies. Because of the resource availability of large companies and their more frequent actions to be disclosed, we can expect higher ESG disclosure scores for larger firms. Following the relevant literature, we anticipate that our size variable, which is equal to the net sales of the firms (in hundred million US dollars, adjusted for inflation), will get a positive coefficient.

X also includes the financial leverage of rail companies. In line with the comparable research, the leverage variable, which we measure by dividing the total debt by total assets, is expected to be positively associated with the ESG disclosure score.

Tangibility is the last financial explanatory variable in X. Based on the theoretical expectation and previous academic evidence, we anticipate getting a negative coefficient for the tangibility of rail companies, which we measure by dividing fixed assets by total assets.

Because we can expect that the legal system can be a significant determinant of the ESG reporting performance of companies, we try to capture in X the association between the legal system of countries and the ESG reporting performance of rail companies founded in those countries. In our study, we employ a dummy variable to take the effect of the legal system into account. Our dummy variable, common law, is equal to 1 for rail companies established in common law countries. Because the literature reports the strengths of both legal systems, we anticipate that the coefficient of the common law dummy variable can be either positive or negative.

We use the Bloomberg database to compile our sample. It consists of 33 publicly traded rail companies from 9 countries (Table 2 in the Appendix). We are able to collect the statistics from financial statements starting from as early as 1987 and board-structure variables starting from 2007. However, because the ownership statistics start from 2010, we limit our analyses to the 2010–2017 period. Table 3 in the Appendix depicts the definitions and the descriptive statistics of the variables used in our analyses.

The correlation matrix of the variables is shown in Table 4 in the Appendix. We calculated the variance inflation factor (VIF) of the variables to control for the multicollinearity. Our calculations reveal that the VIF scores range from 1.38 to 5.41, and the mean VIF is equal to 2.52. Based on these results, we can conclude that the degree of multicollinearity is acceptable.

Empirical Results

Table 1 presents the results of the econometric estimations. The first column of Table 1 presents the ordinary least squares (OLS) model. We also included the year dummies (not shown in Table 1) to take the time effects into account in the OLS model. The second estimation is a random effect (RE) model. The last three columns depict the results of the generalized least squares (GLS) models. The coefficients of the explanatory variables in all of our estimations are in the same direction except profitability and tangibility. We use the GLS models when we interpret the findings and discuss policy implications, since their estimates tend to be more efficient when compared to those of both OLS and RE models. We use robust standard errors to handle heteroskedasticity. Another possible problem might be the endogeneity. Because, on the one hand, the profitability of rail companies might affect their ESG reporting performance. On the other hand, ESG disclosure performance might influence profitability. To control for endogeneity, we first regress ROA on other explanatory variables and predict the residuals. Then, we regress ESG on the explanatory variables including the residual. Since the coefficient of the residual variable is not statistically significant ($P > |z| = 0.77$), we conclude that there is no endogeneity between ESG and ROA.

Table 1 Regression results where the dependent variable is the ESG disclosure score

	OLS (1)	*RE* (2)	*GLS* (3)	*GLS* (4)	*GLS* (5)
Government share	0.129***	0.061	0.131***	–	–
	(4.16)	(1.46)	(4.94)		
Government minority stake	–	–	–	2.052***	–
				(2.68)	
Government majority stake	–	–	–	–	8.255***
					(3.01)
Board size	0.923***	−0.208	0.861***	1.046***	0.903***
	(3.85)	(1.04)	(5.01)	(5.57)	(5.08)
Independent directors	0.290***	0.123***	0.289***	0.222***	0.274***
	(7.17)	(2.63)	(11.03)	(8.04)	(10.00)
Profitability	−7.223	24.553*	−15.758**	−18.358**	−16.244**
	(0.45)	(1.80)	(2.05)	(2.00)	(2.04)
Size	0.179***	0.193***	0.176***	0.163***	0.176***
	(7.60)	(4.22)	(13.31)	(10.44)	(12.59)
Financial leverage	20.707***	7.468	17.867***	7.530***	15.792***
	(5.40)	(1.34)	(5.94)	(2.79)	(4.94)
Tangibility	−11.611*	19.802**	−12.506***	−15.146***	−12.652***
	(1.69)	(2.28)	(3.29)	(3.81)	(3.23)
Common law	−6.892***	−1.578	−6.084***	−3.162**	−5.207***
	(2.93)	(0.40)	(4.57)	(2.07)	(3.66)
Constant	0.235	−0.892	3.952	13.305***	5.808
	(0.03)	(0.10)	(0.83)	(3.01)	(1.19)
R^2 statistic	0.56	–	–	–	–
F statistic	34.39	–	–	–	–
Prob > *F*	0.0000	–	–	–	–
Wald test	–	44.39	655.54	523.59	590.65
Prob > Chi²	–	0.0000	0.0000	0.0000	0.0000
Number of groups	–	33	33	33	33
Number of observations	228	228	228	228	228

We start with the government ownership variable, which is the focus of our study. To analyze the possible effects of government ownership, we employed three different government ownership variables. The first one is the government share, which is equal to the percentage share of government ownership. Our first GLS estimation (column 3) reveals that there is a positive association between the percentage of shares held by the government and the ESG disclosure performance of rail companies. Particularly, holding other variables constant, a 10-percentage-point increase in the government stake should increase the ESG disclosure score of rail companies by 1.31 points, and this finding is statistically significant at the 1% level. When we replace the government share variable with dummy variables representing the minority and majority government stakes, we see that the positive association remains unchanged. According to the fourth and fifth columns of Table 1, rail companies with minority government stake are expected to have higher ESG scores by 2.05 points, whereas ESG scores should increase by 8.26 points in the case of majority government ownership. We should note that these coefficients are statistically significant at the 1% level.

Regarding the board-structure variables, almost all estimations produced statistically significant (at the 1% level) and positive coefficients for both board size and board independence. The findings of our GLS estimations suggest that a one-member increase in the board of directors is expected to increase the ESG disclosure score of publicly traded rail companies in the range of 0.86–1.05 points. With respect to the share of the independent directors on the board, a 10-point increase in the ratio of independent directors to total number of directors on the board is likely to increase the ESG disclosure score in the range of 2.22–2.89.

The next four explanatory variables are the financial ones. In relation to profitability, we document that a 0.1-point increase in ROA is expected to decrease the ESG disclosure score in the range of 1.58–1.84 points. We should note that this finding is against our earlier expectation. About the size of rail companies, our findings suggested that a 100 million US dollar increase in the size (measured by net sales) of a rail company should be associated with an increase of 0.16–0.18 points in its ESG disclosure score (significant at the 1% level). Regarding the financial leverage, we document that a 0.1-point increase in the total liabilities to total assets ratio is likely to increase the ESG disclosure score in the range of 0.75–1.79 points. With respect to the tangibility, we can expect a 1.25- to 1.51-point decrease in ESG disclosure scores of rail companies if they increase their tangibility ratios by 0.1 points.

Lastly, our finding reveals the negative association between the common law system and ESG disclosure scores of rail companies. Holding other variables constant, the ESG disclosure score of rail companies founded in a common law country was expected to be lower, in the range of 3.16–6.08 points, than that of a comparable rail company from a civil law country.

Conclusion and Policy Implications

The goal of this study is to test the effect of government ownership on ESG disclosure scores of publicly traded rail companies. Our sample consists of 33 rail companies from 9 countries over the 2007–2017 period. Apart from the policy variables, we employ a set of control variables representing corporate governance (board size and share of independent directors on the board), a country-specific macro variable (law system), and financial variables (net sales, ROA, financial leverage, and tangibility) derived from balance sheets and income statements of rail companies.

Regarding our policy variable, our analyses reveal that government ownership has a statistically significant and positive effect on the ESG reporting performance of publicly traded rail companies. Our GLS estimations suggest that this association is valid for each of the three government ownership variables we use.

This study also presents noteworthy results on other determinants of ESG performance. Regarding the board structure, our analyses suggest that both larger boards and higher shares of independent directors on the board have a positive association with ESG disclosure scores of rail companies. This finding is coherent with those of Chen and Jaggi (2000), Said et al. (2009), Siregar and Bachtiar (2010), Samaha et al. (2012), and Giannarakis (2014b). With respect to the financial variables, our estimations reveal that larger and more leveraged rail companies are more likely to get higher ESG disclosure scores, whereas we report that higher profitability and tangibility ratios tend to reduce ESG reporting performance. These findings are consistent with what Baldini et al. (2018) indicate for profitability; Wallace et al. (1994), Meek et al. (1995), Zarzeski (1996), Ahmed and Courtis (1999), Cormier and Magnan (1999), Klapper and Love (2004), Barako et al. (2006), Khanchel (2007), Reverte (2009), da Silva Monteiro and Aibar-Guzmán (2010), A. Bokpin (2013), Giannarakis (2014b), Branco and Rodrigues (2008), Samaha et al. (2012), Giannarakis (2014a), Chiu and Wang (2015), and Velte (2016) suggest for firm size; Ahmed and Courtis (1999), Jaggi and Low (2000), Barako et al. (2006), and Khanchel (2007) indicate for financial leverage; and Himmelberg et al. (1999), Klapper and Love (2004), and Khanchel (2007) show for tangibility. Lastly, our common law dummy variable has a negative impact on ESG disclosure performance.

Our analyses suggest crucial policy implications. Assuming that our findings are valid, rail companies, which would like to benefit from an improved ESG disclosure performance, should enlarge their boards and recruit more independent directors from the corporate governance point of view. Financially, they need to increase their sales and financial leverage while reducing their tangibility ratios. With respect to the government ownership, which is the focus of this study, rail companies should attract government as a partner. Our analyses suggest that the positive effect of government ownership is increasing with the increasing government stake, but even a minority government stake can help perform better in terms of ESG disclosure.

Obviously, such actions are easier said than done. For example, increasing sales necessitates a well-prepared business strategy and significant financial resources. It also depends on factors (such as competition and macroeconomic conditions) beyond the control of the management of companies. Likewise, decreasing the tangibility ratio in the rail industry, which is quite capital-intensive, may be unattainable to some degree. Financial leverage can be increased to some extent, but this will clearly increase the financial risk of rail companies. When compared with such actions, changes in corporate governance variables, like increasing the number of board members and employing more independent directors, might be more easily implemented. Regarding the ownership structure, having the government as a shareholder, even with a minority stake, can contribute to the ESG disclosure performance of publicly traded rail companies.

The major limitation of this study is its relatively smaller sample when compared to comparable studies. In addition, a control variable to measure the quality of the management would be useful, as Waddock and Graves (1997) pointed out before. For future work, one can analyze the effect of ESG reporting scores on the accounting and stock market performance of rail companies. In addition, a survey examining how the managements of rail companies evaluate ESG activities can complement empirical studies.

Appendix

Table 2 Sample railway companies

Rail company	*Country*
Aurizon Holdings Ltd	Australia
Canadian National Railway Co	Canada
Canadian Pacific Railway Ltd	Canada
Central Japan Railway Co	Japan
CSX Corp	USA
Daqin Railway Co Ltd	China
East Japan Railway Co	Japan
Firstgroup PLC	UK
Genesee & Wyoming Inc	USA
Getlink SE	France
Go-Ahead Group PLC	UK
Grupo Mexico SAB de CV (Grupo Mexico)	Mexico
Guangshen Railway Co Ltd	China
Kansas City Southern	USA
Keikyu Corp	Japan
Keisei Electric Railway Co Ltd	Japan
Kobe Electric Railway Co Ltd	Japan
Kyushu Railway Co	Japan
MTR Corp Ltd	Hong Kong
Nagoya Railroad Co Ltd	Japan
Nankai Electric Railway Co Ltd	Japan
National Express Group PLC	UK
Nishi-Nippon Railroad Co Ltd	Japan
Norfolk Southern Corp	USA
Odakyu Electric Railway Co Ltd	Japan
Providence & Worcester Railroad Co	USA
Sanyo Electric Railway Co Ltd	Japan
Shin-Keisei Electric Railway Co Ltd	Japan
Stagecoach Group PLC	UK
Tobu Railway Co Ltd	Japan
Tokyu Corp	Japan
Union Pacific Corp	USA
West Japan Railway Co	Japan

Table 3 Descriptive statistics

Variable	*Definition*	*Expected sign*	*Mean*	*Std. dev.*	*Minimum*	*Maximum*
ESG	ESG disclosure scores of publicly traded rail companies published by Bloomberg database		32.173	12.139	7.85	56.61
Government share	The percentage of shares held by the government	+	7.427	21.118	0	96.93
Government minority stake	Dummy variable which is equal to 1 if the share of the government is more than 0% and less than 50%, 0 otherwise	+	0.596	0.492	0	1
Government majority stake	Dummy variable which is equal to 1 if the share of the government is more than 50%, 0 otherwise	+	0.058	0.234	0	1
Board size	The number of board members	+	12.484	3.498	5	26
Independent directors	The share of the independent members of the board	+	45.493	31.820	0	92.86
Profitability	The ratio of pretax income to total assets	+	0.058	0.044	−0.024	0.274
Size	The net sales of each rail company (in hundred million US dollars, adjusted for inflation)	+	32.786	30.521	0	137.467
Financial leverage	The ratio of total liabilities to total assets	+	0.653	0.186	0.123	1.041
Tangibility	The ratio of fixed assets to total assets	−	0.855	0.101	0.370	0.953
Common law	Dummy variable equal to 1 for the airport companies established in a common law country	+ −	0.418	0.494	0	1

Table 4 Correlation matrix

	ESG	*Government share*	*Government minority stake*	*Government majority stake*	*Board size*	*Independent directors*	*Profitability*	*Size*	*Financial leverage*	*Tangibility*	*Common law*
ESG	1.0000										
Government share	0.0754	1.0000									
Government minority stake	0.2984	−0.2174	1.0000								
Government majority stake	0.0460	0.9808	−0.3005	1.0000							
Board size	0.2629	0.0839	−0.1451	0.0530	1.0000						
Independent directors	0.3310	0.0058	0.3114	0.0261	−0.4688	1.0000					
Profitability	0.2352	0.1702	0.2006	0.2022	−0.1524	0.4059	1.0000				
Size	0.5790	−0.0214	0.1787	−0.0163	0.4598	0.0430	0.2962	1.0000			
Financial leverage	0.1123	−0.4522	0.2142	−0.4767	0.1263	−0.2579	−0.3197	0.0399	1.0000		
Tangibility	0.0307	0.0495	−0.1298	0.0455	0.3371	0.0233	−0.1838	0.1175	−0.2655	1.0000	
Common law	0.2500	0.0363	0.3125	0.0606	−0.4507	0.8549	0.2942	0.0153	−0.0901	−0.1142	1.0000

References

Adnan, S. M., Hay, D., & van Staden, C. J. (2018). The Influence of Culture and Corporate Governance on Corporate Social Responsibility Disclosure: A Cross Country Analysis. *Journal of Cleaner Production, 198*, 820–832.

Ahmed, K., & Courtis, J. K. (1999). Associations between Corporate Characteristics and Disclosure Levels in Annual Reports: A Meta-Analysis. *The British Accounting Review, 31*(1), 35–61.

Amran, A., & Susela Devi, S. (2008). The Impact of Government and Foreign Affiliate Influence on Corporate Social Reporting: The Case of Malaysia. *Managerial Auditing Journal, 23*(4), 386–404.

Baldini, M., Dal Maso, L., Liberatore, G., Mazzi, F., & Terzani, S. (2018). Role of Country-and Firm-Level Determinants in Environmental, Social, and Governance Disclosure. *Journal of Business Ethics, 150*(1), 79–98.

Barako, D. G., Hancock, P., & Izan, H. Y. (2006). Factors Influencing Voluntary Corporate Disclosure by Kenyan Companies. *Corporate Governance: An International Review, 14*(2), 107–125.

Bhojraj, S., & Sengupta, P. (2003). Effect of Corporate Governance on Bond Ratings and Yields: The Role of Institutional Investors and Outside Directors. *The Journal of Business, 76*(3), 455–475.

Bokpin, G. A. (2013). Determinants and Value Relevance of Corporate Disclosure: Evidence from the Emerging Capital Market of Ghana. *Journal of Applied Accounting Research, 14*, 127–146.

Branco, M. C., & Rodrigues, L. L. (2008). Factors Influencing Social Responsibility Disclosure by Portuguese Companies. *Journal of Business Ethics, 83*(4), 685–701.

Chen, C. J., & Jaggi, B. (2000). Association between Independent Non-executive Directors, Family Control and Financial Disclosures in Hong Kong. *Journal of Accounting and Public Policy, 19*(4–5), 285–310.

Chen, K. C., Chen, Z., & Wei, K. J. (2009). Legal Protection of Investors, Corporate Governance, and the Cost of Equity Capital. *Journal of Corporate Finance, 15*(3), 273–289.

Chiu, T. K., & Wang, Y. H. (2015). Determinants of Social Disclosure Quality in Taiwan: An Application of Stakeholder Theory. *Journal of Business Ethics, 129*(2), 379–398.

Collett, P., & Hrasky, S. (2005). Voluntary Disclosure of Corporate Governance Practices by Listed Australian Companies. *Corporate Governance: An International Review, 13*(2), 188–196.

Cormier, D., & Gordon, I. M. (2001). An Examination of Social and Environmental Reporting Strategies. *Accounting, Auditing & Accountability Journal, 14*(5), 587–617.

Cormier, D., & Magnan, M. (1999). Corporate Environmental Disclosure Strategies: Determinants, Costs and Benefits. *Journal of Accounting, Auditing & Finance, 14*(4), 429–451.

Dhaliwal, D., Li, O. Z., Tsang, A., & Yang, Y. G. (2014). Corporate Social Responsibility Disclosure and the Cost of Equity Capital: The Roles of Stakeholder Orientation and Financial Transparency. *Journal of Accounting and Public Policy, 33*(4), 328–355.

El Ghoul, S., Guedhami, O., Kwok, C. C., & Mishra, D. R. (2011). Does Corporate Social Responsibility Affect the Cost of Capital? *Journal of Banking & Finance, 35*(9), 2388–2406.

Eng, L. L., & Mak, Y. T. (2003). Corporate Governance and Voluntary Disclosure. *Journal of Accounting and Public Policy, 22*(4), 325–345.

Feigenbaum, H. B. (1982). Public Enterprise in Comparative Perspective. *Comparative Politics, 15*(1), 101–122.

Ferguson, M. J., Lam, K. C., & Lee, G. M. (2002). Voluntary Disclosure by State-Owned Enterprises Listed on the Stock Exchange of Hong Kong. *Journal of International Financial Management & Accounting, 13*(2), 125–152.

Giannarakis, G. (2014a). Corporate Governance and Financial Characteristic Effects on the Extent of Corporate Social Responsibility Disclosure. *Social Responsibility Journal, 10*(4), 569–590.

Giannarakis, G. (2014b). The Determinants Influencing the Extent of CSR Disclosure. *International Journal of Law and Management, 56*(5), 393–416.

Himmelberg, C. P., Hubbard, R. G., & Palia, D. (1999). Understanding the Determinants of Managerial Ownership and the Link Between Ownership and Performance. *Journal of Financial Economics, 53*(3), 353–384.

Hsu, P. H., Liang, H., & Matos, P. P. (2017). Leviathan Inc. and Corporate Environmental Engagement. Research Collection Lee Kong Chian School Of Business.

Ilkhanizadeh, S., & Karatepe, O. M. (2017). An Examination of the Consequences of Corporate Social Responsibility in the Airline Industry: Work Engagement, Career Satisfaction, and Voice Behavior. *Journal of Air Transport Management, 59*, 8–17.

Inchausti, B. G. (1997). The Influence of Company Characteristics and Accounting Regulation on Information Disclosed by Spanish Firms. *European Accounting Review, 6*(1), 45–68.

Jaggi, B., & Low, P. Y. (2000). Impact of Culture, Market Forces, and Legal System on Financial Disclosures. *The International Journal of Accounting, 35*(4), 495–519.

Jensen, M. C. (1993). The Modern Industrial Revolution, Exit, and the Failure of Internal Control Systems. *Journal of Finance, 48*(3), 831–880.

Karaman, A. S., & Akman, E. (2018). Taking-off Corporate Social Responsibility Programs: An AHP Application in Airline Industry. *Journal of Air Transport Management, 68*, 187–197.
Karaman, A. S., Kilic, M., & Uyar, A. (2018). Sustainability Reporting in the Aviation Industry: Worldwide Evidence. *Sustainability Accounting, Management and Policy Journal, 9*(4), 362–391.
Khanchel, I. (2007). Corporate Governance: Measurement and Determinant Analysis. *Auditing Journal, 22*(8), 740–760.
Klapper, L. F., & Love, I. (2004). Corporate Governance, Investor Protection, and Performance in Emerging Markets. *Journal of Corporate Finance, 10*(5), 703–728.
Kuo, T. C., Kremer, G. E. O., Phuong, N. T., & Hsu, C. W. (2016). Motivations and Barriers for Corporate Social Responsibility Reporting: Evidence from the Airline Industry. *Journal of Air Transport Management, 57*, 184–195.
Lipton, M., & Lorsch, J. W. (1992). A Modest Proposal for Improved Corporate Governance. *The business lawyer, 48*(1), 59–77.
Meek, G. K., Roberts, C. B., & Gray, S. J. (1995). Factors Influencing Voluntary Annual Report Disclosures by US, UK and Continental European Multinational Corporations. *Journal of International Business Studies, 26*(3), 555–572.
Monteiro, S., & Aibar-Guzmán, B. (2010). Determinants of Environmental Disclosure in the Annual Reports of Large Companies Operating in Portugal. *Corporate Social Responsibility and Environmental Management, 17*(4), 185–204.
Özcan, İ. Ç. (2018). Halka Açık Demiryolu Şirketlerinin Yönetişim Aydınlatma Notlarının Belirleyicileri. *İşletme Araştırmaları Dergisi (Journal of Business Research-Turk), 10*(4), 1242–1254.
Plumlee, M., Brown, D., Hayes, R. M., & Marshall, R. S. (2015). Voluntary Environmental Disclosure Quality and Firm Value: Further Evidence. *Journal of Accounting and Public Policy, 34*(4), 336–361.
Reverte, C. (2009). Determinants of Corporate Social Responsibility Disclosure Ratings by Spanish Listed Firms. *Journal of Business Ethics, 88*(2), 351–366.
Said, R., Hj Zainuddin, Y., & Haron, H. (2009). The Relationship between Corporate Social Responsibility Disclosure and Corporate Governance Characteristics in Malaysian Public Listed Companies. *Social Responsibility Journal, 5*(2), 212–226.
Samaha, K., Dahawy, K., Hussainey, K., & Stapleton, P. (2012). The Extent of Corporate Governance Disclosure and its Determinants in a Developing Market: The Case of Egypt. *Advances in Accounting, 28*(1), 168–178.
Sarkar, P. (2011). Common Law vs. Civil Law: Which system provides more protection to shareholders and promotes financial development. *Journal of Advanced Research in Law and Economics, 2*(4), 143–161.

Seo, K., Moon, J., & Lee, S. (2015). Synergy of Corporate Social Responsibility and Service Quality for Airlines: The Moderating Role of Carrier Type. *Journal of Air Transport Management, 47*, 126–134.

Siregar, S. V., & Bachtiar, Y. (2010). Corporate Social Reporting: Empirical Evidence from Indonesia Stock Exchange. *International Journal of Islamic and Middle Eastern Finance and Management, 3*(3), 241–252.

Skouloudis, A., Evangelinos, K., & Moraitis, S. (2012). Accountability and Stakeholder Engagement in the Airport Industry: An Assessment of Airports' CSR Reports. *Journal of Air Transport Management, 18*(1), 16–20.

Stiglitz, J. E. (1996). *Whither Socialism?* Cambridge, MA/London: MIT Press.

Sukcharoensin, S. (2012). The Determinants of Voluntary CSR Disclosure of Thai Listed Firms. *International Proceedings of Economics Development & Research, 46*(p), 61–65.

Velte, P. (2016). Women on Management Board and ESG Performance. *Journal of Global Responsibility, 7*(1), 98–109.

Waddock, S. A., & Graves, S. B. (1997). The Corporate Social Performance–Financial Performance Link. *Strategic Management Journal, 18*(4), 303–319.

Wallace, R. S. O., Naser, K., & Mora, A. (1994). The Relationship Between the Comprehensiveness of Corporate Annual Reports and Firm Characteristics in Spain. *Accounting and Business Research, 25*(97), 41–53.

Wang, K., Sewon, O., & Claiborne, M. C. (2008). Determinants and Consequences of Voluntary Disclosure in an Emerging Market: Evidence from China. *Journal of International Accounting, Auditing and Taxation, 17*(1), 14–30.

Wang, P., Wang, F., Zhang, J., & Yang, B. (2012). The Effect of the Ultimate Owner and Regulation Policy on Corporate Social Responsibility Information Disclosure: Evidence from China. *African Journal of Business Management, 6*(20), 6183–6193.

Wang, Q., Wu, C., & Sun, Y. (2015). Evaluating Corporate Social Responsibility of Airlines Using Entropy Weight and Grey Relation Analysis. *Journal of Air Transport Management, 42*, 55–62.

Zarzeski, M. T. (1996). Spontaneous Harmonization Effects of Culture and Market Forces on Accounting Disclosure Practices. *Accounting Horizons, 10*(1), 18–37.

İsmail Çağrı Özcan is an assistant professor at Ankara Yıldırım Beyazıt University. His research focuses on (i) transportation economics, finance, and policy, (ii) project finance and privatizations and (iii) regional economics. He has his work published in the *Journal of Air Transport Management, European Journal of Transport and Infrastructure Research, International Journal of Transport Economics*, and *Case Studies on Transport Policy*, among others.

Integrated Reporting in Municipally Owned Corporations: A Case Study in Italy

Spiridione Lucio Dicorato, Chiara Di Gerio, Gloria Fiorani, and Giuseppe Paciullo

Introduction

Municipally owned corporations (MOCs) are organisations 'with independent corporate status, managed by an executive board appointed primarily by local government officials with majority public ownership' (Voorn et al. 2017). Corporatisation places municipally owned entities 'on a commercial basis in a competitive environment. It allows the government, as the owner, to intervene by providing broad direction in key performance targets and community service obligations' (Teo 2000). Municipally owned corporations have become the primary type of entity responsible for the production and provision of several public services in the past decade. Even now, despite extensive privatisation, they are crucial in societies and economies throughout the world (World Bank 2014; OECD 2015).

S. L. Dicorato (✉) • C. Di Gerio • G. Fiorani • G. Paciullo
University of Rome "Tor Vergata", Rome, Italy
e-mail: dicorato@economia.uniroma2.it

F. Manes-Rossi, R. Levy Orelli (eds.), *New Trends in Public Sector Reporting*, Public Sector Financial Management,
https://doi.org/10.1007/978-3-030-40056-9_9

An oversight mechanism to improve governance and accountability is necessary for MOCs. Integrated reporting (IR) could address this due to its ability to present a holistic perspective of the factors that create value for an entity. The increasing focus among stakeholders on social, environmental, and governance issues is the root source of the growth observed in integrated reports that are produced by entities (Adam and Simnett 2011). Integrated reporting presents numerous advantages, as information is aligned more accurately to stakeholders' needs, with more significant non-financial information becoming available; this provides for better resource allocation by investors and stakeholders alike (Frías-Aceituno et al. 2014).

These companies, 'in the balance between private law companies and organisational extension of public authorities' (Maltoni 2017), are called to assess the desirability of integrating corporate governance tools in corporate social responsibility (CSR) programmes (Decree No. 175/2016). Integrated reporting can assist state-owned companies in achieving accountability (KPMG 2012). This is because integrated reporting can be adapted to take the goals of state-owned companies into account (KPMG 2012).

Citizens are mainly interested in understanding and verifying how the administration fulfils its mandate and manages its services, the priorities and objectives of the intervention, the (expected and realised) levels of performance, and particularly the effects produced by its action. The adoption of an integrated reporting system in public administrations and, in particular, in the MOCs appears to respond to the transparency and external communication of choices and results in greater effectiveness.

This chapter aims to delineate the trends in the literature regarding the implementation of an integrated reporting system in municipally owned corporations and the existing frameworks applicable to them. To analyse this objective through a single case study methodology, we focus on a significant example of IR implementation in Italy.

Accountability in Municipally Owned Corporations

The term most frequently used by academics and practitioners to define 'enterprises where the state, regional governments or cities have significant control, through full, majority, or significant minority ownership' (OECD 2010) is state-owned enterprises (e.g. Aharoni 1981; OECD 2010; Bruton et al. 2015). Instead, we posit that municipally owned corporations (MOCs) are autonomous organisations owned by municipalities, used to produce or deliver local public services outside of the local bureaucracy (Voorn et al. 2017). They have proliferated during the past two of three decades, and many municipalities have utilised them for public service provision (Whincop 2005; Grossi and Reichard 2008; Florio and Fecher 2011) to perform certain missions of their own, such as to seek flexibility outside of bureaucratic structures and related constraints on the use of public money. Corporatisation also may increase budget flexibility, enterprise outputs and revenues, cost-efficiency, and employee productivity (Cambini et al. 2011; Lindlbauer et al. 2015) and allow major cost savings (Domberger and Rimmer 1994; Domberger and Jensen 1997).

Several approaches regarding MOCs' accountability focus on analysing corporate governance in a public environment and performance measures that account for the noneconomic goals of MOCs (e.g. Goldeng et al. 2008; Abatecola and Poggesi 2010; Bhasa 2015; Ting and Lean 2015).

Due to the social, economic, and technological forces arising from the use of taxpayer money (Hoque and Moll 2001), fostering the accountability of MOCs is particularly important for preventing the loss of control by the core administration, which can result from MOCs' greater autonomy (Schillemans 2008; Whincop 2005; OECD 2015). Additionally, changes in the institutional arrangements of public service provision have precipitated new requirements in terms of accountability and transparency (Grossi and Thomasson 2015).

Chiu and Hung (2004) assert that minimal research has investigated the topic of the accountability of MOCs, and Sinclair (1995) confirms that accountability in the public sector is often perceived as difficult to achieve. However, the accountability of MOCs is developing and is a continual work in progress (Sands 2004).

Integrated Report: A Literature Review

Integrated reporting (IR) has gained attention in recent years due to the necessity of highlighting information and content regarding an organisation's performance. In the past, the focus was on financial information only, although several studies have demonstrated that the capability of traditional financial reporting to satisfy the information-related needs of a broad range of stakeholders has been deemed insufficient to explain the value of an entity (Guthrie et al. 2017). In recent decades, studies have focused on different forms of reporting for accountability (Gray et al. 1988; Bebbington et al. 2014; Guthrie et al. 2017) and legitimacy

(Deegan et al. 2002; Beddewela and Fairbrass 2015) and on supporting and promoting stakeholders' engagement (O'Riordan and Fairbrass 2008, 2014). The integrated report is issued by an organisation for investors, and more generally all stakeholders, to assemble financial and non-financial information (de Villiers et al. 2014, 2017), including social, environmental, and governance-related issues, with qualitative information (Adam and Simnett 2011) focusing on future value creation. However, more critical voices have emerged to defend social and environmental stakeholders' concerns (Brown and Dillard 2014; Flower 2015; Beck et al. 2017). IR has also been criticised because of a perceived risk of pressures exercised by lobby groups and larger players in the industry (Lodhia 2015) and because of the possibility that IR has been captured by investors and accountants (van Bommel 2014; Strong 2015).

In accordance with the provisions of the International Integrated Reporting Council (IIRC), an integrated report is defined as a report that 'demonstrates the linkages between an organisation's strategy, governance and financial performance and the social, environmental and economic context within it operates. By reinforcing these connections, IR can help the business to take more sustainable decisions and enable investors and other stakeholders to understand how an organisation is performing' (IIRC 2011). Additionally, the integrated report guarantees the perfect matching of information from traditional budget and sustainability reports with internal management mechanisms, performances, risks, strategies, and future perspectives of the organisation (IIRC 2013). The long-term vision of the IIRC is concerned with integrated thinking as an element of the main business practices and integrated reporting as a standard instrument that can grant stability, financial sustainability, and efficient and productive allocation of capital.

Consequently, the key element of IR involves gathering an enhanced range of an entity's performance information, including that gathered from organisations where performance is measured through traditional reporting (Surty et al. 2017). Furthermore, IR aids in the identification of risks and opportunities by an entity so that it may allocate resources more efficiently. Also, IR enhances the commitment of stakeholders by achieving a greater level of amalgamation between financial and non-financial information (Frías-Aceituno et al. 2014). Therefore, the commitment can reinforce the organisation's reputation, trust, and consensus and the entity's social legitimacy.

Integrated Report and MOCs: The IIRC's Framework

In accordance with the Chartered Institute of Public Finance and Accounting (CIPFA), IR can help guide public bodies in their day-to-day reasoning, decision-making, and actions to consider the resulting impact across different timeframes (not only in terms of a short or medium timeframe). IR explains how sustainable outcomes will be delivered to satisfy the requirements of stakeholders over time; it also extracts and consolidates the substance of what matters, ensuring that there is integrity in what is reported and the alignment of reporting requirements against associated risks, opportunities, and performance (CIPFA 2016).

The adoption of the Integrated Reporting Framework (IRF) supported by the IIRC should imply a range of internal changes aimed at producing an integrated report and using this information for internal decisions. Previous research has highlighted the internal aspects of the IRF, including management accounting systems and processes and the effects of the IRF on the engagement of senior executives in internal processes and on management orientation and decision-making (de Villiers et al. 2014). Additionally, the IRF has been analysed in terms of integrating sustainability into the strategic process (Eccles and Saltzman 2011; Steyn 2014), in relation to contextual factors (Dragu and Tiron-Tudor 2013; Frías-Aceituno et al. 2013), and addressing increasing demands for non-financial disclosure (Stubbs and Higgins 2015). A further stream of research has focused on the management accounting changes in organisations' adoption of IR; this research has applied institutional theory (Lounsbury 2008) and the literature on management accounting change (Burns and Scapens 2000; Lapsley and Wright 2004; Miller and Power 2013) to explore the adoption of IR results in strategic thinking.

Municipally owned corporations (MOCs) must comply with rules and regulations in reporting activities. IR can assist state-owned companies in achieving accountability, and this is because IR can be adapted to account for the goals of MOCs, focusing on their objectives (KPMG 2012). Integrated reporting brings governance, financial capital, intellectual capital, social capital, and environmental capital onto a common platform (Abeysekera 2013). Furthermore, IR will enable MOCs to address factors that are important to vast numbers of stakeholders who are interested in their performance (Nkonki 2014). Finally, it can also assist in ensuring that companies make sustainable decisions, as stakeholders of the organisation possess greater insight into the objectives and performance of those decisions through reporting disclosures (Nkonki 2014), not only in terms of profit. Indeed, stakeholders can perceive the value that MOCs create by reporting more holistically, based on financial and non-financial information. The use of IR better prepares MOCs to analyse their long-term strategic objectives in light of stakeholders' needs (Nkonki 2014). IR can be achieved through the application of the IIRC's Integrated Reporting Framework guidance regarding the application and preparation of IR (Surty et al. 2017). This framework, updated in 2013, aims at providing both effective shareholder accountability (Solomon and Maroun 2012) and information that can aid providers of financial capital in making investment decisions. The framework also seeks to address accountability in relation to the entity's use of all of the various sources of capital and also grants to stakeholders a clear understanding of how this inseparable link among capital creates value for the entity, not only in the short term but in the medium and long term as well (IIRC 2013). Feng et al. (2017) highlight the application of the IIRC in IR to sustain and promote the so-called integrated thinking, defined as 'the active consideration by an organisation of the relationships between its various operating and functional units and the [six] capitals that the organisation uses or affects' (IIRC 2013, p. 33).

Integrated reports should illustrate the linkages and connectivity between financial and non-financial information such as management commentary and governance matters (Dumitru et al. 2013); the IRF requires that 'an integrated report should show a holistic picture of the combination, interrelatedness and dependencies between the factors that affect the organization's ability to create value over time' (IIRC 2013). The connectivity of information is driven by integrated thinking and will provide insight into how integrated thinking is applied across the entity and allows for concerns to be considered collectively by each department within the entity (Surty et al. 2017). This framework contains two elements: first, the guiding principles, which indicate the content of and the method with which information is prepared and presented in the integrated report, and secondly, the content element, which provides guidance as to what should be contained within the integrated report (IIRC 2013). The implementation of the IRF guiding principles has caused publicly owned companies to perceive the necessity of employing this method, since they have decided to involve opposing objectives to not only make a profit but also meet certain social and environmental objectives (Luke

2010). IR in public sector organisations is a new phenomenon with a limited number of adopters (Guthrie et al. 2017).

The Global Reporting Initiative (GRI) (2011) is a comprehensive guideline for implementing and developing voluntary reporting systems across environmental, economic, and social sustainability dimensions (e.g. Hussey et al. 2001; Morhardt et al. 2002; Li et al. 2011). Each sustainability dimension included in the GRI guidelines is organised into aspects which comprise one or more sustainability indicator applicable in holistic view measurements (GRI 2011). The GRI was launched for the first time in the late 1990s; currently, a growing number of companies globally implement their reporting according to the GRI guidelines (Petera and Wagner 2015). The IRF and GRI can communicate with each other from two different angles. From an institutional perspective, the relationship between the two 'editors' bodies' has continuously been strengthened because the IIRC and GRI are considered more effective as collaborators rather than as competitors. From an operational perspective, this liaison has precipitated a revision of the GRI guidelines (GRI Sustainability Reporting Standards 2016 version has become effective from 1 July 2018). Given that before 2015, the two standards appeared to exclude each other, since 2016, this has changed; the GRI has been made potentially complementary and combined with the IRF; in practice, the IRF can be used to set up and structure reporting processes and then adopt the GRI standards for measuring, monitoring, and evaluating performance, which is also a component of the Integrated Reporting Framework.

Methodology

In this chapter, we employ the IIRC's Integrated Reporting Framework using a qualitative single case study method; this is a useful research method because there are not clearly evident boundaries between the contemporary phenomenon and the context (Yin 2002). Case studies investigate the properties, actions, attitudes, and social structures of institutions by applying one or more methods, such as participant observation, interviews, and analysis of documents. We have analysed the case study of 'Farmacie Comunali Pomezia S.p.A.' (FCP) as one of the first Italian MOCs to apply the IIRC's guidelines and principles. The company is entirely owned by the Municipality of Pomezia and is responsible for the management of pharmacies with the licence of the same municipality. The core business is not limited to the pharmaceutical service, although it includes the following: (1) the management of municipal pharmacies, including the sale of drugs and related products; (2) the provision of socio-sanitary services useful to the community according to the rules regulating pharmaceutical services; (3) the wholesale distribution of pharmaceutical products and articles; (4) socio-sanitary, dietetic, and medical education activities involving the citizens; and (5) functional activities with the pharmaceutical services.

The case was executed through two different steps: a study concerning the activities performed by FCP through document and website analysis, followed by a structured interview with the chief executive officer (CEO). The first one consisted of a deep analysis of the activities on the basis of both the types of capital identified by the IIRC and the dimensions (social, environmental, and economic) postulated by the GRI. Entities applying the GRI will find that it can provide important input for many aspects of the six capitals within the IRF. Sustainability disclosure provides 'a broader view of a company's performance than financial disclosure alone. When used in integrated reporting, it can reveal value creation across six capitals: human, social and relationship, manufactured, intellectual, financial, ad natural'. Through the frameworks of the GRI and IIRC, the FCP integrated report aims to clarify how the application of both guidelines can provide insight into value creation across the six capitals and drive transparency.

The interview provides enhanced insight into the subject of the study, as it allows for more personal and insightful access to information, playing an important role in data collection (Yin 2002; Wilkinson and Birmingham 2003). The interview is structured as a face-to-face interview and was conducted at the beginning of February 2018. The length of the interview was about 45–60 minutes. The interview was recorded and transcribed through extensive notes undertaken in Italian and later translated to English. To ensure correct information gathering, we sent the notes back to the interviewee for him to check. The related questions were intended to understand the significance of IR for FCP and the reasons provided in the implementation of IR in the internal processes, systems, and structures of the organisation. The interview contains a series of 12 questions dealing with the reporting process led by the IRF of the International Integrated Reporting Council (IIRC), which allows stakeholders a broader view of business activity relative to the traditional annual financial statement, which detects merely the economic sector. Therefore, to account for the social sector and the environmental one, the integrated report of FCP also uses a further reporting standard, the Global Reporting Initiative (GRI). Indeed, the GRI and IIRC work together as strategic partners, since 'they share a vision for the evolution of corporate reporting in which alignment and clarity of corporate reporting frameworks, standards and requirements drive consistency and comparability, leading to improved efficiency and effectiveness in corporate reporting practices'. Both organisations will continue to proactively communicate to the market the role, nature, and alignment of each other's framework, guidelines, and standards to ensure clarity in the corporate reporting environment.[1]

Findings

According to previous research dealing with case studies (Havlová 2015; du Toit et al. 2017; Macias and Farfan-Lievano 2017), the process employed by FCP in adopting the IRF was intended to clarify how value has been created across the capital classification on the basis of the GRI's dimensions (GRI 2017). The main reasons for adopting the GRI standard while preparing integrated reports were explained by the CEO and revolved around four aspects: (1) *readability*, to make the reporting process more intelligible and transposable and to ensure greater clarity of information to stakeholders; (2) *comparability*: given the expanding use of the GRI guidelines in integrated reporting, the adoption of its standards allows for a better comparability of the information provided; (3) *reliability*: considering the GRI standards as a consolidated source, standards allow the construction of a correct reporting process, with particular reference to key performance indicators (KPIs), which are well combined with the objectives of the integrated report; (4) *completeness*, to enrich its corporate reporting with some qualitative-quantitative information suitable to represent, in addition to the economic-financial dimension, the social dimension and the environmental dimension through a holistic approach. In the explanation of the results, we structured the FCP activities identified through the interviews and the document analysis, spreading the three GRI dimensions using the IRF and demonstrating how the existing frameworks are applicable to MOCs.

[1] Visit https://www.globalreporting.org/information/current-priorities/integrated-reporting/Pages/default.aspx

GRI: Social Dimension

The analysis of the social dimension of FCP is classified into human and social capital, based on du Toit et al. (2017). It attempted to obtain a holistic view of the level of reporting of social, environmental, and ethical information:

- *Human capital analysis*: Respecting the principles of social sustainability, FCP adopts a policy of management of the human resources which guarantees growth and employment stability, engaging in the construction of a positive, cooperative, healthy, and safe company climate where people can grow, develop their skills, and exploit their talents. Specifically, the Municipality of Pomezia is composed of a staff of 47 employees and follows an ethical code which is intended to respect the human rights of the employees.
- *Social and relationship capital analysis*: FCP operates in a multidimensional context, characterised by the interaction and the comparison with a broad and diversified audience of stakeholders (customers, suppliers, staff, shareholders, and the external environment). Each brings specific experiences and expectations that the MOC manages through both an open approach to dialogue and listening to their needs, and '*with the intention to give centrality to people at every step of the process*' (CEO), promoting stakeholders' engagement (O'Riordan and Fairbrass 2008, 2014) and aligning with stakeholders' needs for better resource allocation by investors and stakeholders alike (Frías-Aceituno et al. 2014). FCP provided a profound review of the service offered to users from a perspective that presents not only a typically commercial purpose, but also a social nature that is promoted through a series of initiatives complying with statutory obligations and with the integrated report in favour of the community. These main initiatives include the following: (1) the development of the FCP App, which allows users to book medical examinations and medicines to pharmacies, to ask questions concerning their inherent doubts related to the use of drugs (by the means of a specific live chat), and to be informed about shifts, promotions, and events offered by pharmacies; (2) the issue of fidelity

cards for public employees and ASL[2] employees; (3) tender procedure opening to suppliers and wholesalers of pharmaceutical companies towards FCP; (4) activities of social intervention such as days of socio-sanitary education and prevention days about specific pathologies (e.g. diabetes); and (5) the monitoring of personnel needs, in quantitative and qualitative terms, to develop a remuneration policy linked to commercial results and productivity, since continuous training and staff motivation are regarded as determining factors for the growth of the company asset.

GRI: Economic Dimension

Some authors (Havlová 2015; Dumay et al. 2017; du Toit et al. 2017; Macias and Farfan-Lievano 2017) have regarded the economic dimension analysis of organisations as fundamental. In the FCP context, the economic analysis can be structured, according to the IRF, into manufactured and financial capital classification:

- *Manufactured and intellectual capital analysis*: FCP encompasses six pharmaceutical stores in the territory of the Municipality of Pomezia, playing a prominent role in the territorial economy. This is a challenge that the MOC identifies as (1) ethical, by adopting principles and rules of integrity that allow the management of important economic interests that revolve around the management of the assistance service in a transparent manner; (2) that is aimed at people, through a continuous improvement of the services offered, as well as by helping to create employment growth; and (3) that is performed by identifying the appropriate professional partnerships necessary and by activating a series of activities aimed at improving the market appeal of the six pharmaceutical branches.
- *Financial capital analysis*: Regarding the economic aspect, the information on the subsidiary company has been systematically summarised and integrated to compare its profitability (economic) and financial indicators in 2016 and 2017. In the analysis of the compa-

[2] ASL or Azienda Sanitaria Locale is namely the Italian definition of local health authorities, a public body of the Italian public administration, deputy to the provision of health services.

ny's economic structure, we proceed in understanding the contribution made by typical, ancillary, and extraordinary management in achieving the overall economic result (the six pharmacies). The main economic profitability indicators used to measure economic performance are as follows: ROE, return on equity, or equity profitability rate, which is a synthetic indicator that measures the convenience of investing money in business management in relation to capital risk (Cavalieri 2010). ROE evaluates the management's work in turning all of the investments made in return. Therefore, a high ROE describes a company with high performance but does not provide guarantees regarding the conditions of economic durability. The second is ROI, or return on investment, which highlights the profitability and economic efficiency of the management (operating result) regardless of the sources used, expressing effectively what the capital invested yields in that company. ROI can be interpreted as a measure of the efficiency and effectiveness level in relation to the typical management and represents a fundamental assumption of business profitability. ROS, or return on sales, is the rate of return or profitability of sales and expresses the percentage of wealth, after deducting the coverage of all the costs of the typical management, that the company was able to generate relative to the value of sales. Its value is strongly influenced by the dynamics of the supply markets and by the choices related to the degree of rigidity of the production structure (Cavalieri 2010). Net financial position is a structural margin determined as the difference between financial assets and liabilities.

Based on the social and financial analysis of the integrated report of FCP, it is important to consider risks to pursue the company's objectives and subsequently involve the creation of value. Risks highlighted in the integrated report may be classified into financial and non-financial ones, based on the source of the risk itself. FCP, which is entirely owned by the Municipality of Pomezia, must undertake the direction and coordination of the municipality and harmonise the relationships between the local authority, company administration, and employees. In compliance with the existing regulations and statutes governing relationships among these parties, it can be noted that there are no significant non-financial risks of internal sources. Regarding the risks related to the effectiveness and efficiency of the processes, the integrated report contains a critical and timely analysis aimed at addressing the appropriate future corrective changes. Among the risks of an external nature, the integrated report states the need to cope with the following: (1) a possible highly competitive market in the area; (2) legislation which demands stringent obligations to the company (public), since private competitors often have advantages of less stringent regulatory links; and (3) a political-social context that imposes, in such a critical area, an attitude that is invariably in line with the citizens' needs.

GRI: Environmental Dimension

The natural capital asset is concerned with value creation in organisations (du Toit et al. 2017; Macias and Farfan-Lievano 2017) dealing with environmental dimensions. The same line has been followed by linking the GRI environmental dimension to the natural capital evidence in FCP:

- *Natural capital analysis*: Not all capitals are equally relevant or applicable to all organisations. While most organisations interact with all capitals to some extent, these interactions might be relatively minor or so indirect that they are not sufficiently important to include in the integrated report (IIRC 2013). In the case of FCP, the environmental dimension '*has not been a relevant theme for the understanding by investors – and the stakeholders in general – of the company's ability to create value in the short, medium and long term*' (CEO).

Conclusions

A strategic, continuous, multichannel, and differentiated reporting activity for stakeholders that integrates the environmental and social behaviour of organisations with their governance (Eccles et al. 2012) allows an enhanced analysis of an organisation's performance. This aspect is also true for those companies (municipally owned corporations or state-owned enterprises, as defined principally by the literature) wherein the organisational structure is more complex to analyse. To report in a more transparent manner the activities of these organisations, because of the interests and stakeholders involved, instruments such as the general budget, the social balance, or the sustainability report are not sufficient to fulfil those interests. Consequently, the adoption of the integrated report within the MOCs could represent the right compromise that allows for a clearer, more transparent and effective reporting. The integrated report, in fact, is oriented to the creation of a shared value, or the set of policies and operational practices which can strengthen the competitiveness of a company and improve economic and social conditions of a community in which the MOC operates. Integrated reporting can assist municipally owned corporations (MOCs) in achieving accountability and in taking their goals into account (KPMG 2012). Although the creation of shared value focuses on the interconnection between economic and social progress, companies have only occasionally faced social issues from a value perspective, regarding them as, in almost every case, ancillary aspects and contributing in this manner to the reduction of visibility of the connections between the two pillars.

The analysis of the literature about MOCs' performance, the related implementation of IR, an instrument which can provide a multidimensional picture of public organisations' accountability, and the analysis of existing frameworks find application in the proposed case study. The integrated report experienced by the MOC analysed was based on both types of capital identified by the IIRC and the dimensions (social, environmental, and economic) postulated by the GRI. This brand new methodology should allow a proper fit between the previous literature framework regarding IR and the real implementation of the integrated report in municipally owned corporations. In realising and describing such interconnections, FCP's first integrated report renders the following: (1) the opportunity to establish a best practice in the referring market, (2) the consideration of citizens as an active part of the process: from a simple consumer to an actor who can direct the company's activity, (3) the basis for setting strategic objectives and consequent actions, thereby merging together the economic, social, and environmental aspects of the entire organisation.

While this study provides support for the use of the IRF in MOCs, there are some limitations in our case study, indicating avenues for further research. First, FCP is at the first edition of its IR, and consequently, it has been not possible to make any comparison with the previous years. Second, the analysis has been conducted only for FCP, and a comparative analysis among other organisations has not been conducted. These two limitations cannot allow both an internal and an external appraisal in terms of improvements of the IIRC's types of capital and competitiveness. For this reason, future research should focus on an analysis of IR which can yield a longitudinal examination and a comparison with other MOCs (or organisations in general), with the aim of verifying several changes from economic, social, and environmental perspectives.

References

Abatecola, G., & Poggesi, S. (2010). Corporate Governance and Performance: Evidence from the Italian Listed Local Public Utilities (2000–2008). *International Journal of Public Administration, 33*(11), 534–540.

Abeysekera, I. (2013). A Template for Integrated Reporting. *Journal of Intellectual Capital, 14*(2), 227–245.

Adam, S., & Simnett, R. (2011). Integrated Reporting: An Opportunity for Australia's Not for Profit Sector. *Australian Accounting Review, 21*(3), 292–301.

Aharoni, Y. (1981). Performance Evaluation of State-Owned Enterprises: A Process Perspective. *Management Science, 27*(11), 1340–1347.

Bebbington, J., Unerman, J., & O'Dwyer, B. (2014). *Sustainability Accounting and Accountability*. London/New York: Routledge.

Beck, C., Dumay, J., & Frost, G. (2017). In Pursuit of a 'Single Source of Truth': From Threatened Legitimacy to Integrated Reporting. *Journal of Business Ethics, 141*(1), 191–205.

Beddewela, E., & Fairbrass, J. (2015). Seeking Legitimacy Through CSR: Institutional Pressures and Corporate Responses of Multinationals in Sri Lanka. *Journal of Business Ethics, 136*(3), 503–522.

Bhasa, M. P. (2015). Ownership Structure and Performance of Listed State-Owned Enterprises vis-à-vis Comparable Private Enterprises: Evidence from India. *IUP Journal of Corporate Governance, 14*(3), 7–24.

Brown, J., & Dillard, J. (2014). Integrated Reporting: On the Need for Broadening Out and Opening Up. *Accounting, Auditing and Accountability Journal, 27*(7), 1120–1156.

Bruton, G. D., Peng, M. W., Ahlstrom, D., Stan, C., & Xu, K. (2015). State-Owned Enterprises Around the World as Hybrid Organisations. *The Academy of Management Perspectives, 29*(1), 92–114.

Burns, J., & Scapens, R. W. (2000). Conceptualizing Management Accounting Change: An Institutional Framework. *Management Accounting Research, 11*(1), 3–25.

Cambini, C., Filippini, M., Piacenza, M., & Vannoni, D. (2011). Corporatization and Firm Performance: Evidence from Publicly-Provided Local Utilities. *Review of Law and Economics, 7*(1), 195–217.

Cavalieri, E. (2010). *Economia Aziendale Volume I – Attività Aziendale e Processi Produttivi*. Torino: Giappichelli Editore.

Chiu, S., & Hung, E. (2004). Good Governance or Muddling Through? Layoffs and Employment Reform in Socialist China. *Communist and Post-Communist Studies, 37*(3), 395–411.

de Villiers, C., Rinaldi, L., & Unerman, J. (2014). Integrated Reporting: Insights, Gaps and an Agenda for Future Research. *Accounting, Auditing and Accountability Journal, 27*(7), 1042–1067.

de Villiers, C., Venter, E., & Hsiao, P. (2017). Integrated Reporting: Background, Measurement Issues, Approaches and an Agenda for Future Research. *Accounting and Finance, 57*, 937–959.

Deegan, C., Rankin, M., & Tobin, J. (2002). An Examination of the Corporate Social and Environmental Disclosures of BHP from 1983–1997: A Test of Legitimacy Theory. *Accounting, Auditing and Accountability Journal, 15*(3), 312–343.

Domberger, S., & Jensen, P. (1997). Contracting Out By the Public Sector: Theory, Evidence, Prospects. *Oxford Review of Economic Policy, 13*(4), 67–78.

Domberger, S., & Rimmer, S. (1994). Competitive Tendering and Contracting in the Public Sector: A Survey. *International Journal of the Economics of Business, 1*(3), 439–453.

Dragu, I. M., & Tiron-Tudor, A. (2013). The Integrated Reporting Initiative from an Institutional Perspective: Emergent Factors. *Procedia – Social and Behavioral Sciences, 92*, 275–279.

du Toit, E., Schütte, G., & van Zyl, R. (2017). Integrated Reporting by South African Companies: A Case Study. *Meditari Accountancy Research, 25*(4), 654–674.

Dumay, J., Bernardi, C., Guthrie, J., & La Torre, M. (2017). Barriers to Implementing the International Integrated Reporting Framework: A Contemporary Academic Perspective. *Meditari Accountancy Research, 25*(4), 461–480.

Dumitru, M., Glavan, M. E., Gorgan, C., & Dumitru, V. F. (2013). International Integrated Reporting Framework: A Case Study in the Software Industry. *Annales Universitatis Apulensis: Series Oeconomica, 15*(1), 24–39.

Eccles, R. G., & Saltzman, D. (2011). Achieving Sustainability Through Integrated Reporting. *Stanford Social Innovation Review, 9*(3), 56–61.

Eccles, R. G., Krzus, M. P., & Casadei, A. (2012). Report Integrato. *Rendicontazione integrata per una strategia sostenibile*. Forlì: Edizioni Philantropy.

Farmacie Comunali Pomezia S.p.A. (2018). *Bilancio Integrato – Anno contabile 2017*. Pomezia. http://www.farmaciepomezia.it/amministrazione-trasparente.php.

Feng, T., Cummings, L., & Tweedie, D. (2017). Exploring Integrated Thinking in Integrated Reporting: An Exploratory Study in Australia. *Journal of Intellectual Capital, 18*(2), 330–353.

Florio, M., & Fecher, F. (2011). The Future of Public Enterprises: Contributions to a New Discourse. *Annals of Public and Cooperative Economics, 82*(4), 361–373.

Flower, J. (2015). The International Integrated Reporting Council: A Story of Failure. *Critical Perspectives on Accounting, 27*, 1–17.

Frías-Aceituno, J. V., Rodríguez-Ariza, L., & García-Sánchez, I. M. (2013). Is Integrated Reporting Determined By a Country's Legal System? An Exploratory Study. *Journal of Cleaner Production, 44*, 45–55.

Frías-Aceituno, J. V., Rodríguez-Ariza, L., & García-Sánchez, I. M. (2014). Explanatory Factors of Integrated Sustainability and Financial Reporting. *Business Strategy and the Environment, 23*(1), 56–72.

Goldeng, E., Grünfeld, L. A., & Benito, G. R. G. (2008). The Performance Differential Between Private and State-Owned Enterprises: The Roles of Ownership, Management and Market Structure. *Journal of Management Studies, 45*(7), 1244–1273.

Gray, R., Owen, D., & Maunders, K. (1988). Corporate Social Reporting: Emerging Trends in Accountability and Social Contract. *Accounting, Auditing and Accountability Journal, 1*(1), 6–20.

GRI. (2011). *GRI Sustainability Reporting: How Valuable Is the Journey?* https://www.globalreporting.orgresourcelibrary/GRI-Reporting-Stats-2010.pdf.

GRI. (2017). *Focusing a Path to Integrated Report.* https://www.globalreporting.org/resourcelibrary/GRI-CLG_IntegratedReporting.pdf.

Grossi, G., & Reichard, C. (2008). Municipal Corporatization in Germany and Italy. *Public Management Review, 10*(5), 597–617.

Grossi, G., & Thomasson, A. (2015). Bridging the Accountability Gap in Hybrid Organisations: The Case of Copenhagen Malmö Port. *International Review of Administrative Sciences, 81*(3), 604–620.

Guthrie, J., Manes-Rossi, F., & Orelli, R. L. (2017). Integrated Reporting and Integrated Thinking in Italian Public Sector Organizations. *Meditari Accountancy Research, 25*(4), 553–573.

Havlová, K. (2015). What Integrated Reporting Changed: The Case Study of Early Adopters. *Procedia – Economics and Finance, 34*, 231–237.

Hoque, Z., & Moll, J. (2001). Public Sector Reform – Implications for Accounting, Accountability and Performance of State-Owned Entities – an Australian Perspective. *International Journal of Public Sector Management, 14*(4), 304–326.

Hussey, D. M., Kirsop, P. L., & Meissen, R. E. (2001). Global Reporting Initiative Guidelines: An Evaluation of Sustainable Development Metrics for Industry. *Environmental Quality Management, 11*(1), 1–20.

International Integrated Reporting Council. (2011). *Towards Integrated Reporting. Communicating Value in the 21st Century.* https://integratedreporting.org/wp-content/uploads/2012/06/discussion-paper-summary1.pdf.

International Integrated Reporting Council. (2013). *The Integrated Reporting Framework. II Framework.* http://www.discussionpaper2011.theiirc.org/wpcontent/uploads/2011/DP/discussionpaper2011_print_version.pdf.

International Integrated Reporting Council (IIRC) and CIPFA. (2016). *Focusing on Value Creation in the Public Sector*. http://integratedreporting.org/wpcontent/uploads/2016/09.

KPMG. (2012). *Integrated Reporting Issue 2: Performance Insight Through Better Business Reporting*. https://integratedreporting.org/wp-content/uploads/2012/06/KPMG-Integrated-Reporting-Performance-Insight-Through-Better-Business-Reporting-Issue-2.pdf.

Lapsley, I., & Wright, E. (2004). The Diffusion of Management Accounting Innovations in the Public Sector: A Research Agenda. *Management Accounting Research, 15*(3), 355–374.

Li, N., Toppinen, A., Tuppura, A., & Xiong, Y. (2011). Corporate Responsibility and Strategic Groups in the Forest-Based Industry: Exploratory Analysis based on the Global Reporting Initiative (GRI) Framework. *Corporate Social Responsibility and Environmental Management, 19*(4), 191–205.

Lindlbauer, I., Winter (née Hinz), V, & Schreyögg, J. (2015). Antecedents and Consequences of Corporatization: An Empirical Analysis of German Public Hospitals. *Journal of Public Administration Research and Theory, 26*(2), 309–326.

Lodhia, S. (2015). Exploring the Transition to Integrated Reporting Through a Practice Lens: An Australian Customer Owned Bank Perspective. *Journal of Business Ethics, 129*(3), 585–598.

Lounsbury, M. (2008). Institutional Rationality and Practice Variation: New Directions in the Institutional Analysis of Practice. *Accounting, Organizations and Society, 33*(4), 349–361.

Luke, B. (2010). Examinig Accounting Accountability Dimensions in State-Owned Enterprises. *Financial Accountability and Management, 26*(2), 134–162.

Macias, H., & Farfan-Lievano, A. (2017). Integrated Reporting as a Strategy for Firm Growth: Multiple Case Study in Colombia. *Meditari Accountancy Research, 25*(4), 605–628.

Maltoni, A. (2017). Le società in-house nel T.U. sulle partecipate pubbliche, *Urbanistica e Appalti, 1*, 7–23.

Miller, P., & Power, M. (2013). Accounting, Organizing, and Economizing: Connecting Accounting Research and Organization Theory. *The Academy of Management Annals, 7*(1), 557–605.

Morhardt, J. E., Baird, S., & Freeman, K. (2002). Scoring Corporate Environmental and Sustainability Reports Using GRI 2000, ISO 14031 and Other Criteria. *Corporate Social Responsibility and Environmental Management, 9*(4), 215–233.

Nkonki. (2014). Insights into State-Owned Companies Integrated Reporting; Trends in South Africa. *Southern African Business Review*. https://doi.org/10.25159/1998-8125/3841.

O'Riordan, L., & Fairbrass, J. (2008). Corporate Social Responsibility (CSR): Models and Theories in Stakeholder Dialogue. *Journal of Business Ethics, 83*(4), 745–758.
O'Riordan, L., & Fairbrass, J. (2014). Managing CSR Stakeholder Engagement: A New Conceptual Framework. *Journal of Business Ethics, 125*(1), 121–145.
OECD. (2010). *OECD Corporate Governance – Accountability and Transparency: A Guide for State-Owned Ownership*. Paris: OECD Publishing.
OECD. (2015). *OECD Guidelines on corporate governance of State-Owned Enterprises*. Paris: OECD Publishing.
Petera, P., & Wagner, J. (2015). Global Reporting Initiative (GRI) and its Reflections in the Literature. *European Financial and Accounting Journal, 10*(2), 13–32.
Sands, J. (2004). Regulatory Independence, Public Accountability and the Victorian Prison System. *Australian Journal of Public Administration, 63*(4), 50–58.
Schillemans, T. (2008). Accountability in the Shadow of Hierarchy: The Horizontal Accountability of Agencies. *Public Organization Review: A Global Journal, 8*(2), 175–194.
Sinclair, A. (1995). The Chameleon of Accountability: Forms and Discourses. *Accounting, Organizations and Society, 20*(2), 219–237.
Solomon, J., & Maroun, W. (2012). *Integrated Reporting: The New Face of Social, Ethical and Environmental Reporting in South Africa*. London: Association of Chartered Certified Accountants.
Steyn, M. (2014). Organizational Benefits and Implementation Challenges of Mandatory Integrated Reporting: Perspectives of Senior Executives at South African Listed Companies. *Sustainability Accounting, Management and Policy Journal, 5*(4), 476–503.
Strong, P. (2015). Is Integrated Reporting a Matter of Public Concern? Evidence from Australia. *The Journal of Corporate Citizenship, 60*, 81–100.
Stubbs, W., & Higgins, C. (2015). Stakeholders' Perspectives on the Role of Regulatory Reform in Integrated Reporting. *Journal of Business Ethics, 147*, 489–508.
Surty, M., Yasseen, Y., & Padia, N. (2017). Trends in Integrated Reporting: A State-Owned Company Analysis. *Southern African Business Review*. https://doi.org/10.25159/1998-8125/3841.
Teo, S. (2000). Evidence of Strategic HRM Linkages in Eleven Australian Corporatized Public Sector Organisation. *Public Personnel Management, 29*(4), 557–575.
Ting, I. W. K., & Lean, H. H. (2015). Does Government Ownership Matter? Comparative Study Between GLCs and NGLCs in Malaysia. *The Singapore Economic Review, 60*, 2.

van Bommel, K. (2014). Towards a Legitimate Compromise? An Exploration of Integrated Reporting in the Netherlands. *Accounting, Auditing and Accountability Journal, 27*(7), 1157–1189.
Voorn, B., van Genugten, M., & van Thiel, S. (2017). The Efficiency and Effectiveness of Municipally Owned Corporations: A Systematic Review. *Local Government Studies, 43*(5), 820–841. https://doi.org/10.1080/03003930.2017.1319360.
Wilkinson, D., & Birmingham, P. (2003). *Using Research Instruments. A Guide for Researchers* (1st ed.). London: Routledge.
Whincop, M. J. (2005). *Corporate Governance in Government Corporations.* Aldershot: Ashgate.
World Bank. (2014). *Corporate Governance of State-Owned Enterprises: A Toolkit.* Washington, DC: World Bank Group.
Yin, R. K. (2002). *Case Study Research, Design and Methods* (3rd ed.). Newbury Park: Sage.

Spiridione Lucio Dicorato is a post-doctoral research fellow at the University of Rome "Tor Vergata". His research is focused on public accounting, financial management, and local public groups.

Chiara Di Gerio is a PhD candidate in Public Management and Governance track at the University of Rome "Tor Vergata". Her research project is focused on sustainable development in higher education and social reporting in Italian universities.

Gloria Fiorani is Associate Professor of CSR (Corporate Social Responsibility) and Accountability at the University of Rome "Tor Vergata". She is an expert in sustainable development and Third Mission. She teaches courses on corporate social responsibility, public administration, and social innovation and common goods. She is the director of the executive Master MARIS (Reporting, Innovation, and Sustainability).

Giuseppe Paciullo is a PhD candidate in Public Management and Governance track at the University of Rome "Tor Vergata". His research project is focused on the use of performance information in public administration and how performance information is disclosed in Italian hospitals.

Reflections on New Trends in Public Sector Reporting: Integrated Reporting and Beyond

Francesca Manes-Rossi and Rebecca Levy Orelli

The Accountability Challenge: The Need for Alternative Reporting Formats

Public sector organisations (PSOs) today are urged to act within an extremely complex 'web of accountability' (Page 2006). Discharging hierarchical and legal accountability is no longer sufficient: satisfying the information needs of superordinate bodies and obeying disclosure requests as mandated by laws and regulations are both seen as merely complying with obligations. Public accountability is something more; it is considered a crucial element of democratic behaviour, and public sector organisations increasingly need to explain their decisions and disclose their performance

F. Manes-Rossi (✉)
Department of Economics, Management and Institutions, University of Naples Federico II, Napoli, Italy
e-mail: manes@unina.it

R. L. Orelli
Department of Management, Alma Mater Studiorum, University of Bologna, Bologna, Italy
e-mail: rebecca.orelli@unibo.it

F. Manes-Rossi, R. Levy Orelli (eds.), *New Trends in Public Sector Reporting*, Public Sector Financial Management,
https://doi.org/10.1007/978-3-030-40056-9_10

in a wide range of 'accountability forums' (Bovens et al. 2014). Politicians, public agencies, central governments and international institutions, courts of audit, financial institutions, standard-setters, media, citizens and public services clients are all entitled to and demand understandable information. However, research has identified several downsides related to accountability, in particular dysfunctional effects related to over-exposure, which can limit public managers' autonomy (Pollitt 2003; Schillemans 2016).

A recent strand of research (Biondi and Bracci 2018; Cohen and Karatzimas 2015; Guthrie and Farneti 2008; Manes-Rossi 2019) focuses on accountability tools specifically addressing citizens' needs for information, which range from sustainability reporting to integrated reporting (IR) and from service reporting to other citizen-centric reports (for instance, popular reporting and integrated popular reporting). The underlying concept is to meet the information needs of those stakeholders for whom traditional reports based on accounting numbers do not provide useful information (Brusca 1997), as well as to identify the public value created by the organisation (Guthrie and Martin-Sardesai 2020).

This book aims to contribute to this strand of research, investigating the emergence of integrated reporting in public sector organisations, as well as of other alternative reporting tools that may be better tailored to communication with citizens and other non-specialist stakeholders. It also considers alternative reporting formats that can better support politicians and mangers in their decision making. The book also investigates how strategies, management activities, routines and procedures may need to change in order to provide information to and create new opportunities for dialogue with stakeholders, including citizens, public sector entities, supervising organisations and financial institutions. Ultimately, through case studies, stories of pioneers in the field, comparisons to existing frameworks and critical discussions, the book aims to outline the benefits and consequences of public sector organisations adopting innovative reporting, and key lessons related to its implementation.

New Trends in Public Sector Reporting

The most recent tool to make a splash in the reporting world is integrated reporting (IR). Promoted by the International Integrated Reporting Council (IIRC) through a specific framework published in 2013, IR is 'concise communication about how an organisation's strategy, governance, performance and prospects, in the context of its external environment, lead to the creation of value over the short, medium and long term' (IIRC 2013, p. 7). Despite some doubts about adopting a tool originally designed for the needs of investors, public sector organisations around the world have explored using IR, including universities (Veltri and Silvestri 2015), cities (Manes-Rossi 2018) and state-owned enterprises (Guthrie et al. 2017; Montecalvo et al. 2018). The merit of IR is its ability to bring together financial and non-financial information, focusing on the value creation process. This makes IR suitable for promoting deeper engagement with all stakeholders and increasing clarity about relations with and commitment to the public, thus promoting better decision making by external stakeholders (Katsikas et al. 2017). Aggestam and Sonnerfeldt, in their chapter, analyse the emergence of IR in the public sector through a multi-stakeholder approach and from a governance perspective. Considering the roles of and interactions between different actors involved in policy making, they contend that the adoption of IR is part of the shift from hierarchical to networked governance in public sector reporting. Building on research into transnational governance interactions (Eberlein et al. 2013), the authors analyse the regulatory governance process. They find that the need for IR in the public sector is framed in the context of climate change and sustainability, combined with the need to address reporting problems. The IR regulatory process involves the main actors in financial reporting, including the International Federation of Accountants (IFAC), the Chartered Institute of Public Finance and Accounting (CIPFA), and the World Bank, and means adhering to IR principles in the production of key policy documents. The authors conclude that effective IR implementation in the public sector requires interacting with other, non-financial reporting frameworks, standards and schemes that are relevant to the organisation.

Public sector entities' increased attention to sustainability issues has been at the core of a growing strand of literature over the last 13 years. Public sector organisations are responsible for more than 40% of worldwide economic activities, and because they deliver public services and public goods, they play a central role in pushing communities to work for a more sustainable future (Ball and Grubnic 2007; Guthrie and Farneti 2008). Consequently, sustainability reporting practices have consistently seen growing adoption by public sector organisations all around the world. Taking into account this trend, in their chapter, Frei, Lubinger and Greiling investigate universities' stakeholder engagement processes and compliance to the Global Reporting Initiative (GRI) G4 guidelines in their sustainability reporting. Driven by stakeholder theory and neo-institutionalism, the authors review the literature on sustainability reporting practices in the university sector and on stakeholder engagement processes. The results of the literature review constitute the basis for their content analysis of sustainability reports produced worldwide. The authors' results offer evidence of a selected embrace of accountability by universities, with low involvement of external stakeholders in developing and validating sustainability reports. One of their more surprising findings is that universities do not provide full coverage of those communication topics identified in the stakeholder engagement process. Furthermore, most of the reports analysed make selective use of GRI indicators, with an overall level of compliance of around 54%, and only a limited number of universities publish their reports in the GRI database.

Communicating with citizens is gaining importance and attention in view of their role as co-producers in the shift to public governance (Sicilia et al. 2016). Scholars have discussed at length the poor information often provided to citizens on fiscal and budgetary issues (Beckett and King 2002). In an effort to overcome the institutionalised 'one-way' approach to public sector reporting, participatory budgets were popularised in the 1990s. In their chapter, Lorson and Haustein discuss potential strategies for making public sector reporting more citizen-oriented, taking into account what can be learned from experiences with participatory budgeting. The authors discuss the strengths and drawbacks of participatory budgets and identify the implications for actors involved in citizen-centric public sector reporting (e.g. administrative staff, local councillors, third parties and citizens) and how they can inform report content and complexity. They conclude by suggesting the use of simplified reports characterised by conciseness and connectivity, focused on specific projects and prepared using jargon-free language and a dialogic style. The pivotal point is to nourish dialogue with citizens through consultation, both online and in person, and to favour democratic participation and citizens' membership in the decision-making process.

Other alternative reporting formats have also been adopted by public sector entities with the aim of communicating their financial situation and their overall performance to a wider audience. Reforms have developed throughout Europe (Brusca et al. 2016) aimed at innovating accounting and performance measurement systems, involving deep changes in both budgeting and reporting systems. These reforms are supposed to facilitate a better understanding of reporting results for both internal and external stakeholders. Saliterer and Korac, in their chapter, examine the relative advantages and usefulness of the new reporting tools introduced by the

Austrian central government after the federal budgeting and accounting reform of 2017. They examine the tools from the perspective of public managers and politicians. Combining results obtained through a gap analysis, a quantitative survey and interviews with directors of ministries, legislators and politicians, the authors find that the new reporting tools are more comprehensive and more understandable than the previous tools. However, the new tools do have limitations; for example, accrual figures are more difficult to interpret in comparison to modified cash data. Furthermore, the new reports are not perceived to be of high value for internal management purposes, although they are useful for accountability purposes. Performance information was welcomed by directors and is considered a useful approach to popular reporting or similar citizen-centric reporting. However, legislators criticised some shortcomings of performance reporting, in particular the time lag between financial and non-financial information, which prevented them from seeing an integrated view of the government's performance. Overall, the Austrian experience showed increasing engagement of internal stakeholders with accrual accounting, while at the same time highlighting that there is still room for improvement in communicating central government performance to citizens.

Practices in IR Reporting

The practices of IR include a wide variety of different experiences (La Torre et al. 2019). There are two primary reasons for this variation. The first is that IR is based on responding to demands for accountability and the needs of stakeholders, which are unique to each relationship; the second is related to the relatively low number of specific laws and rules governing IR. IR can communicate information in a variety of different formats, including narratives, numbers and pictures. Davison (2008) observed that a large part of non-financial reports communicate concepts which are not immediately translatable to numbers. Despite its prevalence, the cognitive impact of visually presenting reporting information (Carruthers 2008) has not been deeply investigated (Quattrone 2009). Ruggiero addresses the turn to visual accounting in IR for public sector organisations (PSOs) and aims to analyse the visual dimension of the annual reports of PSOs in order to understand how they can contribute to improved accountability processes. In particular, the chapter focuses on the images used by Hera, a public multi-utility preparing sustainability/

integrated reports, and presents a longitudinal analysis of the reports since 2003. Using a Barthesian (1977) perspective to consider the effect of messages coming from images, Ruggiero uses the Hera case to demonstrate continuous improvement in emotional interpretation of IR published in visual form. Images are used as a means to recall and reconnect with IR contents, with an evolution of sustainability/integrated reporting characterisation through images, and to transform numbers into images, producing a non-quantitative accounting message. The visual dimension of reporting practices could represent a way of reducing the complexity of managerial and accountability issues.

Within the public sector, higher education institutions (HEIs) offer a specific perspective in terms of their interactions with stakeholders and their impact on society. Recent studies have highlighted the key developments and implementation perspectives related to the use of IR in the public universities field (Guthrie et al. 2020). The relationships between the main activities of HEIs (teaching, research and Third Mission) and the environment they operate in, as well as their stakeholders, still need to be deeply investigated (Ramirez et al. 2016; De Villiers et al. 2014), as few studies have studied IR adoption by HEIs (Brusca et al. 2018). In their chapter, Tiron-Tudor, Zanellato, Oprisor and Farcas investigate the enabling conditions that allow HEIs to prepare integrated reports and the results that can be achieved, taking into account the experience of the Babeş-Bolyai University in Romania. Their results show that IR capitals are extensively disclosed in the Babeş-Bolyai University annual reports and that the reports strike a good balance between financial and non-financial information, include the fundamental elements required by the IIRC, and are fed by a coherent information system. The chapter shows that HEIs can sustain integrated thinking and reporting discourse in a specific and coherent manner.

By nature, IR encompasses insights into the environmental, social and governance (ESG) aspects of organisations. The term ESG is commonly used with the same meaning as sustainability, and both terms are seen as encompassing the broad set of environmental, social and governance considerations that can impact a company's ability to execute its business strategy and create value. The chapter by Ozcam examines the factors that determine publicly traded rail companies' ESG disclosure performance, based on a sample of 33 rail companies from 9 countries over the period 2007–2017, with a particular focus on government ownership. The analyses reveal that government ownership has a statistically significant and positive effect on the ESG reporting performance of publicly traded rail companies. The analyses also suggest that larger boards and higher shares of independent directors have a positive association with ESG disclosure scores. With respect to financial variables, the study reveals that larger and more leveraged rail companies receive higher ESG disclosure scores, while higher profitability and tangibility ratios are correlated with reduced ESG reporting performance. The analysis suggests several policy implications. Rail companies which would like to benefit from improved ESG disclosure performance should attract government as a partner, enlarge their boards, recruit more independent directors and increase sales and financial leverage while reducing their tangibility ratios.

Public sector organisations of all types, including public corporations, may benefit from implementing IR. In the case of state-owned companies and municipally owned corporations (MOCs), IR can assist them in achieving accountability because it can be adapted to take into account the goals of MOCs (KPMG 2012). Dicorato, Di Gerio, Fiorani and Paciullo, in their chapter, study the use of IR in MOCs that produce or deliver local public services. MOCs are required to pursue multiple objectives in addition to profit, such as social outcomes, innovation and employment. The case study of *Farmacie Comunali Pomezia S.p.A.* looks at one of the first Italian MOCs to apply the IIRC's guidelines and principles. The case shows how IR can provide a holistic overview of a MOC's performance, enhancing the visibility of both financial and non-financial information, and steering attitudes towards long-term thinking.

The research shows how the IIRC's framework can help organisations pursue accountability policies. The authors also reveal benefits related to the implementation of IR, including heightened consideration of citizens in the process of service delivery and a more balanced consideration of the economic, social and environmental impacts of strategic decisions and related actions.

Conclusion and Directions for Further Research

The book aimed to analyse the role of new public sector reporting tools from two different perspectives. First, how they can impact the provision of information to and creation of opportunities for dialogue with various stakeholders, including citizens, public sector entities, supervising organisations and financial institutions. And second, how they can change the defined strategies and management activities, thus affecting routines, procedures and reports.

Public services are created and provided in complex contemporary environments in which climate change, sustainable economic development, biodiversity and many other emerging issues constitute the driving forces of environmental and human developments (Guthrie and Martin-Sardesai 2020). As a consequence, the set of information that public sector organisations are required to be accountable for nowadays is not limited to their financials, but encompasses their environmental and social impacts as well as the intersections between financial, social and environmental elements. At the same time, the influence of public management reforms in recent decades has produced a variety of organisational forms for public service delivery, operating at the edge between the public and private spheres, which require specific forms of service reporting.

As a response to contemporary challenges, public sector organisations introduced new reporting forms (e.g. integrated reporting, sustainability reporting, participatory budgeting). These forms were applied and deployed in a variety of ways, which means they must be analysed in context to be deeply understood. Citizens, elected officials, public managers and public agencies can benefit from these new forms of reporting, performance measurement and management systems and their enhancement of accountability and value creation.

The book used case studies, critical discussion, comparisons to existing frameworks, insights from those who have implemented new reporting tools and the experiences of the pioneers of integrated reporting to summarise key lessons related to implementing innovative reporting forms and to highlight the benefits and consequences of adopting these communication tools.

The book is of interest to academics, researchers, policymakers, public managers, international organisations and standard-setters who are involved in or are responsible for disclosure and communication of information concerning public entities.

The book represents a starting point for further investigation into several big questions that are still unresolved. First, the issues of how the future evolution of IR will influence the regulation of other reporting tools in the public sphere, and what role specific guidelines will play in public sector entities' integrated reporting need to be explored. Second, the quality of stakeholders' engagement in sustainability reporting needs to be investigated, and the development of reports addressing all categories of stakeholders must be promoted. Third, the issue of timely reporting, or how to align the publication of different reports (financial reporting, performance information, etc.) to gain an integrated view of financial and non-financial performance, must be addressed. Fourth, research should study the emergence of other frameworks that directly address how to report on the sustainable development of organisations (like the United Nations' Sustainable Development Goals) and their use in practice to report on public services achievement. Finally, further study is needed on citizen-centric reports, their characteristics and regulations, and how past experiences can illuminate the future of alternative reporting.

References

Ball, A., & Grubnic, S. (2007). Sustainability Accounting and Accountability in the Public Sector. In J. Unerman, J. Bebbington, & B. O'Dwyer (Eds.), *Sustainability Accounting and Accountability*. London: Routledge.

Barthes, R. (1977). *Image, Music, Text*. Glasgow: Fontana Press.

Beckett, J., & King, C. S. (2002). The Challenge to Improve Citizen Participation in Public Budgeting: A Discussion. *Journal of Public Budgeting, Accounting & Financial Management, 14*(3), 463–485.

Biondi, L., & Bracci, E. (2018). Sustainability, Popular and Integrated Reporting in the Public Sector: A Fad and Fashion Perspective. *Sustainability, 10*(9), 3112.

Bovens, M., Schillemans, T., & Goodin, R. E. (2014). Public Accountability. In M. Bovens, R. E. Goodin, & T. Schillemans (Eds.), *The Oxford Handbook of Public Accountability* (pp. 1–20). Oxford: Oxford University Press.

Brusca, I. (1997). The Usefulness of Financial Reporting in Spanish Local Governments. *Financial Accountability and Management, 13*(1), 17–34.

Brusca, I., Caperchione, E., Cohen, S., & Manes-Rossi, F. (Eds.). (2016). *Public Sector Accounting and Auditing in Europe: The Challenge of Harmonization*. UK: Palgrave Macmillan.

Brusca, I., Labrador, M., & Larran, M. (2018). The Challenge of Sustainability and Integrated Reporting at Universities: A Case Study. *Journal of Cleaner Production, 188*, 347–354.

Carruthers, M. (2008). *The Art of Memory. A Study of Memory in Medieval Culture* (2nd ed.). Cambridge, UK: Cambridge University Press.

Cohen, S., & Karatzimas, S. (2015). Tracing the Future of Reporting in the Public Sector: Introducing Integrated Popular Reporting. *International Journal of Public Sector Management, 28*(6), 449–460.

Davison, J. (2008). Rhetoric, Repetition, Reporting and the "dot.com" Era: Words, Pictures, Intangibles. *Accounting, Auditing and Accountability Journal, 21*(6), 791.

De Villiers, C., Unerman, J., & Rinaldi, L. (2014). Integrated Reporting: Insights, Gaps and an Agenda for Future Research. *Accounting, Auditing & Accountability Journal, 27*(7), 1042–1067.

Eberlein, B., Abbott, K. W., Black, J., Meidinger, E., & Wood, S. (2013). Transnational Business Governance Interactions: Conceptualization and Framework for Analysis. *Regulation & Governance, 8*(1), 1–22.

Guthrie, J., & Farneti, F. (2008). GRI Sustainability Reporting by Australian Public Sector Organizations. *Public Money & Management, 28*(6), 361–366.

Guthrie, J., & Martin-Sardesai, A. (2020). Contemporary Challenges in the Public Sector and Services Reporting, Integrated Reporting and Beyond. In F. Manes-Rossi & R. L. Orelli (Eds.), *Reflections on New Trends in Public Sector Reporting: Integrated Reporting and Beyond*. Palgrave.

Guthrie, J., Manes-Rossi, F., & Orelli, R. L. (2017). Integrated Reporting and Integrated Thinking in Italian Public Sector Organisations. *Meditari Accountancy Research, 25*(4), 553–573.

Guthrie, J., Domingues, A. R., Manes-Rossi, F., & Orelli, R. L. (2020). Integrated Reporting and Sustainable Development Goals in Universities. In C. de Villiers (Ed.), *Handbook of Integrated Reporting*. London: Routledge.

IIRC. (2013). *The International Integrated Reporting Framework*. London, UK: IIRC.

Katsikas, E., Manes-Rossi, F., & Orelli, R. L. (2017). *Towards Integrated Reporting: Accounting Change in the Public Sector*. Cham: Springer.

KPMG. (2012). *Integrated Reporting Issue 2: Performance Insight through Better Business Reporting*. UK: KPMG.

La Torre, M., Bernardi, C., Guthrie, J., & Dumay, J. (2019). Integrated Reporting and Integrating Thinking: Practical Challenges. In S. Arvidsson (Ed.), *Challenges in Managing Sustainable Business*. Cham: Palgrave Macmillan.

Manes-Rossi, F. (2018). Is Integrated Reporting a New Challenge for Public Sector Entities? *African Journal of Business Management, 12*(7), 172–187.

Manes-Rossi, F. (2019). New Development: Alternative Reporting Formats: A Panacea for Accountability Dilemmas? *Public Money and Management, 39*(7), 528–531.

Montecalvo, M., Farneti, F., & De Villiers, C. (2018). The Potential of Integrated Reporting to Enhance Sustainability Reporting in the Public Sector. *Public Money and Management, 38*(5), 365–374.

Page, S. (2006). The Web of Managerial Accountability: The Impact of Reinventing Government. *Administration & Society, 38*(2), 166–197.

Pollitt, C. (2003). *The Essential Public Manager*. Maidenhead: Open University Press/McGraw-Hill.

Quattrone, P. (2009). Books to Be Practiced: Memory, the Power of the Visual, and the Success of Accounting. *Accounting, Organizations and Society, 34*(1), 85.

Ramirez, Y., Tejada, A., & Manzaneque, M. (2016). The Value of Disclosing Intellectual Capital in Spanish Universities: A New Challenge of Our Days. *Journal of Organizational Change Management, 29*(2), 176–198.
Schillemans, T. (2016). Calibrating Public Sector Accountability: Translating Experimental Findings to Public Sector Accountability. *Public Management Review, 18*(9), 1400–1420.
Sicilia, M., Guarini, E., Sancino, A., Andreani, M., & Ruffini, R. (2016). Public Services Management and Co-Production in Multi-Level Governance Settings. *International Review of Administrative Sciences, 82*(1), 8–27.
Veltri, S., & Silvestri, A. (2015). The Free State University Integrated Reporting: A Critical Consideration. *Journal of Intellectual Capital, 16*(2), 443–462.

Francesca Manes-Rossi is Associate Professor of Accounting in the Department of Economics, Management and Institutions at the University of Naples, Federico II, where she teaches and conducts research on public accounting and management. She is an experienced educator and researcher specializing in international public sector accounting standards as well as international financial reporting standards and other accounting issues related to management accounting, performance measurement and audit. In the last few years she has researched intensively on intellectual capital and integrated reporting in public sector entities. Francesca is co-chair of XII Permanent Study Group of the European Group for Public Administration (PSG EGPA) and member of the EGPA Steering Committee.

Rebecca Levy Orelli is Associate Professor of Accounting at the Alma Mater Studiorum, University of Bologna. Her research interests lie in the field of accounting in the European public sector and accounting as social and institutional practice, and are focused on performance measurement and reporting of financial, sustainability and integrated information in different contexts. She has extensively published her work on representation and effects of accounting in local governments, cultural organisations and health care in many international journals, book chapters and books. She acts as reviewer for several international journals and joins international networks in the field of public sector accounting and sustainability. She has also trained government officials in Italy and has been active in providing consulting services to public sector entities.

Index[1]

[1] Note: Page numbers followed by 'n' refer to notes.

F. Manes-Rossi, R. Levy Orelli (eds.), *New Trends in Public Sector Reporting*, Public Sector Financial Management,
https://doi.org/10.1007/978 3-030-40056-9

F

G

H

I

The manufacturer's authorised representative in the EU is Springer Nature Customer Service Centre GmbH, Europaplatz 3, 69115 Heidelberg, Germany. If you have any concerns regarding our products, please contact ProductSafety@springernature.com

Printed and bound by CPI Group (UK) Ltd, Croydon, CR0 4YY
30/09/2026
02225460-0001